THE HOLY SPIRIT AND CHRISTIAN MISSION
IN A PLURALISTIC CONTEXT

THE HOLY SPIRIT AND CHRISTIAN MISSION
IN A PLURALISTIC CONTEXT

EDITED BY

ROJI T. GEORGE

WIPF & STOCK · Eugene, Oregon

Wipf and Stock Publishers
199 W 8th Ave, Suite 3
Eugene, OR 97401

The Holy Spirit and Christian Mission
In a Pluralistic Context
By George, Roji T.
Copyright©2017 SAIACS
ISBN 13: 978-1-5326-9308-3
Publication date 5/29/2019
Previously published by SAIACS, 2017

Dedicated to my mother,

Mrs. V.C. Aleyamma,

for her sacrificial love and prayerful guidance in my life.

TABLE OF CONTENTS

Acknowledgement — v

Abbreviations — vi

Foreword: One Spirit, Many Faiths — 1
          Myk Habets

Introduction — 11
          Roji T. George

1. The Anointing Spirit and the Servant Mission of the Church — 21
          Christopher J.H. Wright

2. The Spirit and Mission in Ephesians — 36
          Idicheria Ninan

3. Holy Spirit and Christian Mission in a Religious Pluralistic Context — 60
          Timothy C. Tennent

4. Holy Spirit in Pentecostal Mission Praxis in India: A Paradigm for Mission in Pluralistic Context — 84
          Shaibu Abraham

5. Prophetic Speech and Action as Witness to Christ's Resurrection — 105
          Gary Tyra

6. Has the Catholic Charismatic Renewal Movement 122
   helped in building a more just society?
   Reginald Alva SVD

7. Calvin's Theology of the Holy Spirit and 138
   Christian Mission in a Pluralistic Context
   Matthew Ebenezer

8. The Shift from *Missio Dei* to *Missio Spiritūs* 152
   in Recent Mission Thinking: The Indian
   Contribution
   Kirsteen Kim

9. Holy Spirit And Christian Mission: A Re-Reading 165
   of Stanley J. Samartha's Theology of the
   Holy Spirit in the Pluralistic Context of India
   Samuel George

10. The Holy Spirit and the Church as the 187
    Ordinary Means of Salvation
    Steven Griffin

11. Third Article Theology and Apologetics 202
    Aruthuckal Varughese John

12. Holy Spirit and Christian Mission in a 223
    Pluralistic Context
    Paul Swarup

13. Christ-Devotee Movement: A Pentecost 244
    at Banaras
    Cyril Kuttiyanikkal

14. Indigenous Spirituality and the Holy Spirit 258
    in a Pluralistic Context
    Atola Longkumer

Index 276

ACKNOWLEDGEMENT

First and foremost, I am indebted to the Source of All Wisdom, the Almighty God, who granted me strength and wisdom to undertake and accomplish the task of publishing this edited volume on the theme, "The Holy Spirit and Christian Mission in a Pluralistic Context." The theme had always remained close to my heart and mind throughout my academic journey; hence, the book is very special to me. I am grateful to God who, by His divine provision, brought together an elite and accomplished team of contributors together to write different chapters on the given theme. They have recognized the importance and relevance of the chosen theme for the life and mission of the Church and have gladly contributed a chapter each from his or her field of specialization. Surely, this volume would not have become a reality without their sacrificial participation in the project. I wish to express my gratitude to Myk Habets for writing Foreword and to the eminent theologians, missiologists, and biblical scholars, who have graciously endorsed this volume after carefully reading the manuscript. I am thankful to SAIACS Press for extending every expert support in publishing and marketing this book. I am also, especially, grateful to Mrs. Laldinmoi P. for copy-editing the manuscript and giving vital suggestions in preparing the final manuscript for publication. Finally, I owe immeasurable gratitude to my beloved wife, Anjana, and our two lovely daughters, Joanne and Janet, who stood beside me encouraging and supporting, at all times.

Abbreviations

AD	*Anno Domini*/in the year of the Lord Jesus
AIDS	Acquired Immunodeficiency Syndrome
ANTC	Abingdon New Testament Commentaries
BC	Before Christ
BST	Bible Speaks Today
ed./eds.	Edition, editor, edited by/editors
ET	English Translation
HIV	Human Immunodeficiency Virus
ISPCK	Indian Society for Promoting Christian Knowledge
LNTS	Library of New Testament Studies
NICNT	New International Commentary on the New Testament
PNTC	Pillar New Testament Commentary
rev. edn.	Revised edition
SAIACS	South Asia Institute of Advanced Christian Studies
SCM	Student Christian Movement
Trans.	Translator(s)
WBC	Word Biblical Commentary
WUNT	Wissenschaftliche Untersuchungen zum Neuen Testament
ZECNT	Zondervan Exegetical Commentary on the New Testament

FOREWORD

ONE SPIRIT, MANY FAITHS

Myk Habets

Christianity has always been a polarizing faith. Indeed, all the Abrahamic faiths are polarizing for they claim exclusivity and total commitment. To "outsiders" of these three religious movements, such exclusive and totalizing claims appear arrogant, aggressive, and intolerant. This creates unwanted but perhaps not unwarranted tensions between families, tribes, cities, and societies. Jesus' teaching in Luke 12:49–53 has never appeared as true as it does today:

> I have come to bring fire on the earth, and how I wish it were already kindled! But I have a baptism to undergo, and what constraint I am under until it is completed! Do you think that I came to bring peace on earth? No, I tell you, but division. From now on there will be five in one family divided against each other, three against two and two against three. They will be divided, father against son and son against father, mother against daughter and daughter against mother, mother-in-law against daughter-in-law and daughter-in-law against mother-in-law.

These are not the only words from Jesus about judgment of course. Jesus was no Marxist revolutionary or wild despot. Those familiar with the Christian scriptures know that the Father carries out his judgment through the Son (John 5:22). This same Gospel tells us that the Father and Son are one (John 10:30). That oneness between Jesus Christ on earth and the heavenly Father has always been considered the very essence of Christianity. John is concerned in his Gospel to make it clear that what Jesus does on earth is in complete agreement with what God the Father does, and who the Father is (John 5:17–26). The Christian gospel in its entirety rests upon the connection between Jesus Christ and God—it is the very substance of the faith. It is worth pausing briefly to consider the relationship between Jesus and the Father before making any comments on the work of the Holy Spirit in the world today.

As I write, it is Advent (2016) and I can't help but reflect upon the coming of Christ. In the 1970s, Scottish theologian and presbyterian minister Thomas F. Torrance preached an Advent sermon to the kirk he formally pastored, wherein he reflected upon the text of John 5:17–27.[1] I would like to take my bearings from his thoughts before offering a word of my own on the topic of the Holy Spirit and Christian mission in a pluralistic context.

A MEDITATION ON JOHN 5

It is not uncommon today to hear reflected the thought that Jesus and the Father are different, and radically so. God the Father is thought to be a rather grumpy individual, remote and aloof, acting in solitary judgment. Jesus on the other hand, is said to be a kindly sage, with words of love and mercy on his lips. Already from our reference to Luke 12, we see this is a caricature. God the Father and God the Son are, as the Nicene Creed so clearly states, *homoousios*, or one in substance and being. What we see then, in the incarnate Son, Jesus Christ, is God in the flesh—God as man, not God in a man—as Athanasius was fond of saying. In John 5, we see Christ doing at least three things in concert with the Father.

First, Jesus and the Father are one in their work of healing (John 5:17). Thomas Torrance reminds us that, "Jesus was saying that in His own work of healing He was continuing the creative work of God Himself when He made the world."[2] As it was in the beginning so it was in the incarnation, "[f]orgiveness, properly understood, is a stupendous act, for it is the undoing of sin."[3] God is for us! This is the message of Scripture and that means that God the Father and God the Son are for us and our

---

[1] Thomas F. Torrance, "Sermon on John 5.17: Advent Sermon" (Scotland: Beechgrove Church, c.1970s), in The Thomas F. Torrance Manuscript Collection, Special Collections, Princeton Theological Seminary Library, Box 44, 1–9.

[2] Torrance, "Sermon on John 5.17," 2.

[3] Torrance, "Sermon on John 5.17," 2.

salvation. "Yes, the glorious, good news of our text is that *Jesus is the hand of God Himself* stretched out to heal and save. *Jesus is the eternal Word of God made flesh*, so that what He says God says, and when He forgives, it is the everlasting God Himself who forgives."[4] It is important that this word of love, mercy, grace, and healing are first. God is for us in Christ Jesus. But this very particular and emphatic claim cannot stand without further clarification.

The second thing we see from John 5 is that Jesus and the Father are one in judgment (John 5:22). Love is given freely, mercy is offered without the need for qualifications, and grace is extended to all; but a response is required. Acceptance of Christ's offer of salvation is essential, and that requires both an epistemological repentance and a personal commitment. A decision is called for, a *metanoia*, a turning. As Torrance articulates it, "[t]his means that face to face with Jesus we are confronted with the divine judgment. God the Judge of all the earth is none other than God who comes to us in Jesus Christ; so that the way that Jesus exercises judgment is none other than the way God exercises judgment."[5]

This should not surprise us. When offered a choice between two alternatives, a decision has to be made. Christ offers a way and that offer demands response; no one is neutral and no one can opt out. If there is truth, then there is error; if there is a right way then there is a wrong way; and if Christ is God in the flesh and demands our total allegiance, then one must either accept or reject this.

In his Advent sermon, Torrance gave the illustration of a discussion he had with a man he met on a train. The man was brought up in a pluralistic context where right and wrong had no objective basis and one followed their own path without judgment, right, or wrong. The problem was that the man was to be married soon and he keenly felt a sense of guilt over some of his actions and wanted to enter his marriage with a keen slate. Torrance explains,

> It was not difficult to explain to that man the difference between a right and wrong idea of divine judgment. His parents had revolted against a harsh 'god' painted by human fear, but instead they had contrived for

---

[4] Torrance, "Sermon on John 5.17," 3, (Emphasis original).
[5] Torrance, "Sermon on John 5.17," 4.

> themselves the kind of 'god' they wanted, at the expense of reality. It is a very different God whom we meet in Jesus Christ. He is the God of infinite love, but His love is so pure that it judges all that is not-love. He is the God of free and total forgiveness, who forgives and judges it by forgiving it. In Jesus the voice of divine judgment and the voice of forgiving mercy are one and the same, for God has committed all judgment to the Son. There is no judgment behind the back of Jesus, and yet the forgiveness mediated to us by Jesus comes out of the very heart of judgment—that is why it is so real and why it pacifies the conscience. Yes, unless the one who forgives is the one who judges you, it is all finally an empty sham, and you are left alone with your sins and imaginations, locked up in yourself and your memories unforgiven and unemancipated.[6]

Even in judgment God is for us and our salvation. The uniqueness, the specificity, and the scandal of particularity associated with Jesus and his revelation of the Father are reasons for rejoicing and the basis for dialogue with those in pluralistic contexts. The message is good news, no matter how scandalous and divisive it may at first appear.

Third and finally, in John 5:26 we see that Jesus and the Father are one in the resurrection of the dead. "You see, Jesus Christ and the heavenly Father are so close, so united, so one," writes Torrance, "that even in the ultimate matters of final destiny, they are not divided—in fact, the executive authority is put in the hands of Jesus (verse 27)—and therefore the future of every man and woman is determined through relation to Jesus."[7]

Such are the consistent claims of Christianity. God the Father and Son work in unison to reconcile and redeem the world through their mutual work of healing, judging, and bringing all things to their rightful end. When such claims confront pluralistic contexts, however, things become complicated, or at least contested. One way to confront this contested context is by appeal to the Spirit.

SPIRIT, SPIRITUALITY, AND THE SPIRIT OF CHRIST

Spirituality has become a plastic word in (post)modern contexts; it is malleable to a conflicting host of definitions and applications, many of

---

[6] Torrance, "Sermon on John 5.17," 6.
[7] Torrance, "Sermon on John 5.17," 7.

which are mutually exclusive. The use of "spiritual but not religious" now dominates religious discourse, and along with it the classical claims of Christianity are pushed ever-more to the periphery of popular sentiment. The Christian claim that Jesus is the way, the truth, and the life (John 14:6) is at best quaint, and at worst offensive. Appeal is no longer made to Christ in much of ecumenical discourse, for Christ divides as much as he unites. When seeking ecumenical agreement, appeal has never been made to God the Father, for that is as divisive as the appeal to the Son. Today, we are told, we must appeal to the S/spirit if we are to make any ecumenical headway, and we must appeal to the S/spirit if we are to be relevant for the contemporary world.[8] This, at least, is what the recent history of the Christian ecumenical and interreligious movements suggests. Across the spectrum of philosophy, economics, sociology, education, politics, and religion, the S/spirit is seen as the way forward for the third millennium. What are Christians to make of this?

Recent attempts to relate to or even to unite Christianity with other religions have often resulted in pluralistic and syncretistic theologies. From the perspective of historical Christianity, this is to be pitied. But for all their faults, the modern ecumenical movement and recent attempts at contextualization have at least recognized the fact that the Spirit is doing a universal work within God's creation and is calling all creatures and all creation toward a holy and perfected *telos*. So far so good, one might say. The great fault in such recent pluralistic and syncretistic theologies has been, however, not the attempt or even the focus on the S/spirit, but, rather, ambiguity over what or who the S/spirit being appealed to is. This is precisely the problem. The urgent requirement and unique contribution Christianity can make to missional and contextual theology is to speak clearly about who it is we name when we invoke the Holy Spirit.

The appeal to the S/spirit, as ambiguous as it may at first appear, is not without biblical and theological merit. In a kind of trinitarian inversion, we find that upon Christ's coronation he (with the Father) sends the Holy Spirit to his church at Pentecost in order to bring to fulfilment all that the Son has accomplished for us and our salvation. From the

---

[8] I use "S/spirit" here to indicate the confusion of what is actually being referred to, the third person of the Trinity or a general principle.

sending of the Spirit to the great Parousia of the Lord, the Spirit is our first point of contact with the triune God. It is the Holy Spirit who works in the world and within humanity to speak the Word, to enact the Father's will, and to bring God's works to perfection. The Spirit is God's presence in creation, God's immanent presence with his creatures. Awareness of the closeness of the Spirit and the universal scope of the Spirit's work has led to significant advancements in ecumenical dialogue, missional hermeneutics, and contextual theology.[9] Mission endeavour that starts with Christ often asks people to come to a decision, or confronts those of other faiths or none with a crisis point. This, of course, is necessary, as we have seen in our brief meditation on John 5, but is it the starting point? Many contend that starting with Christ is but one way to engage in mission, another is to start with the Spirit. When appeal is made to the Spirit then mission can start from below, as it were, and work its way up. Human experiences, cultures, and even religious intuitions become the seedbed for the gospel to be communicated. As someone has said, "there are many ways to Christ but only one way to the Father (through Christ)." The Spirit's work is manifold but ultimately coalesces around bringing glory to the incarnate Son and his purposes in the world.

However, real advancement will only come when Christianity holds its ground, as it were, and enters into pluralistic contexts confident of its own message and content. In a recent work on pneumatology, I outlined a series of theses on what it might look like to start our theology with pneumatology, a Third Article Theology, thesis 8 of which was:

> [Third Article Theology] highlights the eschatological nature of God's Trinitarian mission in the world and proleptically incorporates such eschatology throughout its pneumatological dogmatics, whereby the mission of God in Christ remains the center of the divine drama. An emphasis upon the eschatological ministry of the Spirit comes with at least two corollaries, one christological, the other ecclesiological. Christologically, it is Christ's resurrection, ascension, and current session that render the ministry of the Spirit effective and cosmic. It is in Jesus' words, works, and continuing ministry that the presence of the

---

[9] For both an overview and constructive analysis of the Spirit and ecumenism, see Kirsten L. Guidero, "'In the Unity of the Spirit': A Third Article Theology of Receptive Ecumenism" in Myk Habets (ed), *Third Article Theology: A Pneumatological Dogmatics* (Minneapolis: Fortress Press, 2016), 463-478.

Spirit is most keenly felt. The Spirit is about proclaiming and bringing in the kingdom of God, of which Christ is the King. Ecclesiologically, the eschatological work of the Spirit is even now being progressively realized in and through the church, the body of Christ and temple of the Holy Spirit. 'Thus, in a fundamental sense, the Spirit is both present—already having introduced the coming reign of God—and yet also absent—not yet fully having established the righteousness of God,'[10] writes Amos Yong. On this basis Yong helpfully speaks of a 'pneumatological prolepsis', whereby the inclusion of a missio Spiritus will result in 'an enriched patrology and christology, while simultaneously comprehending the full scope of God's redemptive work, both across space (cosmic) and across time (diachronic).'[11] [12]

Not only are patrology and christology affected, as Yong avers above, but also a theology of religions, missional theology, and the task of contextualization, to name but a few.[13]

Christian theologians, missiologists, and contextual theologians do no good to the church of Christ when they abandon the fundamental substance of the faith in the name of ecumenism, or tolerance, or some other quest for relevancy in the contemporary world. It is only by naming the Spirit as the Spirit of the risen and ascended Lord Jesus Christ, that appeal to the category of S/spirit or the spiritual will yield any substantive results. Christianity, like Islam and like Judaism, is an intellectually robust and existentially rewarding religion that, like its Abrahamic cousins, claims total allegiance and with that allegiance, it claims to witness to the Reality and Truth of the universe. Unlike other religions, Christianity finds the locus of these claims in the Lord Jesus Christ, eternal Son of the Father, as witnessed to by his Holy Spirit. When Christianity brings such totalizing claims into the public sphere, with humility and winsomeness, only then will ecumenical and missional effectiveness become a reality. Many suggest that the way to do this today is to start with the Holy Spirit.

---

[10] Amos Yong, "Primed for the Spirit: Creation, Redemption and the *Missio Spiritus*," *International Review of Mission* 100 (2011), 363.

[11] Yong, "Primed for the Spirit," 364.

[12] Myk Habets, "Prolegomenon: On Starting with the Spirit" in *Third Article Theology: A Pneumatological Dogmatics*, 17–18.

[13] For a comprehensive attempt at a Third Article Theology see *Third Article Theology: A Pneumatological Dogmatics*.

CHRISTIAN MISSION IN PLURALISTIC CONTEXTS

The modern West finds itself well and truly ensconced in secularity. Exclusive religious claims have been relegated to private belief and orthodox theology has been all but evacuated from the public square. Christianity struggles to find a voice amidst such secularity, as its institutions seek legitimacy, or search for a way to exist amidst such a changing culture. Outside the West, religion still dominates most cultures and Christianity faces a different struggle—that of differentiating itself from other religions and making its central claims understood without changing its central message in the process. For East and West, North and South alike, the church in the twenty-first century is struggling with the issue of contextualization. India has produced some of the most stimulating and intriguing works on contextualization and this volume adds to that important work. By focussing on, or starting with the Spirit, the contributors to the present volume have each understood both the changing religious contexts within which Christianity now finds itself, and they have sought to address that challenge head on by starting precisely at the point at which God acts in the world, by his Holy Spirit.

The volume is too big and covers too much ground to comment on all the essays. However, the sweep and scope of the work is impressive. Each contributor appeals, not to a vague concept of "spirit" but, rather, to the Holy Spirit, the third person of the triune God, who works in the world to bring all things to their appointed end. The Christian tradition, both East and West, North and South, ancient and modern, is appealed to, and the contributors never lose their vision of the uniqueness and exclusivity of the Christian gospel.

Several contributors turn first to the Holy Scripture for their foundations, and rightly so, they turn their attention to the book of Acts. Timothy Tennent, no stranger to India, returns to the experience of the Spirit as seen in the Acts of the Apostles, and from that narrative he unearths three key themes: the Spirit empowers the church for mission, the Spirit endues the church with God's authority, and the Spirit gifts the church with powerful signs and wonders. Tennent argues that in this regard, the book of Acts is prescriptive for the church today and points to the 600 million Charismatic/Pentecostal Christians globally who attest to this. The chapter by Shaibu Abraham bears witness to this same Charismatic/Pentecostal phenomenon within India itself, and the chapter by Samuel George examines the work of Stanley Samartha to the same end. In radically pluralistic contexts, we require the manifestations of the Holy Spirit to once again bear witness to the working of the triune God in the world.

Paul Swarup situates the issues of contextualization and mission within the Indian context specifically, and catalogues the various challenges to missions faced within India. While his focus is clearly on India, the issues he deals with are surely not limited to the Indian subcontinent. Swarup focusses on the work of the Holy Spirit in the face of the caste system, a hostile environment, and amidst persecution. Swarup concludes that the Spirit works within the midst of each of these challenges as he affirms the truth of Jesus Christ as Lord, leads the church into all truth, makes people righteous, and empowers believers for the works of service.

Seasoned missiologist and pneumatologist, Kirsteen Kim, chronicles the recent move amongst Christian missions from the concept of a *missio Dei* to that of a *missio Spiritūs*. According to Kim, the development of mission pneumatology in the context of religious pluralism is a particular Indian contribution to a *missio Spiritūs*. Kim returns to the theology of religious pluralism developed by Stanley Samartha and then of Jacques Dupuis, both of whom adopt a distinctly pneumatological approach to the issue of religious pluralism, and interrogates their work in the light of the World Council of Churches policy statement *Together towards Life* (TTL), composed in 2013. Kim concludes her chapter affirming the trinitarian framework required for all Christian theology and the requirement for Jesus Christ to be the criterion for what Christians recognize as the fullness of life and as the embodiment of the Spirit of God.

Varughese John examines what apologetics might look like when a Third Article Theology is adopted. The epistemological role of the Spirit is explicated as are the insights of Søren Kierkegaard who forcefully argued that the Spirit is both the provider of the truth and the condition to receive the truth when it is encountered. John provides a form of relational apologetics that is both faithful to the great tradition and yet contemporary. In short, he provides an insight into what an apologetic suitable for pluralistic contexts might look like.

Each of the contributors to this volume are working from a robustly trinitarian, christological, and biblical foundation and from this vantage point, they are starting with questions of the Spirit in order to further the work of the Church on earth, and to bear witness and proclaim the Lordship of Jesus Christ. Paul's injunction in Ephesians 4:4–6 is clearly upheld: "[t]here is one body and one Spirit, just as you were called in one hope when you were called; one Lord, one faith, one baptism, one God and Father of all, who is over all and through all and in all." And yet each is sensitive to the pluralistic contexts within which the gospel is found and each seeks to contribute to the work of Christian missions today. Starting with the Spirit is proving to be a fruitful task for theology and missions today, and with this volume we have much to ponder and much more to apply.

Dr. Myk Habets

Dean of Faculty,
Head of Carey Graduate School,
Lecturer - Systematic Theology,
Carey Baptist College,
Auckland, New Zealand.

Advent, 2016

INTRODUCTION

Roji T. George

Often, we hear the words of Emil Brunner repeated loud and clear: "The church exists by mission as fire exists by burning."[1] It sets the order right: Mission must be prioritized as the church exists and grows by and for the mission of God in the world. The church is the body of the redeemed sinners by the blood of Jesus Christ according to God's salvific mission but she is energized to actualize her transformational potency and sustained to extend God's rule, the kingdom of God, here and now by the missional work of the Holy Spirit. Hence, Jesus at the point of ascension commanded his disciples to "wait for the gift my Father promised, which you have heard me speak about. For John baptized with water, but in a few days you will be baptized with the Holy Spirit" (Acts 1:4-5). The purpose of one being baptized by the Holy Spirit is entirely missional: "But you will receive power when the Holy Spirit comes on you; and you will be my witnesses in Jerusalem, and in all Judea and Samaria, and to the ends of the earth" (Acts 1:8). The Lukan testimony to the birth and growth of the church in the Acts of the Apostles cannot be fully appreciated without recognizing the significance of the Holy Spirit, the third person of the Trinity.

The command of Jesus in Acts 1:8 assumes two important things for our interest, at present: (i) The pluralistic context of doing Christian mission, i.e., plurality of cultures, religions, ethnic groups, etc, articulated in the words, "the ends of the earth." (ii) The sufficiency of the Spirit in equipping the disciples to fulfil the task of bearing witness to Jesus

---

[1] Emil Brunner, *The Word and the World* (London: Student Christian Movement Press, 1931), 108.

Christ irrespective to every wall of difference. Was Jesus oblivious to the potential challenges of pluralistic contexts? Was he undermining the problems his disciples would face at the mission frontiers? Not at all! Jesus himself undertook his mission in Palestine, predominantly a Jewish context but surely pluralistic to a great extent. The evidence pointing to a pluralistic context and Jesus' interaction with the people of other religions and cultures is present within the canonical testimony to Jesus, the four gospel narratives. However, having conducted his own mission in harmony with the Spirit from the beginning of his mission (Luke 4:16-18) to the end when he imparted his Spirit to his disciples (John 20:22), Jesus appears to be convinced of the undisputed necessity and sufficiency of the Spirit's assistance, enabling, and empowering for his disciples to effectively execute God's purpose in and through their lives.

In the past, the church has struggled to understand the persona of the Holy Spirit and his continuing role in the life of the church. While some have limited it to the function of regeneration, sanctification, and transformation of an individual, others have disputed the availability of his gifts promised to carry out an effective mission today. It is in this context that one needs to revisit the biblical teaching on the missional role of the Holy Spirit, a biblical truth, in general, assumed to be true without intentionally engaging the Holy Spirit in one's day-to-day mission activities. Luke appears to be clear about it in Acts 1:4-5, 8. He sees the bestowal of the Holy Spirit as:

- A gift promised by the Father of our Lord Jesus Christ.
- Jesus has *taught* about it in the hearing of the disciples. He recognizes the truth that the reception of the Spirit is purely *to appoint his follower as his witness* ("*my* witnesses") beyond every geopolitical boundary.
- It is a *Spirit empowering experience* of a disciple to bear witness to the Son transhistorically, transtemporally, and transgeographically.

On these terms, Luke narrates the earliest Christian mission as a model for the church in later centuries to follow. Interestingly, the outpouring of the Holy Spirit, for Luke, is not a one-time event but that which repeats at least two more times in Acts 10:44-46 and 19:6. The truth that undergirds his portrayal of the early Christian (Gentile) mission is the trinitarian basis of the pneumatic missiology: It is the activity of the Spirit, according to the promise of God, to bear witness to the Son both among Jews and the nations. For Luke, the missional significance of the Holy Spirit is constant, undisturbed, and uncontested across the cultural boundaries. In other words, the early Christians bore witness to the Son, Jesus Christ, in pluralistic (Hellenistic, Roman, and Greek) socio-cultural and religio-political contexts by the guidance (e.g., Acts 8:26; 16:6-10) and empowerment (e.g., Acts 4:8-13) of the Spirit. Every action of the early church and her apostles, for Luke, were inspired and regulated by the Holy Spirit. In fact, the boldness of the apostles to bear testimony to Jesus before the Sanhedrin in Acts 4:13-14 is the fulfilment of the words of Jesus in Luke 12:11-12: "When you are brought before synagogues, rulers and authorities, do not worry about how you will defend yourselves or what you will say, for the Holy Spirit will teach you at that time what you should say."

However, the history of Christian theology does not present a very encouraging picture of the church's appreciation of the Spirit's role in her life and mission through the centuries until the modern times. A renewed appreciation and affirmation of the central role of the Holy Spirit in Christian mission started with modern Pentecostalism, though earlier to it there has been some interest in the Holy Spirit within the church. In recent missiological discussions while *missio Dei* and *missio Christi* have played a dominant role, there have been renewed calls from isolated corners to speak about *missio Spiritūs*. The present volume, as a collection of articles from varied ecclesial-theological persuasions, desires to reaffirm the necessity and urgency of a pneumatic missiology. It does not simply speak of God's salvific mission as that which: (i) originates from God, (ii) materializes in and through the Christ event, or (iii) is divinely mandated to the Church to continue doing it in the world. Instead, it highlights the central role of the Spirit in the effective mission of the church. Perhaps, in Lukan fashion, we ought to learn to speak theologically about Christian mission and the charismatic-missional role of the Holy Spirit in one breath where the activity of the church *is* the activity of the Holy Spirit. The two must remain inseparably intertwined always. In other words, the *pneumatic missiology* (i.e., the theology of mission saturated by the theology of the Holy Spirit) and *missional pneumatology* (i.e., the theology of the Holy Spirit conceived missionally) are to be built in relation to/for one another.

To this end, the contributors of the articles from varied ecclesiastic traditions attempt to contribute to the larger theme: "Holy Spirit and Christian Mission in a Pluralistic Context." **Christopher J.H. Wright** discusses the Old Testament roots of "the anointing" (of the Holy Spirit) idea in the New Testament as used to define the ministry of Jesus and the Church. He argues that the root lies in the Isaiahnic prophecies concerning the ministry of the future Servant-King figure (Isa 11:1-5; 42:1-7; 61:1-3). Wright locates it in its wider context of the mission of God, Israel, and Servant in order to exemplify its universal significance. He demonstrates that God desired to bless the nations through Israel in which the historical Israel desperately failed. However, God's mission *to* and *of* Israel is fulfilled by the Servant of the LORD. The Servant is said to fulfil the will of God by the anointing of the Spirit that has four dimensions—justice, compassion, enlightenment, and liberation. It is this multidimensional mission of the Servant that is, finally, fulfilled in the Spirit-filled mission of Jesus (Luke 4:16-21). Hence, the mission of the church by the anointing of the Holy Spirit ought to resemble the Christ's mission as the true inheritor of the mission of God, Israel, and the Servant.

Along the same lines, **Idicheria Ninan** contends that in the letter to the Ephesians, Paul articulates a Holy Spirit-empowered messianic and spiritual identity of the eschatological community of God's people from the vantage of the new covenant. Her missional significance is evident in the multi-ethnic community formation. For Paul, the missional existence of the community is implied in its *berakha*, the prayer report, and *Pax Christi*. Such a communitarian existence of the people as the temple of God and the royal priesthood is said to have direct access to God through the Spirit's indwelling to enable both centripetal and centrifugal witnessing. This twin-forked witness is emboldened by the Holy Spirit controlled counter cultural moral identity that is perfectly modelled in Jesus.

The three chapters that follow focus on different aspects of the modern Pentecostal mission resembling the Spirit-empowered charismatic mission of the earliest community of believers in Acts. While Shaibu Abraham describes the liberative significance of the Pentecostal

Introduction

mission praxis in India, Timothy Tennent and Gary Tyra give a clarion call to non-Pentecostal-Charismatic churches/theologians to show an unbiased openness to learn and adopt important aspects of the pneumatic missiology and missional pneumatology. The core contention of **Timothy C. Tennent** based on Acts is that the earliest church's Holy Spirit-propelled missional existence is rightly encapsulated in the modern Pentecostal understanding of the Spirit active mission of the church. Critically probing both the Lukan account in Acts and the birth and growth of the global Christianity through the Pentecostal revival, he highlights the failure of the traditional western church to grant due importance to missional pneumatology from the patristic period down to the mighty outpouring of the Holy Spirit at the beginning of the Pentecostal movement. In other words, during this large span of time in the ecclesiastic history, the role of the Holy Spirit has been limited to Christian soteriology. Tennent maintains that it created a wide gap between the life and mission of the community described in Acts and the later western church. Although he is painfully aware of the "'mote' in the Pentecostal eye,"[2] he contends to invoke Pentecostal missional pneumatology as a corrective to the traditional western church's blind spots. In continuation, **Shaibu Abraham** exemplifies how the Holy Spirit's active mission praxis of Pentecostals could be an effective model to engage in mission among the rich and poor, educated and uneducated, etc. He maintains, the key reason for the rapid growth of Pentecostal churches in the pluralistic context of India is the use of charismata that liberates people from both spiritual and physical bondages. Such charismata enabled mission is arguably not just liberative but transformative by nature. However, in the light of sporadic violent responses toward Pentecostal mission activities from certain quarters of religious fundamentalists, the need of the hour demands a pneumato-centric theology of mission that avoids confrontational approach towards other religions but honours neighbouring religious traditions without compromising its own missional stance.

Gary Tyra calls the western evangelical Christians to have an open-minded approach "to a *pneumatologically real* version of prophetic speech and action, suggesting that the same kind of missional fruitfulness evident in the book of Acts and currently being experienced by Pentecostal-

---
[2] Chapter 3, 82.

Charismatic disciples living and ministering in the urban centres of the Global South can be experienced in the industrial West as well."[3] In dialogue with his conversation partners, Bevans and Schroeder, Tyra treats the Spirit empowering experience and the Spirit prompted speech and action as firmly founded in the Scripture. Drawing from the Scripture, he recounts three forms of the Spirit enabled mission of the church—prophetic evangelism, prophetic edification, and prophetic equipping—which tremendously characterize the Pentecostal-Charismatic missional pneumatology. Echoing the call of Tennent in his chapter, as mentioned earlier, Tyra too convincingly argues the need for all Christians to actively adopt this type of missional praxis, which is capable of importing immense vitality to the mission of the church in a pluralistic context. He urges us to undertake a respectful Spirit-empowered prophetic speech and act into the lives of our contemporaries that are also a powerful witness to Christ Jesus.

At this point, **Reginald Alva**'s critical reflection upon the widespread Catholic Charismatic Renewal Movement (CCRM) becomes vital. As a Roman Catholic priest-theologian who is sensitive to the significance of the Spirit-empowered missional engagement of the church in a pluralistic context, Alva discusses the charismatic role of the Spirit in the growth of the Roman Catholic church beside the larger Pentecostal-Charismatic mission movement. However, he calls upon CCRM to move beyond the trap of a naive and limited understanding of the role of the Spirit in an individual's life to the Spirit initiated inner conversion experience to flow out to create a just society. It ought to be a movement that operates for the greater good of all by sharing their own resources to build a harmonious society. This is possible only by establishing social equality.

The following cluster of five articles explores the significance of the Holy Spirit in modern ecclesial traditions and theological discussions. As a Reformed theologian, **Matthew Ebenezer**, reiterating that the appropriate place for pneumatology in Christian theology was denied until the emergence of Pentecostalism (a fact that Tennent points out earlier in his essay), undertakes to investigate carefully Calvin's theology and his interest in the Holy Spirit with regard to soteriology. He attempts

---

[3] Chapter 5, 105.

Introduction

to find its relevance for Christian mission in the pluralistic context of India. Hence, he delineates Calvin's theology of the Holy Spirit in relation to his thought on the deity of the Holy Spirit, his relationship with salvation, faith, Scripture, etc. Defending Calvin's "limited" pluralistic context, Ebenezer contends that Calvin emphasized the significant role of the Holy Spirit in mission (without obliterating the fact that he did have a certain degree of negative thought about papists and Muslims of his time) when talking about his role in initiating conversion according to God's sovereign will, in teaching the elect, and in making our preaching effective.

Kirsteen Kim focuses on the works of Stanley Samartha's inter-religious dialogue and Jacques Dupuis' religious pluralism to elaborate the emerging recent shift in the theology of mission from a *missio Dei* to *missio Spiritūs*. She contends, the Indian pluralistic context is integral to such an important paradigm shift in the academic discourse including the formation of the WCC document *Together towards Life* (TTL). By this, she, in a sense, pays tribute to the Indian contribution to the current paradigm shift in the world missiological discourse and in the formation of TTL. Similarly, **Samuel George** attempts to read Samartha's pneumatology in the pluralistic context of India to propose its missional relevance for India today. He explores Samartha's pneumatology in conjunction with his theology of dialogue. Samuel argues that, for Samartha, inter-religious dialogue takes place in the context of the Spirit that seeks to identify the presence of the Spirit beyond the boundary of the church. Thereby, its missional significance is recognized in learning to practice missions in the spirit of respect for neighbouring religions and faith traditions.

Steven Griffin in his article, "The Holy Spirit and the Church as the Ordinary Means of Salvation," discusses different positions in the Christian theological discussion with regard to the role of the church in extending salvation to the world. Moving beyond Karl Rahner, based on the view of Popes Paul VI, John Paul II, and Benedict XVI, Griffin demonstrates that the church is an ordinary means of salvation to the sinful world by the work of the Holy Spirit. It is the body of those who profess faith in Christ as Lord and remain founded upon the apostolic teachings.

Aruthuckal Varughese John seeks to present Christian "apologetics within a pneumatological framework by envisioning Spirit as a starting point for Christian ministry in general and for evangelism undergirded with apologetics in particular."[4] It is an important step towards a balanced theology of missions as it takes the Spirit (the Third Article) in equal seriousness as God the Father and the Son. It corrects the theological obsession with God the Father (the First Article) and the Son (the Second Article) in the history of western theological engagements, a point stated by both Tennent and Ebenezer in their respective articles in the present volume. In fact, apologetics itself as the product of its spirit of the age repeats the mistake of the Spirit-exorcized enslavement to the modernistic intellectual framework. John views it as evidence to the challenges of contextualization of apologetics. Hence, in order to begin within a context of where the question of the Holy Spirit's significance to the Christian mission is, he pursues to answer the question, "what happens if we intentionally begin our apologetics with the Spirit?"[5] John answers this key question by firmly rooting his argument upon the epistemic role of the Spirit in missions and apologetics. He argues that every bit of the knowledge of God is the Spirit mediated knowledge. The Spirit is an active agent of God-knowledge impartation in every circumstance, then the Spirit shaped apologetics is essentially trinitarian in nature, participating in/with the Spirit, aiming at one's re-birth in Christ, and fulfils both the objective (incarnation) and subjective (personal experience of God) aspects of the Christian faith.

Three important areas of identifying the contextual significance of the Holy Spirit are discussed in the final group of articles. **Paul Swarup** paints a macro picture of a complex and challenging pluralistic context of Christian mission in India. In his effort to identify two pertinent challenges arising out of the complex Indian context (theologically, a challenge to the exclusivistic claims of the church, and, missionally, a misrepresentation of Christian charity as an ill-intended and unethical means of conversion), he discusses in detail the recent emergence of religious fanaticism among some in the majority religious community and the promulgation of anti-conversion laws in various Indian states, the age old oppressive

---

[4] Chapter 11, 204.
[5] Chapter 11, 209.

caste system, the ever increasing threat to Indian secularism, etc. The present deteriorating state, despite the Indian constitutional provision for the freedom of religion, is worrisome. He argues that amidst such a conflicting situation, the helping, empowering, and guiding missional role of the Holy Spirit is important to establish social equality and the affirmation of human dignity of the dehumanized, effective evangelism, and strengthening of the church to withstand instances of persecution while boldly confessing the Lordship of Jesus.

Cyril Kuttiyanikkal, a Roman Catholic priest-theologian, introduces the charismatic outworking of the Holy Spirit in and through the Roman Catholic Christ-devotee movement in Banaras. Based on the characteristic representation of the Holy Spirit as "fire" and "wind," Kuttiyanikkal demonstrates the charisma of the Holy Spirit visible outside the strict western Christianity in the proliferation of the gospel among the Christ-devotees in the rural villages of Banaras. He describes the way the work of the Spirit in and through the church attracts devotees to *Christi/masihi satsang* regularly. Kuttiyanikkal explains in detail how the recognition of the work of the Spirit among the seekers of Christ is a viable option to nurture Christ seekers in their own social locations without causing social uprootedness and social dislocation. In several respects, his contention of the charismatic role of the Holy Spirit in effective mission of the church to produce disciples of Jesus is similar to Shaibu Abraham's contention in an earlier chapter in this volume. Surely, the Roman Catholic Christ-devotee movement, as per Kuttiyanikkal, appears to be much more culturally rooted in the native soil than the Pentecostal missions praxis which, though it has been contextual in approach, was suspicious and resistant to cultural adaptation.

Finally, **Atola Longkumer** reflects upon the activity of the Holy Spirit from an indigenous Naga spirituality perspective. She argues that the Spirit-empowering experiences among the Naga Baptist Christians, especially women, presents the role of the Holy Spirit as a gender equalizer in an ecclesial context that was and is a patriarchal society. The re-invented role of women in Naga spirituality as the Spirit-empowered mediators between God and humans is congruent with the all-embracing missional function of the Spirit who breaks gender stereotypes within the ecclesial context.

To conclude, every chapter in the volume upholds the trinitarian understanding of the Godhead with a firm conviction that the primary task of the church in the world is to be the light to the nations. It is with this conviction that the authors engage in theological-missiological discussion to highlight the need to affirm missional pneumatology beyond denominational boundaries in fulfilling the mission of God in this world and to bear witness to Jesus Christ, the Son of God, as the sole means of salvation to humankind. I hope the varied viewpoints represented in this volume together highlight the need for affirming, practicing, and teaching the role of the Holy Spirit in the mission of the church today in a pluralistic context, lest we continue in our Spirit-blindness forever.

1

THE ANOINTING SPIRIT AND THE SERVANT MISSION OF THE CHURCH

*Christopher J.H. Wright**

The experience of "the anointing" is often popularly connected with powerful Christian ministry. In this paper, however, we trace the language of anointing back to its Old Testament roots, particularly in relation to the mission of the Servant-King, and ask what relevance the anointing of the Holy Spirit has to the mission of Jesus and the mission of the church.

ANOINTING AND THE COMING SERVANT-KING

There are several texts in Isaiah which speak of the future ministry of a coming figure. Among the most prominent and theologically significant of these are: Isaiah 11:1-5; 42:1-7; 61:1-3. It would be good to pause and read all of them at this point. There are at least three things that these great passages all have in common:

1. They all speak of a coming one – sometimes in the language of *kingship* (son of David), coronation and rule; sometimes in terms of a *servant*.

---

* **Christopher J.H. Wright**, PhD, is the International Ministries Director of Langham Partnership. This chapter is taken and adapted from *Knowing the Holy Spirit through the Old Testament* by Christopher J.H. Wright. Copyright (c) 2006 by Christopher J.H. Wright. Used with permission of InterVarsity Press, P.O. Box 1400, Downers Grove, IL 60515, USA. <www.ivpress.com>

2. They all speak of the role of the *Spirit of Yahweh* (the LORD) in relation to that person and the tasks he will carry out. He will manifestly be filled with the power of God's Spirit.

3. They all speak of God achieving his own *mission* or purpose through this Servant-King – this figure who will come. God will accomplish things through this person. He is anointed by God's Spirit for a task that God wants to be done.

Here, then, is clearly an "anointed one" *par excellence*. Like the historical kings of Israel, who were literally and physically anointed with oil, he too will be anointed, but there is a mystery in that his kingship will be unlike most human kings ever known. He will be characterized by the humility and gentleness of a servant. Like the kings, his anointing will symbolize the power and presence of God's Spirit, but in his case there is detailed description of what that will include. And above all, his anointing is essentially his commissioning to carry out God's ultimate mission and purpose for the world – not just for Israel, but "to the ends of the earth."

Now as Christians, we know that this prophetic vision leads ultimately to Jesus Christ, our anointed Servant-King. But before we look at Jesus, we need to put this prophetic picture that points to him in its wider context. We need to see it in the light of the whole sweep of God's mission in the Bible. So, we shall look at the mission of God, the mission of Israel and the mission of the Servant. Only then can we fully understand the mission of Jesus and the mission of church. And of course, we will be linking the role of the Spirit of God to all of these dimensions.

THE MISSION OF GOD

God's purpose for human beings, made in God's own image, was that they should rule the earth (Gen 1:26-28). But if they were to be like God (in his image), then they would exercise that rule through care and service (Gen 2:15). Kingship exercised through servanthood is the very nature of human relationship to creation, as described in Genesis 1-2. This was God's intended pattern for life on earth. That is why God made the earth. That is why God put us in it. That was the creational mission of God.

But we rebelled against God's authority, distrusted God's word, and disobeyed God's commands (Gen 3). As a result we plunged ourselves and the earth into the chaos of sin and evil, violence and corruption, strife and suffering, that we find ourselves in still. The story of the accumulating grip of sin in the human race runs through Genesis 3-11, climaxing in the story of the tower and city of Babel in chapter 11. It is a bleak picture indeed. What hope is there now for the mission of God in creation?

But God decided, not to abandon nor to destroy his creation, but rather to redeem it. So, he called Abraham, and with Abraham we enter the next major phase of the mission of God – God as redeemer.

Genesis 12:1-3 records God's call, command, and promise to Abraham. God promised three things to Abraham: a) that he would have descendants and become a great people; b) that God would bless this people in a special relationship which is later called a covenant; and c) that God would give them a land to live in. These promises provide a framework for the following major sections of the Old Testament story, as bit by bit, God fulfilled them.

But the bottom line of the covenant with Abraham widens the scope of the promise out far beyond Israel as a nation: "through you all nations on the earth will find blessing." The vision is universal. In fact, this promise to Abraham in Genesis 12 is God's answer to the problems posed by human sin in Genesis 3-11. In Genesis 11, we find the nations scattered under God's curse. Now, we hear that God's intention is that the nations should once again be blessed, as the earth and humanity were at creation. So, Abraham is actually a fresh start for the world. This promise is God's great manifesto. This text is God's declaration of his mission, which is nothing less than the blessing of all nations.

So important is this promise to Abraham in the Bible, that Paul actually calls it the gospel. We may have thought that the gospel begins with Matthew, but Paul says it begins in Genesis.

> Consider Abraham: 'He believed God, and it was credited to him as righteousness.' Understand, then, that those who believe are children of Abraham. The Scripture foresaw that God would justify the Gentiles by faith, and announced *the gospel in advance* to Abraham: 'All nations will

be blessed through you.' So, those who have faith are blessed along with Abraham, the man of faith. (Gal 3:6-9, Emphasis added)

The mission of God, then, is to bless all nations on earth. But how? Well, we need the whole of the rest of the Bible to answer that, including of course the New Testament. But the first part of the answer lies in Genesis also – the promise of a people. Out of Abraham's descendants, at first physical, and then also his spiritual seed, God would create a whole community of people, through whom his blessing would come to the nations.

THE MISSION OF ISRAEL

The people of Israel in the Old Testament knew that they had been chosen by God. A chosen people, that is one of their most fundamental beliefs. But they were not chosen for a unique and exclusive privilege that would forever belong to them alone. No, their mission was to fulfil God's mission, by being the vehicle of his blessing to the nations. Or, to use the language of Isaiah, to be a light to the nations, that God's salvation should go to the ends of the earth. Israel in the Old Testament was not chosen *over against* the rest of the nations, but *for the sake of* the rest of the nations.

How was Israel to fulfil this mission? Did it mean that they were supposed to set off on missionary journeys to the other nations? I don't think so. I do not find evidence in the Old Testament itself that God ever intended Israel to *go to* the rest of the nations, during that era. Occasionally, an individual might be sent – as for example Jonah was sent to Nineveh. But on the whole, the mission of Old Testament Israel was a matter of *being* rather than *going*.

So, if Israel were not meant to *go*, but to *be*, what exactly were they to be? Exodus 19:4-6 gives the answer. They were to be a *priestly* people – representing God among the nations, just as their priests represented God among the people, for the sake of blessing them. They were to be *holy*. Being holy fundamentally means being different, or distinctive. God wanted Israel to be a model of how human life ought to be. He wanted Israel to be a society that was visibly, socially, economically, politically and religiously different from the nations around. They would be as different from the other nations in their quality of life as Yahweh, the God of Israel, was different from the gods of the other nations in his moral character. So Israel's mission was to reflect Yahweh their God in the midst of the nations – to be holy as God is holy; to be light, as God is light.

In practical terms, this sense of Israel's distinctiveness – of being a contrasting society to the other nations - was expressed often in their law. Read, for example, Leviticus 18:1-3; 19:2; and Deuteronomy 4:6-8.

Sadly, however, we know that the whole history of Israel, as it is told in the great history books of Joshua, Judges, Samuel and Kings, is one of disobedience, rebellion and failure. In fact, Israel simply replicates the story of the fall of humanity. The story of Israel is a recapitulation of the story of Genesis 1-11. Blessing, promise and command, followed by sin and rebellion. Perhaps we should not be very surprised. Israel was God's chosen people, but they were as much part of the sinful human race as the rest of the world.

So, the history of Israel finally ran into the buffers of God's judgment, and into the sands of exile. The northern kingdom of Israel was destroyed by Assyria and the people scattered in 721 BC. And in 587 BC, Nebuchadnezzar came down on Jerusalem with his Babylonian armies. The city was besieged and destroyed after terrible suffering. The temple was burnt down, and the king was carried off into exile along with most of the population of Judah. And all the prophets of the time interpreted these events clearly as the judgment of God.

So, was it 'The End'? Was their history at a full stop? Had Israel finally stepped off the stage into the graveyard of oblivion, never to rise again? Many in Israel thought so, and sank into despair. But not God. Certainly, it was the end for that generation, but it was not the end of God's covenant promise to his people as a whole. And it was certainly not the end of God's mission to bless the nations through this people.

The great prophecies that we sampled earlier from Isaiah were addressed to the exiles, and they spoke of *hope beyond judgment*. The time of God's punishment would end, and the word would be "Comfort, comfort my people, says your God" (Isa 40:1). Israel was still God's servant, still called and chosen in Abraham, still intended to be for the blessing of "all flesh" who would ultimately see God's glory (Isa 41:8-10).

So, there would be a future for God's people. God's mission for Israel would still go on. God's promise to Abraham was not dead. The nations will still be blessed.

But the massive question was, how could Israel fulfill such a mission now, given their situation? In exile, Israel was a *failed* servant. They were disabled and disqualified by their sin and rebellion. They were historically paralyzed. This is the utterly realistic assessment of their condition. The same prophet's dire description of Israel in exile is devastating - they are blind, deaf, plundered, looted, trapped, and imprisoned (Isa 42:18-22). How could their mission ever be fulfilled? Enter the Servant of the Lord.

THE MISSION OF GOD'S SERVANT

And so, in that context of Israel as God's *failing* servant, God announces a new beginning, a new arrival – one who would come and embody that mission of Israel by taking it on himself. He is announced as "my Servant," or "the Servant of the LORD." The Servant of the LORD, in Isaiah, would have a mission *to* Israel – to restore Israel again to God – and would also embody the mission *of* Israel by bringing God's blessing to the nations. This was a task that only the unique Servant of the LORD could accomplish.

So, we need to look carefully at this Servant figure in the prophecies of Isaiah, this anointed Servant of the LORD. For this Servant is said to be endowed with God's Spirit. So by looking closely at him, we will see the work of the Spirit at its most profound and transforming.

He is introduced as an individual (as distinct from the reference to Israel as God's servant in Isa 41:8) for the first time in Isaiah 42:1-7. (It would be worth reading that passage carefully at this point).

Immediately we are reminded that he will have the Spirit of God upon him, in order to carry out the mission entrusted to him. So, the anointing power of Yahweh's Spirit, which readers of this prophecy would have associated with the power of God in the lives of the judges and kings like David, will be the hallmark of this Servant. Whatever the Servant does, it will really be God doing it through him. Whatever mission the Servant has, he has received from God. Whatever the Servant will accomplish, God will be accomplishing through him. That is the point of being anointed with God's Spirit. It is a commitment and commissioning to do the will and purpose of God. Many of the historically anointed judges and kings of Israel lost the plot of their own anointing and went off to do their own thing, with disastrous results. *This* anointed Servant, however, will be the perfectly obedient one. By the Spirit of God, *he* will fully accomplish what God intends. So what is that?

There are four main dimensions to the Spirit-filled mission of the Servant that we can see in Isaiah 42:1-7. We can only summarize them here.

- *Justice (vv. 1, 3, and 4)*

    This is the most repeated word in the passage – it occurs three times. The mission of the Servant is, above all, a mission to bring justice. In Old Testament terms, to do justice means putting things right. It includes putting an end to situations that are unfair, situations of exploitation and violence, and restoring those who are the victims of such behavior. It includes what we mean when we speak of "human rights." God says that the work of his Servant will ultimately bring about these things for the nations. So, the mission of the Servant is very much in the public arena and ultimately international in scope. It is not just a matter of putting people right with God, or even only of putting things right for Israel. The text speaks rather of a comprehensive and universal achievement of God's justice on earth.

- *Compassion (vv. 2-3)*

    Verses 2 and 3 stand in sharp contrast to what has been said about Cyrus, the king who would conquer and crush nations beneath his feet (in chapter 41). The Servant will be equally effective, but without noise and violence. His will be justice with gentleness, strength with compassion. He will be filled with *my* Spirit, promises the LORD, so he will share the LORD's tenderness for the weak and vulnerable. The Servant's mission will be successful, but not coercive. His method will not be to solve the problem of the weak and poor by eliminating and crushing the people themselves, but by restoring them in compassionate justice.

- *Enlightenment (v. 7)*

  The Servant will bring light and sight to the eyes of those in darkness and blindness. In the immediate context, this was a word of hope for Israel, who were "blind" and in the darkness of exile. But in the wider horizon of this Servant's global mission, it must include bringing enlightenment to all who live in the darkness of sin without the light of the revelation of God's saving love.

- *Liberation (v. 7)*

  Again, this would originally have brought joy to the exiles, to know that their Babylonian prison would finally be opened to set them free. But it is the language used of God's liberating intention for human beings in all forms of oppression and bondage, not least to the sin and rebellion that lies at the root of all human suffering.

All of these were important and resonant words for the exiles, to whom the prophet's words were first addressed. But the scope of the Servant's Spirit-filled mission, we are told, goes beyond Israel to the nations. The Servant will bring the blessing of God's justice *to the nations* – which echoes the Abrahamic mission of Israel itself.

So, in Isaiah 49:1-6, the Servant speaks and addresses the nations in his own right. Notice the important transition that takes place between verse 5 and verse 6. The Servant's mission is to restore Israel to God. But, God says, that is not all. That is not nearly enough. In addition to his mission to Israel, God's long range purpose for his Servant is to bring God's salvation *to the ends of the earth!* So, the Servant, then, has a mission *to Israel*. And yet, he also embodies the mission *of Israel*, by being commissioned to take the blessing of God's salvation to the nations.

But this mission of the Servant will be costly. Isaiah 49 speaks of the Servant's frustration and struggle. The next time the Servant speaks, it is to describe his experience of rejection, contempt and physical abuse (Isa 50:6). And the climactic Servant passage, Isaiah 52:13–53:12 describes how the Servant will suffer a travesty of justice in which he is finally executed with great violence. Yet through that death, as a self-sacrifice, God's saving purpose will be accomplished. For God will lay on his Servant the sin of us all, and by his death he will enable many to be counted righteous. The Servant, says our prophet, *will accomplish* all God's purpose; but it will be at the cost of his own life. Yet through paying that ultimate price, the Servant will experience victory and vindication from God, and finally be glorified.

Finally, in Isaiah 61:1-2, the Servant speaks again, in language that echoes our first passage (Isa 42). "Here I am," he says. "This is what I came to do. *This is what the Spirit of the LORD has anointed me to do.*"

Notice again the same claim to the anointing of the Spirit of God. And notice again the same multi-tasking description of the Servant's mission. And of course, notice how this passage brings us very close to our next step – namely to Jesus himself taking these words on his own lips, in a synagogue in Nazareth one Sabbath morning.

But just before we jump across the centuries to Jesus, let's pause to look back over our voyage of discovery so far. We have seen the *mission of God* – which is to bless all nations on earth. We have seen the *mission of Israel* – which was to be the vehicle of that blessing to the nations, as promised to Abraham. But in the context of Israel's historical failure, we have seen the *mission of the Servant of the LORD*– a dual mission of restoring Israel and also bringing justice, compassion, enlightenment and liberation to the ends of the earth. All this was prophesied with Israel still in exile.

Well, the exile came to an end in 538 BC. Or did it? Yes, many Jews (though by no means all) returned from Babylon to Judah, rebuilt Jerusalem, and eventually the temple also. But the centuries passed, and Israel seemed to be still under the heel of foreign oppressors – initially the Persians, then the Greeks, and finally the Romans. In heart and spirit they felt like exiles even in their own land. They felt unforgiven, unliberated, oppressed and in captivity. And so they continued to long for deliverance, for true liberation. They took up these prophecies again, knowing that of course they had been partially fulfilled in the remarkable release from Babylon and return to their own land, and yet knowing also that they spoke of something greater and more magnificent yet to come. They longed for the One who would come and achieve all that God had promised. They longed for the Anointed One, the one on whom God's Spirit would rest, the one who would bring in the longed-for age of God's unhindered rule and the end of the domination of their enemies.

ANOINTING AND THE MISSION OF JESUS CHRIST

And so it was, then, that on a Sabbath morning, in a dusty synagogue in Nazareth, in the backwaters of despised Galilee, a thirty year old local villager took his turn to read from the scroll of the prophets. Jesus read these words that we have since numbered and labelled as Isaiah 61:1-2. Then he sat down. That was the customary posture for explaining the scriptures. The people would have expected Jesus to speak again about their longings that some day, may be even the next day, God would keep that promise and the anointed one would come to rescue them.

But Jesus shatters that weary assumption with words that must have electrified them all. "Today," he quietly begins, "TODAY! this scripture is being fulfilled! Right here among you, as you listen to *me*...!" (Luke 4:16-21, Emphasis added).

Jesus claims the prophetic text as his own. Jesus makes himself the embodied sermon. Jesus makes the mission of God, the mission of Israel, and the mission of the Servant his own mission. As the astonished people listen, the emphatic scriptural word "*me*" in the text of Isaiah has now become the living voice of one of their own young adults from their own town in their own synagogue. Jesus ben-Joseph, son of the village carpenter, dares to claim, "the Spirit of the LORD is upon *me*; the LORD has anointed *me*."

Through this text, Jesus sets out the manifesto of his own mission. Through this text Jesus answers in advance the questions that became more and more insistent as his ministry gathered pace. "Who are you? What do you think you are doing? Why do you feel compelled to act in this way? Why are you no longer minding your own business in your father's carpenter's shop? What is the power by which you do these things?" And Jesus answers: "I have been anointed by no less than the

Spirit of the LORD God himself, and this text sets out the contours of the mission of God that I am to fulfil."

But if Jesus is the one anointed by the Spirit of God, what should we expect to find in his life and ministry? We find exactly those same four key marks of the anointed Servant of the LORD, marks that were spelled out in the Old Testament, and we find them all combined also in the ministry of Jesus.

There was *justice*. That was implicit in his announcement of the reign of God, which all Jesus' contemporaries knew from their Scriptures would bring God's justice to the world. Justice would mean God putting things right, and that is what Jesus went about doing in his personal relationships and teaching. It did not happen in the form of a violent revolution such as some of his supporters wanted. And it did not happen all at once, for the kingdom of God is like a seed growing secretly, or like yeast slowly permeating the dough. But it was a key element in what he taught his disciples to seek. "Blessed are those who hunger and thirst for justice," he said. "Seek first the kingdom of God and his justice" (Matt 5:6; 6:33).

There was *compassion*. Jesus sought out all those whom society rejected and marginalized, and ministered especially to them: the sick, women, children, the morally and politically compromised (prostitutes and tax-collectors), Gentiles, "sinners." He even gained a reputation for such behavior. "Friend of sinners," they called him. They meant it as an insult but Jesus took it as a compliment for it summarized exactly why he came.

There was *enlightenment*. Teaching, teaching, always teaching – that's the picture of Jesus we see in the gospels. Jesus certainly opened the eyes of the physically blind, but on an even greater scale he opened the eyes of the spiritually blind to the truth about God, about sin, judgment and forgiveness, about himself and the significance of his coming in relation to the story of Israel, about how life was to be lived by those who submitted to the reign of God.

There was *liberation*. Jesus went about delivering people: from sickness, from the chains of paralysis; from the burden of sin; from the loneliness of ritual exclusion; from demonic oppression; from the prison of remorse. And of course, as he put it himself, he came ultimately to give his life "as a ransom for many," thus achieving ultimate liberation – forgiveness and salvation for sinners.

But the Gospels show us that Jesus not only fulfilled the *mission* of the Servant in the power of the Spirit, he also accepted the *destiny* of the Servant, as prophesied in Isaiah. And that was to suffer rejection, contempt, unjust trial and bloody execution. And in doing all this, he took upon himself the deepest cause of all injustice, cruelty, blindness and bondage – namely our sinful rebellion against God. So, Jesus went to the cross, and the cross was the cost of all those dimensions of God's mission as itemized in the mission of the Servant.

And Jesus was raised from the dead! As Isaiah 53 had promised, God did not abandon his Servant, but glorified him and enabled him to see the fruit of his suffering. In Christ's death and resurrection, the mission of God was accomplished. "It is finished!"

ANOINTING AND THE MISSION OF THE CHURCH

So, at last, we come to our final step. We are those who claim to follow Jesus. We claim to be filled with the same Holy Spirit. And these are not arrogant claims, for they stand upon clear New Testament statements and promises. But if so, what kind of effect should the presence of the Holy Spirit have in our lives and ministry?

To put it more simply, what is *"the anointing"*? This is a phrase that is much used in some Christian circles. In itself it is a curious abbreviation and easily misunderstood. We ought to talk more fully of "the anointing of the Holy Spirit," since the word "the anointing," when it is used on its own these days, sometimes seems to mean little more than a powerful personality, or a particularly aggressive way of speaking and ministering. As applied to preachers, in some Christian cultures, it seems to be equated with plenty of noise. The greater the volume of shouting, the more proof there is that the preacher has "the anointing." But that seems a long way from the anointing of the Servant of the Lord, for whom the proof of the Spirit of God was precisely the opposite. He would achieve his mission very effectively but he would not "shout or cry out or raise his voice in the streets." In Uganda, during a Langham preaching seminar there, I preached several expositions of the Bible as models that were then evaluated by the participants. One participant's written comment is my favorite. "I could feel the sweet flow of the Spirit without noising up." This encouraged me, not only to be reminded that I didn't have to shout and jump around just to prove the Holy Spirit was speaking through the message, but also that this brother had realized (as an apparent surprise to him!) that "the anointing" is not a matter of decibels.

No, anointing by the Spirit, we have now clearly seen from the Bible, is not primarily an external thing that proves its presence by noise (though, of course, the Spirit of God can make a great deal of noise on occasion, as on the day of Pentecost). Rather, *spiritual anointing is primarily an equipping for mission, a commissioning for service*. Anointing by God's Spirit is what enables people to do what God wants to get done. And for us, who follow Jesus, anointing is enabling us to do what the scriptures have shown so clearly that God wants to get done. Mission for us has to be *mission in Christ's way*, and that means following the pattern of Spirit-filled servanthood that characterized him.

Now of course Jesus was unique. His life was unique. He was *the* Servant of the LORD – the only perfectly obedient one. His death was unique, for he was the only perfect embodiment of the living God in a human life – the unique God-man. And so he alone could take our sin upon himself in such a way that "God was in Christ reconciling the world to himself." Nobody else ever has done, ever could do, or ever needs to do, what Jesus alone has done as the Son and Servant of the living God in the power of God's Spirit. In all these ways Jesus uniquely and perfectly fulfilled the mission of God for the salvation of the world.

Yes, but in another sense, Jesus passed on that mission of God to his disciples. The risen Jesus commanded his disciples to replicate themselves by spreading communities of obedient discipleship throughout all the nations (Matt 28:18-20). For that task he specifically empowers them by the Holy Spirit (Luke 24:45):

> [Y]ou will receive power when the Holy Spirit comes on you; and you will be my witnesses in Jerusalem, and in all Judea and Samaria, and to the ends of the earth. (Acts 1:8)

So, Jesus entrusts to us a participation in the mission of God (to bless the nations of humanity), the mission of Israel (to be a light to the nations and the agent of blessing), the mission of the Servant (to bring salvation to the ends of the earth), and his own mission (that repentance and forgiveness of sins should be preached in his name – Luke 24:47). The church is now the inheritor and agent of all these dimensions of the great biblical mission – and especially the servant mission. And for all those dimensions we need the anointing of the Holy Spirit.

This is how Paul saw his own mission. He was called to be the apostle to the nations (Gentiles), but in that task Paul saw simply the continuation of the mission of God's anointed Servant. In Acts 13:47, he explicitly quotes the Isaiah texts and applies that servant task and responsibility to himself and his small band of church-planting missionaries.

So, in line with Paul, we need to see that the mission of the Spirit-anointed Servant to the nations becomes ours too. We too need to be committed to the same broad and holistic mission as the Servant of Isaiah 42, Isaiah 61 and Luke 4. For it is clear that in his own earthly lifetime Jesus himself did not "complete" the tasks of bringing justice, enlightenment and liberation to the ends of the earth. These same tasks are ours. And they call for the same combination of all dimensions of ministry - of spiritual and physical, personal and social, historical and eternal - as they did in Christ's own ministry. For it is in *all* of these areas that the central good news of the gospel of the kingdom of God is to be heard, applied, trusted, obeyed, and lived out.

Historically the church has indeed seen its mission in these broad terms. It is not a matter of engaging in *both* the gospel *and* social action, as if Christian social action was something separate from the gospel itself. The gospel itself has to be demonstrated in word and deed. Biblically, the gospel includes the totality of all that is good news from God for all that is bad news in human life – in every sphere. So, like Jesus, authentic Christian mission has included good news for the poor, compassion for the sick and suffering, justice for the oppressed, liberation for the enslaved, and forgiveness for the sinner. The gospel of the Servant of God in the power of the Spirit of God addresses every area of human need and every area that has been broken and twisted by sin and evil. And the heart of the gospel, in all of these areas, is the cross and resurrection of Christ.

What then is anointed mission? If it is anointed by the Spirit of God, then it will be mission that reflects the one who quoted the Old Testament and said, "The Spirit of the Lord is upon me, because the Lord has anointed me…." Filled with the Holy Spirit (as Luke stresses often), Jesus ate and drank with the poor and the marginalized, fed the hungry, talked with children, taught the crowds, comforted the bereaved, restored the ostracized, released the demon-oppressed, challenged the rich and the authorities, brought people forgiveness of sins, healed relationships as well as bodies, and in all of this declared that *God reigns* – here and now, and still to come. And all of this was part of *his* anointed mission.

"The Spirit of the Lord is upon *me*," he said, "for the Lord has anointed *me*…." Yes, but he also said, "As the Father has sent me, I am sending *you*." And with that he breathed on them and said, "Receive the Holy Spirit" (John 20:21-22, Emphasis added).

Mission in the way of Christ, then, is mission that is empowered by the anointing Spirit of God, committed to the justice and compassion of God, characterized by the Servant of God, including even suffering and the way of the cross. Before we pray (for ourselves or others) for the anointing of the Spirit, perhaps it would be good to remind ourselves what the Bible says that will mean.

2

THE SPIRIT AND MISSION IN EPHESIANS

*Idicheria Ninan**

Ephesians is one of the less consulted letters in the scholarly discussion of Paul's theology, let alone his theology of missions in it. The primary reason for this neglect is its disputed authorship. Further, the document is allegedly more inward looking than focused on the world at large, zooming in on the community's identity, and moral formation than reaching the world with the gospel.[1] This essay argues otherwise: *That the construction of identity and moral formation precisely constitutes the missional significance of Ephesians.* While Paul's authorship of the letter is not central to the argument, the essay positions itself with Paul's authorship,[2] and the

---

* **Idicheria Ninan**, PhD, is Professor of New Testament at SAIACS, Bangalore, where he is also the Head of Department. He was the founding Principal of IPC Kottayam Theological Seminary, Kottayam, Kerala. He has written a commentary on *Ephesians* in *South Asia Bible Commentary*.

[1] According to MacDonald, "Ephesians reveals a stronger introversionist sectarian response than other Pauline epistles including Colossians." Margaret Y. MacDonald, *Colossians and Ephesians*, Sacra Pagina, vol. 17 (Collegeville, Minnesota: Liturgical Press, 2008), 21.

[2] The idea that majority or 80 per cent of modern scholars argue for non-Pauline authorship, as suggested by L.J. Kreitzer, *Hierapolis in the Heavens* (London: T&T Clark, 2007), 1-9, is a gross overstatement. For a more nuanced view of Pauline authorship see H.W. Hoehner, *Ephesians: An Exegetical Commentary* (Grand Rapids, MI: Baker Academic, 2002), 2-61. See also P.T. O'Brien, *The Letter to Ephesians*, PNTC (Grand Rapids, MI: William B. Eerdmans, 1999), 4-47; A. Kuruvilla, *Ephesians* (Bangalore: SAIACS Press, 2015), 9-13.

Lycus valley churches as recipients, with a potential to be treated as the letter to the Laodiceans.[3]

I.H. Marshall in a short article argued for the missional interest of Ephesians, beyond the lone voice of 6:15.[4] Likewise, Max Turner saw the missional flavour of the letter in its appeal for unity along with ethical instructions.[5] I will, similarly, argue that Ephesians offers a *Messianic and Spiritual* redefinition of the people of God from the vantage of the new covenant.[6] The resultant multi-ethnic Messiah-Spirit people share together with Israel both the status and the responsibilities of the covenant people of God. This eschatological vision of God's family on earth enjoins the shaping of commensurate behavioural patterns in the second half of the letter. Such a refashioning of ecclesiology and ethics on the template of redemptive history points to an inbuilt missional stance despite the absence of formulations like the great commission in Matthew 28:18-20.[7] Both the missional existence and praxis of the eschatological people of God may be actualised only by the empowerment of the Spirit. We will journey through the two halves of the letter, summarising the main themes in the letter and draw out the missional implications of each section.

THE MISSION OF GOD IN THE NARRATIVE SECTION (EPH 1-3)

Majority of scholars have approached Ephesians 1-3 primarily as a discussion of individual and corporate dimensions of soteriology. I shall go on to show that the soteriological themes are built on a salvation

---

[3] That it addresses Laodicea or Hierapolis, see A.T. Lincoln, *Ephesians*, WBC, vol. 42 (Dallas: Word Books, 1990), lxxxii. For Hierapolis, Kreitzer, *Hierapolis in the Heavens*.

[4] I.H. Marshall, "Who were the Evangelists" in Jostein Adna and Hans Kvalbein (eds), *Mission of the Early Church to Jews and Gentiles*, WUNT, 127 (Tubingen: Mohr Siebeck, 2000), 251-263.

[5] Max Turner, "Mission and Meaning in Terms of 'Unity' in Ephesians" in Antony Billington (ed), *Mission and Meaning: Essays Presented to Peter Cotterell* (Carlisle: Paternoster, 1995), 138-166.

[6] Cf. Christopher J.H. Wright, *Knowing the Holy Spirit through the Old Testament* (Downers Grove, IL: InterVarsity Press, 2006), 87-120.

[7] Stephen Bevens, "The Church as Creation of the Spirit: Unpacking a Missionary Image," *Missiology: An International Review* 35/1 (2007), 5-21, argues for the role of the Spirit in the formation and equipment of the church to be a church that highlights the missional function of the Spirit. In his discussion, Ephesians gets two marginal references (4:11; 3:8), although much of what he wishes to highlight can be derived from a study of Ephesians!

historical frame shaped by eschatology, ie, from the vantage point of the messianic events and the outpouring of the promised Holy Spirit.[8] Paul weaves a cosmic plan of redemption pulling out the threads of the Israelite story of the covenant (her faith and hope) with the Messiah and the Spirit as the agents of God's saving acts. [9] This narrative declaration (1:3-2:22) climaxes in an autobiographical reflection on Paul the prisoner's unique calling to be an apostle (3:1-13). The section ends with his apostolic prayer for the church (3:14-21).[10] In as much as Ephesians narrates the triune God's saving story, ie, *missio Dei*, it invites the church to participate in God's mission by becoming what they are called to be.

THE MISSIONAL NUANCES OF *BERAKAH* (1:1-14)

The Ephesian narrative is woven with the same threads that would be employed in a tapestry of Israel's story and mission. First, the readers are addressed as both saints (*hagiooi*) and faithful (*pistoi*) in the Messiah Jesus (1:1,15,18; 3:8; 4:12). This is clearly drawing upon description of Israel, called to be a holy nation and charged to be faithful (Exod 19:6; Lev 11:44; 19:2 cf. 1 Pet 1:16; 2:9).[11] Similarly, the letter ends by referring to the recipients as "all who love our Lord Jesus Christ with an undying love" (6:24) as a community which shares in grace, peace, and love showered by God (6:23-24). One may make an initial comment that Ephesians from the start to finish has a new covenant perspective.

---

[8] Michael J. Gorman, *The Apostle of the Crucified Lord: A Theological Introduction to Paul and His Letters* (Grand Rapids, MI: William B. Eerdmans, 2004), 504. For him, "Ephesians, then, announces the story of this cosmic salvation of God in Christ known in the church."

[9] Commentators have rightly noted the rich Old Testament ideas that explain the various "liturgical," theological terms that denote the people of God. Similarities between the Qumran Literature have also been explored. The passage has been of interest in addition to liturgical, sacramental ideas and discussions on pre-destination. Missing the story of Israel and her eschatology in these discussions tend to be a mistake, as if Paul had relinquished his Jewish faith for an entirely new idea of the church, which ransacked the treasures of Israelite scriptures to define itself as a super-sessionist entity! Cf. Lincoln, *Ephesians*, lxiv. Hoehner, *Ephesians*, 54, disputes Lincoln's claim because Paul does not discuss the case of unbelieving Israel of the future of Israel in Ephesians as in Romans.

[10] Hoehner, *Ephesians*, 62, 65, thinks that 3:1-13 is a parenthetical expansion of the mystery, added to the theological section of God's plan of spiritual blessings. The narrative reading proposed here makes this piece quite central to interpreting Ephesians.

[11] T.G. Gombis, *The Drama of Ephesians: Participating in the Triumph of God* (Downers Grove, IL: InterVarsity Press Academic, 2010), 77-81, seems to find an analogy with Israel as the people of God and the purpose of creation and redemption to be the image of God.

The long and convoluted sentence in Greek (1:3-14) is a *berakah* prayer that praises God by enumerating his blessings on the readers drawn from diverse ethnicities.[12] The list of *Spirit enabled* blessings includes election (1:4; Deut 14:2), adoption to sonship (1:5; 1 Cor 2:7; Rom 8:15, 23, 29-30; 9:4; Gal 4:4-7), redemption (1:7; Exod 6:6; Deut 13:6; 15:15; 24:18; Isa 51:11; Dan 4:34) which is the forgiveness of sins, the revelation of the plan and will of God (1:9), the Messiah as the point of integration of the whole of creation (1:10), the status of the people of God as God's own inheritance (1:11; Deut 32:8-9; 4:20; 9:29; Ps 33:12), the sealing with the promised Holy Spirit and the "yet-to-be" realised but guaranteed hope of future inheritance (1:14). This list overlaps significantly with the themes of Romans 9:4-5 where Paul argues for the legitimacy of covenantal history in the light of the Messiah's mission.[13] Israel's covenantal blessings are now disbursed through the messiah Jesus (1:3-14).[14]

The covenantal blessings of Israel as listed above originally established her unique identity as the people of the one true God. Ephesians points to a universal distribution of Israel's privileged status through the agency of the Messiah and the Spirit. The Messiah's agency is highlighted almost thirteen times in the one long sentence. God's eternal plan was to sum up all things in heaven and earth under one head, that of the Messiah (1:10). In him, the promises to Israel flourish as Gentiles participate in the status and responsibility of Israel through the promised Holy Spirit. The present sharing in the Spirit points to both the "already" and the "yet-to-be" realised aspects of soteriology; the Messiah and the Spirit have inaugurated the grand finale of God's saving acts which still awaits the "yet-to-be" manifested Messianic climax (1:14, 18; 4:4, 13-16, 30; 5:6; 6:6-8).

---

[12] See the use of 1st and 2nd person pronouns here and in chapter 2:1-10, and the Jew-Gentile issue from 2:11 onwards.

[13] An exclamatory praise of God ends the narration of the unique privileges of Israel in Romans 9:5 whereas it begins the list of spiritual blessings in Ephesians 1:3-14. While there is some confusion on the recipient of the eulogy whether it is addressed to the Messiah or God in Romans, in Ephesians, God the Father of our Lord Jesus, the Messiah, is the one who is blessed.

[14] For a titular function of Christ and not merely as a colourless surname see Hoehner, *Ephesians*, 143-144; N.T. Wright, *Paul and the Faithfulness of God* (Minneapolis: Fortress Press, 2013), 817-825.

The very suggestion of an eternal plan culminating in the Messiah and the Spirit through the formation of a people of God as the Messiah-Spirit people, with a future "yet-to-be" enacted, is more than a catena of blessings or soteriological concepts. It is the construction of the identity of the beneficiaries with reference to the new covenant. These appropriations of Israelite faith and hope ought not to be torn away from Israel's story of redemption, ie, from the call of Abraham, Israel's covenantal status as God's family, the hoped for renewal of the covenant through the Spirit, and the eschatological restoration of Israel climaxing in the reconciliation of the world.[15] The Messiah-Spirit people are incorporated into God's redemptive story as it climaxes in the gospel.[16] The underlying meta-narrative that shapes the identity of the Messiah-Spirit people points to *missio Dei*.[17]

This narrative construction of identity has liturgical, didactic, and missional effects. The eschatological people of God have one

---

[15] Most commentaries note the structure of the long passage and the Old Testament background of the concepts. However, they fail to see the story of the covenant as the template of the presentation. Cf. M.Y. MacDonald, *Colossians, Ephesians*, 196-214; C.E. Arnold, *Ephesians*, ZECNT (Grand Rapids, MI: Zondervan, 2010), 76-97; Kuruvilla, *Ephesians*, 20-37. Cf. his recommended sermon outline especially in pages 36-37. Pheme Perkins, *Ephesians*, ANTC (Nashville: Abingdon Press, 1997), 44, finds a "linguistic and metaphoric parallel with the OT." And the surprise spring of 2:11-12 with the Jew-Gentile issue, and the scheme of integration in 2:13-3:13 fails to get its interpretative key. When read in the way proposed here, Paul will be seen not spinning out a theology of salvation using words and concepts from his former Bible, but reimagining his heritage and hopes in the light of the Messiah and his apocalyptic experiences. Cf. Wright, *Paul and the Faithfulness of God*, 609-1268.

[16] E. Best, *A Critical and Exegetical Commentary on Ephesians* (Edinburgh: T&T Clark, 1998), 198, recognises a story line in 2:1-3:13 about how the Gentiles are drawn into the people of God. O'Brien, *Ephesians*, occasionally uses the word salvation history, and richly draws on Jewish sources to explain the text. However, he argues for a salvation historical pattern in both Galatians and Ephesians, elsewhere. See P.T. O'Brien, *Gospel and Mission in the Writings of Paul: An Exegetical and Theological Analysis* (Grand Rapids: Baker Academic, 1993), 1-19. With reference to 1:4-23, most commentators rarely see the story as developed here because they tend to focus on the time frame of eternity to eternity and soteriological enumeration with the church in focus. Gombis, *Drama of Ephesians*, 74-77, while suggesting a historical narration for the people of God to inspire both the sense of identity and behaviour, fails to see a re-imagination of the Israelite story here. I think, N.T. Wright stands out as the exception in seeing the template of Israel and her covenant story, her faith and hopes as reshaped by Paul under the light of the sudden *apocalypse* of the Messiah and the experience of the Spirit.

[17] Christopher J.H. Wright, *Mission of God: Unlocking the Bible's Grand Narrative* (Downers Grove: InterVarsity Press, 2006), 60-62.

primary function, to be the praise of the glory of God (1:6, 12, 14).[18] Their composition is an act of the triune God, ie, with God the Father as the chief actor; the Messiah as chief agent, all the acts of blessings are spiritual in the heavenly places. God in his goodness, grace, faithfulness, wisdom, and love leads the world to flourish as his own inheritance, his children, and his people.[19] The Holy Spirit guarantees the future security of the redeemed.[20] The trinitarian act that culminates in the formation of a unique people showcases *missio Dei*. It is not human efforts but the work of God.[21] It is not at the expense of the church as it shows the formation of God's people.

God's praises articulated here serve a paradigmatic role for shaping the praise-prayers of the early church. Its declaration in worship and catechism while shaping the reader's identity as the member of a unique community promotes a missional orientation for the community.[22] Doxological existence is a missional existence (Ps 105:1-3). Just as Israel's eschatological restoration sought to make her a people with a mission (Isa 43:19-21), this community formed in the Messiah will be a missional community as they declare the praises of God. They are both holy and blameless as a sacrificial animal is (Exod 29:37; Num 6:14; 19:2).

---

[18] O'Brien, *Ephesians*, 116-117, recognises in passing a salvation historical scheme here, where the reclamation of Israel as the inheritance of God is the fulfilment of the song of Moses (Deut 32:8-9). However, he does not go on to develop the implications of restoration eschatology here.

[19] Gombis, *Drama of Ephesians*, 67-70, finds the worship of the church leading to a missional existence. "The church is the gathered people of God who assemble to gain strength and who then wander out into the world to do good, to radiate the life and blessing of Jesus Christ in practical ways"(70). However, his apocalyptic focus, fails to see the meta-narrative that would have fired Paul's pre-Christian existence, and how his conventional world is re-imagined by the Christ event, not to throw the baby out with the bath water!

[20] Lincoln, *Ephesians*, 39. For a theological structure of the passage see Kuruvilla, *Ephesians*, 20-37.

[21] David J. Bosch, *Transforming Mission: Paradigm Shifts in Theology of Mission* (Maryknoll: Orbis Books, 1991), 390-391; Wright, *Mission of God*, 62-64.

[22] Gombis, *Drama of Ephesians*, 1-33, prefers a narrative reading of Ephesians, as more transformational than the traditional patterns which he calls as "a wandering discussion of various theological and doctrinal matters…to construct abstract theologies of the church and its relationship to Christ" (30). He chooses instead to read Ephesians 6:10-20 and the theme of the triumph of Christ as a story of God's triumph against the backdrop of Old Testament war imageries, "Ephesians then, is a drama, portraying the victory of God in Christ over the dark powers that rule this present evil age, and the letter becomes a script for how God's people can continue, by the power of the Spirit, to perform the drama called the triumph of God in Christ" (19).

This blamelessness points forward to the purity gifted to the bride of the Messiah in 5:26 and a relational identity as a bride dedicated to the Messiah. Then again, the community is suggestively engaged in a priestly function just as Aaronic priesthood is to be blameless (Lev 21:16-24). They have become the eschatological kingdom of priests or the royal priesthood. Their induction as God's special people who will receive the Spirit's apocalyptic education (1:17-19) locates them within the missional ambit of the holy apostles and prophets who likewise are privileged to receive special revelation and mandated to proclaim the secret of God to all of creation (3:1-13).[23]

MISSIONAL ECHOES OF THE PRAYER REPORT (1:15-23)

The introductory prayer report (1:15-23) summarises the recipients' identity as those characterised by their faith in the Lord Messiah and love for all the holy ones (1:14).[24] The prayer is addressed to the Father of the Lord Jesus Christ for the donation of the *Holy Spirit* as the tutor of the church (1:17).[25] The primary learning object is the identity of God and what God's call through the gospel offers the church: The hope of the call, the deep estimation of the identity of church as God's own inheritance, and an appreciation of God's great power (1:18-19). These prayer concerns once again revolve around the covenant status of the people formed through the gospel and their privileges, patterned after God's relation to Israel, his promises to Israel, his estimation of Israel, and his revelation of himself as supremely powerful.[26] The prayer, in addition, is studded with the jewels of the new covenant: The trinitarian description and experience of God, the gift of the Holy Spirit, the universal knowledge of God, and the future that is guaranteed in the new covenant. So, they should not have an "other" to compete with their allegiance to the redeemer God.[27]

---

[23] See fn 8 and section on 3:1-13.

[24] Gorman, *Apostle of the Crucified Lord*, 507, finds a reference to the reader's covenant faithfulness in the words faith and love.

[25] For a similar reading of the Spirit as the Holy Spirit see O'Brien, *Ephesians*, 132. The prayer for the gift of Spirit shows the ongoing function of the Spirit.

[26] Even while emphasising Israel as God's inheritance (Deut 9:29; 2 Sam 21:3; 1 Kgs 8:51, 53; 2 Kgs 21:14; Isa 47:6), Arnold, *Ephesians*, 108, fails to see the suggested salvation historical continuity leading to the new covenant. There seems to be a scholarly pattern of christological hijacking of Israel's texts and heritage, which Paul seems to be correcting in Romans 9-11!

[27] Wright, *Mission of God*, 76-77, argues that knowing God is to know him as unique and sovereign (Exod 6:7; Deut 4:32-35).

Chris Wright, developing the theme of knowing God in Israelite history, brings out its missional focus in the following words:

> (T)hrough their major historical experiences of YHWH's grace in redemption and deliverance, Israel believed that they had come to know him as the one and only true and living God. ... Furthermore, they had a *sense of stewardship of this knowledge since it was God's purpose that ultimately all nations would come to know the name, the glory, and the salvation and mighty acts of YHWH and worship him alone as God.*[28]

From 1:20-23, there is a Messianic explanation of the power of God, manifested supremely in the resurrection of the Messiah, his exaltation as the most exalted and powerful, his conquest of all, and his appointment as the head of the church which is his body. Just as the eulogy of 1:3-14, the prayer report has declarative, didactic, and missional functions. It proclaims the kingdom of the Messiah, his resurrection from the dead, and his appointment as the legitimate *ruler of the universe* (1:20-22). The saints identified as the church or the people of God are his body (1:23), his very physical presence on earth and in heaven! Using the words of Psalm 8, all things are subjected to the Messiah. Thus, the creation of humanity as the image of God with a regal function (Gen1:26-28), as recounted in Psalm 8:4-6, is established in the messianic kingdom (cf. Ps 110:1).[29] MacDonald draws attention to similar ideas in Daniel 7 and the saints of the most high participating in the reign of the "one like a son of man."[30] The people of the Messiah, as the very body of the Messiah, share in his cosmic dominion.[31] This is indeed the missional engagement of the church through her being and becoming what she is made to be.[32]

Clinton Arnold's position that the author of Ephesians pastorally addresses the threat of magical practices and witchcraft that were widely

---

[28] Wright, *Mission of God*, 92, (Emphasis added).

[29] Gombis, *Drama of Ephesians*, 85-90, points to the story of the triumph of God shaping the narrative from 1:20 to 2:22.

[30] MacDonald, *Ephesians*, 224-225; Perkins, *Ephesians*, 49-50, posits Daniel 7:13-27 as the key informant to such Christological development.

[31] See Wright, *Paul and the Faithfulness of God*, for an elaborate development of the theme of Adam, Israel, Messiah along the grid of image, royal-priesthood, and the redefinition of the people of God.

[32] The christocentric-ecclesiological missiology is to be noted here as sharing in the dominion of Christ. Thus, *missio Dei* may not be bifurcated as the kingdom of God and the ecclesial routes, but it is integral in the Messiah who is the head of the body, the church.

practised in the Greco-Roman society, particularly in Asia Minor, has received critical acceptance from most commentators.[33] That being one of the reasons behind the composition of Ephesians, the good news of the appointment of Christ above all other powers and authority (1:20-21) is not to be hushed-up within the confines of the house churches. It is meant to be published. Even if it were an intentional whisper, its political nuances would have taken it beyond the confines of the community.[34] As in the eulogy of 1:1-14, here also, there is confession, proclamation, and affirmation of the church as God's special people, the very physical presence of the exalted Messiah. Arnold goes on to suggest that "the church is filled by Christ and is thus the fullness of Christ; as head of Spirit-filled church, Christ is engaging in a mission to 'fill all things, things on earth and things in heaven.'"[35] The church participates in *missio Dei* through the proclamation of the gospel, by sharing in the reign of Christ, by offering exclusive worship to the God revealed in the gospel, by its absolute dependence on him as the primary benefactor, its growth in every place, and transformation resulting from being filled with Christ.[36]

THE MISSIONAL IMPLICATIONS OF THE COMMUNITY OF RESURRECTION (2:1-10)

Ephesians 2:1-3 gives an extremely negative description of humanity outside Christ. The state of alienation from God places human beings as objects of divine wrath (2:3). This is a spirituality marked by slavery to powers that are in opposition to God. Human existence is described as dead in sin, walking in worldly ways of carnality, covetousness and disobedience (2:1-3). Reflections of Eden (Gen 3) and the exile of the covenant people in Babylon (Ezek 36) present the state of alienation from God as living in death. However, God's inalienable character as manifested in the covenant with Israel (Exod 34:6-7) shows itself in

---

[33] C.E. Arnold, *Ephesians Power and Magic: The Concept of Power in Ephesians in the Light of its Historical Setting* (Cambridge: Cambridge University Press, 1989).

[34] See Te-Li Lau, *The Politics of Peace: Ephesians, Dio Chrysostom and the Confucian Four Books* (Leiden: Brill, 2010), 76-156, for an elaborate development of the political nuances of Ephesians.

[35] Arnold, *Ephesians*, 119.

[36] Arnold, *Ephesians*, 119. See also 506-507 where he applies this to 4:11 and refers to the ongoing mission of the church in 6:17. He also suggests Paul's pattern in 3:2, 8 as an example for the church to replicate.

the divine embrace of love, mercy, and grace (2:4, 5, and 7-8), offered to one and all through the Messiah. Israel's covenant God manifests his power (1:20) to give life to the dead (2:5). Three compound verbs—*to make alive together with, to be raised together with, and to be seated together with* Jesus the Messiah (2:5-6)—explain the plan of reconciliation stated in 1:10. Messianic reconciliation is both life to the dead and restoration from exile. It creates the community of resurrection. This new creation in the Messiah is an act of God with no human contribution that can claim to be a co-agent (2:10). Salvation is entirely by divine grace and it is appropriated by humans through faith, not by good works. However, they are saved for the sake of good works. Salvation is participation in the life and resurrection of the Messiah!

What is the missional intent of this soteriology? In as much as it proclaims the gospel of the Messiah with allusion to Genesis 3 and the exile in Ezekiel 36-37, it builds on the narrative framework of 1:3-14 as reaching a critical goal point. The community of resurrection arising out of it, from both Jewish and non-Jewish backgrounds, gets embedded in the story of Israel to share in the missional implications of the creation of Israel. The good works prepared beforehand for those incorporated into Christ primarily points to the display of God's character: The affluence of mercy, greatness of love, and the superabundance of grace. God demonstrates his own identity through the display of his character (2:7), bestowed on the people who participate in the story of the crucified and risen Messiah. Redemption leads to the reclamation of the image of God (Gen 1:26-28). Israel is appointed to be God's special people, a kingdom of royal priesthood (Exod 19:4-6) and the servant of YHWH (Isa 43:7, 21). Similarly, the gracious, merciful, and loving work of God in the Messiah (2:4-9) mandates the redeemed to reveal God. The community is formed for the very purpose of revealing the character of God (2:7). The gross weight of good works (2:10), ie, the demand of a transformed lifestyle issuing from new creation, includes both worship and witness in making God known as his representatives.[37]

---

[37] See the contrasting use of "walk" in the former and present state, and the repetition of walk metaphor for conduct in chapters 4-5.

MacDonald, drawing from social scientific studies on sectarian religious movements, considers Ephesians to be addressing an introversionist sectarian pattern.[38] The soteriology of such groups developed from an extreme negative view of the outside world and that salvation is found only by the membership of the sect. According to MacDonald, this points to a withdrawal from engaging the world. However, early Christianity did not withdraw into ghetto communities. Even if a qualified version of the introversionist model is true to the recipients,[39] sectarian identity is embedded with a passion to recruit new members—for there is no salvation outside that community. The purpose of demonstrating God's character will require of the sect both showcasing it (see below on chapters 4-6) as well as making it known by enlightening those outside the community.

THE MISSIONAL MANDATE OF *PAX CHRISTI* (2:11-22)

The earlier discussion (1:20-2:10) showcased the greatness of God's power working for the benefit of those who believe in two dimensions—the inauguration of the messianic kingdom through the resurrection and exaltation of Jesus (1:2-23), and the inauguration of the new covenant through the resurrection of the Messiah in which believers participate (2:1-10). In this section, the theme is developed in far more corporate terms to show how the messianic era in reconciling all things in heaven and earth (1:10) brings forth a new integrated humanity (2:15). Humanity lives in alienation with one another, a fact symbolised by the religio-social segregation between Jews and Gentiles. From their covenantal standing as the unique people of the true and living God (Exod 19:4-6; Ps 80:8-9; 105), non-Jews are excluded from the community and the promises of God to the community. Outside the covenant there was no scope of salvation and there is no experience of the true God (2:12).[40] The author exposes his soteriological template without any grain of doubt. The celebration of salvation leading to the reconciliation of God and the universe in 1:1-2:10 gains clarity within the grid of the Abrahamic plan of salvation inherited

---

[38] MacDonald, *Ephesians*, 236-240.
[39] MacDonald, *Ephesians*, 236.
[40] Perkins, *Ephesians*, 67, hears the echoes of Romans 9:4-5, stated in negative terms, with reference to those outside the covenant with Israel. See above for a similar suggestion while discussing on 1:3-14.

by Israel. However, Israel's hoped-for Messiah was not considered to be the redeemer of the alien nations in as much as he, the vindicator of Israel, would be their judge. Israel was special and had a distinctive task as God's firstborn bearing the sign of circumcision (2:11). The law of God fenced God's people by giving them their covenantal identity and demarcating those who are inside from those who are outside (2:14).

The advent of the Messiah has made a radical restructuring of such a concept of the people of God. The specific Jewish laws of identity that demarcated them as unique and excluded others have now been pulled down. The unification of all things in heaven and earth under one head, the Messiah, has destroyed the wall of separation (2:14-15). A new humanity is created, by integrating those who were far off and those who were near (2:13, 16), by the one Messiah, who proclaims the gospel of peace (2:17; cf. Isa 52:7). His death was for the specific purpose of integrating humanity as one new entity, as the people of God, thus witnessing both the reconciliation between God and mortals, as well as among mortals (2:15, 18). The messianic proclamation of peace is less of an appeal to which people ought to give their consent than the proclamation of an objective truth—the messianic peace—*Pax Christi*. Unlike *Pax Romana*, the gospel's *Pax Christi* does not subjugate one segment of humanity to another.[41] It is a new humanity where all are integrated as fellow citizens sharing equal status (2:19).[42]

The challenge here is not only to the imperial ideology of Rome but also to the vision of the eschatological pilgrimage of the nations to Israel (Isa 66:18-20 cf. 2:1-5; 56:6-8; 57:19).[43] The Messiah makes a new humanity which is the fulfilment of the covenant promises of God and

---

[41] Arnold, *Ephesians*, 158, denies that there is an intentional contrast between *Pax Romana* and *Pax Christi*. However, through the rubric of the kingdom of God and Messianic reign that looms so large from 1:20-23, it is hard to deny that an ancient reader would have missed the echoes of an anti-imperial polemic here.

[42] D.K. Darko, *No Longer Living as the Gentiles: Differentiation and Shared Values in Ephesians 4:17-6:9* (New York: T&T Clark, 2008), 109-116, lists most of the themes suggested above, and yet denies the prevalence of a salvation historical scheme here. The affluence of the Old Testament themes (faith and hope of Israel) is theologically appropriated in the Messiah and the Spirit to the new humanity.

[43] The juxtaposition of themes like the reign of God, restoration of Israel, the blessing of the nations, the making of the eschatological people out of the dregs of the society leading to the new temple point to restoration eschatology. See B.F. Meyer, *The Aims of Jesus* (London: SCM, 1979), 170-173, 221.

yet something radically new.[44] The nations are gathered in a state of equality with Israel.[45] The body metaphor makes the Messiah the head and all the rest his body (1:23; 4:1-16); there is no Israelite hegemony in the eschatological fulfilment of God's promises.

There is universal and uniform access for all to the presence of God (2:18). This is the covenantal privilege of the priesthood of God's people. There is a democratisation of the notion of royal priesthood pointing away from the hierarchical restrictions of access drawn from ethnicity, tribe, gender, physical disability, conditions of health, or even states of physical purity and impurity.[46] The democratised priesthood denotes both the privileges of personal intimacy and the collective responsibility of the new humanity to represent God to the world and *vice versa*. That is a missional challenge. *This access is in the one Spirit, and the priestly function of the church is a function of the Spirit.*

This egalitarian sect of new creation shares the same relation with the most high God, as his family, his household, his temple, and his residence (2:19-22). The building metaphor of the people of God repudiates the claims of other residences of God on earth (2:21-22).[47] Since the building is growing and not yet completed, there is the idea of addition of members.[48] The presence of God with those who share in *Pax Christi* is not localised in Jerusalem. Gentiles who once did not

---

[44] Arnold, *Ephesians*, 177-178, notes a new covenant theme in 2:11-22. However, it is more of an abrogation of the old covenant (*Ephesians*, 201, with reference to 3:1-13) than is shown in this essay. Perkins, *Ephesians*, 76-78, emphasises that the new people of God do not become a sect within Judaism. The apocalyptic newness in the letter establishes a continuity with the God of the Old Testament, its scriptures, for the new people created under the Messiah, comprising of both Jews and non-Jews. I think the new-covenant pattern shows greater continuity while accounting for the discontinuity, because fundamental newness of this entity was a divine mystery (3:1-13).

[45] For a discussion of the conversion of Gentiles in the restoration of Israel, particularly in Isaiah and the Second Temple Jewish literature, see James P. Ware, *Paul and the Mission of the Church: Philippians in Ancient Jewish Context* (Grand Rapids, MI: Baker Academic, 2011), 57-162.

[46] S. Bevans, "The Church as the Creation of the Spirit: Unpacking a Missionary Image," *Missiology* 35/1 (2007), 18, notes the post Vatican II effect of the formation of "lay ecclesial ministers" in the pyramidal form of structure of Roman Catholic hierarchy. Currently, 80 per cent of such lay ministers are women!

[47] The temple in Jerusalem is the *katoikaeterion* of God (1 Kgs 8:39, 43, 49) which is now the new people of God.

[48] Best, *Ephesians*, 287.

have access to the temple in Jerusalem are now the temple along with the Jews who like them are incorporated in the Messiah, the Lord.[49] In this universalised vision of the temple, God is present as the Spirit, at all times, in all seasons and everywhere the community of God exists. *As the house of God, the community which is signified by the presence of the Spirit becomes a centre of pilgrimage for all nations. Israel's centripetal mission is nuanced with reference to the community of the Spirit.* In addition to this, the metaphor of the church as a building which is still growing clearly endorses a mission to those outside the community. *The Spirit as the central player in both the priestly role of the people of God as well as the presence of God in the Christian gathering becomes the Spirit of mission.*

MISSION AS THE PUBLICATION OF THE MESSIANIC SECRET (3:1-21)

Mission for Paul meant suffering for the glory of the church just as the Messiah suffered for the church (3:1, 13). His appointment as an apostle to the Gentiles was specifically to publish the messianic secret (3:1-2). The messianic secret (3:4) is not about the strangeness of a crucified and risen Messiah (as suggested in the synoptic gospels), but rather about the Messiah people or the new covenant family of God (3:6; 2:11-22): *Gentiles will enter the realm of God's grace on the same terms as that of Israelites.*[50] The incorporation of non-Israelites into the total plan of God is *to share together with Israel* in the promises of God (3:6). The threesome effect of *syn* compounds here (*synklaeronoma, syssooma,* and *symmetocha*) is similar to the threesome pattern of 2:19-22 (*sympolitai, synarmologoumenae, synoikodomeisthe*).[51] Together they are incorporated into the crucified and risen messiah. The resultant Jew-Gentile messianic community is a new entity, and not the one incorporated into historic Israel or the synagogue. Here, salvation history reaches its climax in the blessing of the nations

---

[49] Gombis, *Drama of Ephesians*, 85-106, develops the narrative, however, as an apocalyptic version alone. He refers to the paradigmatic story of Israel to challenge the church's stance towards uncompromising holiness (160-162).

[50] The option between "faith in Jesus" and the "faithfulness of Jesus" does not affect the equality of the criterion that constitutes the people of God. It is God's act, and people share in it by faith.

[51] Attempts to justify the construction of a social identity using an ideological framework, enabling the community to discover their solidarity and difference with the world fails to read the strong promptings of continuity and discontinuity suggested by the deliberately profuse employment of the "together with" verbs in chapters 2 and 3 as shown above. Darko, *No Longer*, 123-128.

through their incorporation: *Isaac and Ishmael, Jacob and Esau, Joseph and the other patriarchs are reconciled in the Messiah.* [52]

Such formation of a new humanity was a carefully guarded secret in the creator God (3:9) which is now apocalyptically revealed. It could not be the outcome of the exegetical exercise of a rabbinic school or even a messianic *midrashic* reading of the old covenant.[53] It has to be a special revelation of God's Spirit to those graced to be apostles and prophets, the bearers of the gospel of the Messiah (3:2, 5, 7, 8). Paul's commission to *evangelise* the Gentiles with the inscrutable riches of the Messiah, and *to bring to light* the administration of God's secret plan to everyone,[54] recalls the mandate of the servant of God in Isaiah. The churches that emerge from the publication of the *messianic secret* will need to share the same mandate of the servant of God in Isaiah. Ministry as a gift of grace (3:2, 7-8) and as the function of the exceeding power of God (3:7b) requires the loyal discharge of the stewardship of the mandate (*oikonomia* 3:2) to make known to every generation the wisdom and secret that God has entrusted to the church. Such continuity is a litmus test of both the church's apostolic and prophetic foundation as well as orientation (2:20; 3:5)! [55]

The apostles publish the triumph of God through the gospel; humanity is no more under the "powers" who have been defeated. The powers are subjugated to the dominion of the exalted Messiah. Rescued humanity shares in the kingdom (1:20-23; 2:1-3, 4 -10) of the Messiah and his life through the Spirit. The church as social reality embodies the message that it witnesses, ie, the proclamation of the gospel as a demonstration piece. Hence, the church is "both a *sign* and an *instrument* of the intimate union with God and the unity of all humanity."[56] This proclamation

---

[52] A.J. Kostenberger and P.T. O'Brien, *Salvation to the Ends of the Earth: A Biblical Theology of Mission* (Downers Grove, IL: IVP, 2001), 166-167.

[53] "It was neither insight into the OT nor a brain wave on his part which led him to see that the Gospel must include Gentiles." Best, *Ephesians,* 300.

54 Turner, "Mission," 146, suggests that "to bring to light" suggests conversion in Acts 26:17-18; 2 Corinthians 4:4-6; 1 Thessalonians 5:4-5; Ephesians 5:8-14 and that this is an ongoing process.

[55] The Pauline pattern of forming communities around him and their task of learning by imitation was similar to methods of philosophical schools. Paul would thus become a model missionary too. See Kostenberger and O'Brien, *Salvation,* 194-195.

[56] Vatican II as summarised by Bevens, "The Church as Creation of the Spirit," 7.

through the demonstration of God's new humanity, affects not only those who are still outside the benefits of the gospel but even the powers that held humanity in the bondage of immorality and alienation from God (3:10; 2:1-3).[57] Their hold over humanity is dismantled by the victorious Messiah and his victory needs to be published and demonstrated.

Paul repeats the universal access of the royal priesthood to the very presence of God without gender or ethnic differences (3:12). Access to God is with this confidence that an "audience with God will not be denied."[58] This messianic integration into the one family of God of all things in heaven and earth (1:10), as the kingdom of priests, issues itself into a prayer that far surpasses all human imagination.[59] The missional mandate to bear his image and fill the earth as given to Adam (Gen 1:26-28; Ps 8) now becomes a prayer for the church. The locus of God's glory in a humanity refashioned as God's glory bearing images is in the Messiah and in the church for all generations to come (3:21). The glory that descended in the Exodus wanderings, in the tabernacle, and the temple of Solomon is now transposed universally to the body of Christ as the people of God. The messianic glorification of the church takes place, as God supplies beyond the wildest imaginations of the human mind (3:20) inner strength through the Spirit with the Messiah living at the very core of their existence (3:17). A community established in the love of God (3:3, 17-19) is filled with all the fullness of God (3:19). The construction of a new humanity flourishing in divine character and empowered by the Spirit is the means to fill the earth with the knowledge and presence of God. Paul further unpacks the missional implications of communities of character in chapters 4 to 6 as discussed below.

MISSION MANDATE OF THE NEW CREATION (4:1-6:20)

Having constructed the identity of the Messiah people, Paul goes on to highlight their God given responsibility, denoted as walking (4:1, 17, 22;

---

[57] See Michael Gorman, *Becoming the Gospel: Paul, Participation and Mission* (Grand Rapids, MI: William B. Eerdmans, 2015), 181-211, chapter 6 for similar development of the missional implications of Ephesians. Gorman points out that Paul embodies the gospel as he suffers for it, just as the church embodies the reconciled community of peace through the gospel.

[58] Best, *Ephesians*, 322.

[59] O'Brien, *Ephesians*, 58-65, argues that unity of the people of God is the central theme of Ephesians. The whole letter may be seen as an interpretation of 1:9-10.

5:2, 8, 15). "Walking implies involvement in the world—mission—not existence in an isolated holy huddle. The church, Paul says, is to be a place of peace and unity sustained by inner, centripetal practices that embody the gospel (4:1-6:9) and external, centrifugal practices that proclaim the gospel (6:10-22). These two sets of missional practices, of course, are not unrelated but overlapping."[60] I shall proceed to highlight these missional practices in Ephesians as empowered by the Spirit.

MISSION THROUGH THE UNITY OF THE SPIRIT AND A GROWING BODY (4:1-16)

Having established the wisdom of God as the messianic summation of all things (1:10), visibly manifested in the new covenant community comprising of Jews and Gentiles (2:11-3:13), it is not surprising that the primary responsibility of the church is to maintain the unity of the Spirit in peaceful union.[61] If *Pax Romana* is held by the might of Rome's military and metal, the unity of the Spirit or *Pax Christi* is to be guarded by the moral transformation of the people who participate in the Messiah's humanity and by sharing in the virtues (4:2) that reflect the image of God (4:20-24). Paul enumerates the essential factors of the unity in theological and ecclesiological terms—there is only one God, one Lord, one Spirit, one body, one faith, one baptism, and one hope to which all are called (4:4-6).

The metaphor of the one body is explained with reference to the diversity of ministerial gifts (4:7-11), the call for every member of the body to be equipped for *ministry (diakonia),* and the resulting growth of the body into maturity (4:12-16). The development of the body to maturity is facilitated by its inter-connectedness, corporate engagement, and absolute surrender to the one head who is the Messiah. The mark of maturity is the Messiah's fullness (4:13) referring back to the prayer of 3:14-21.[62] The

---

[60] Gorman, *Becoming the Gospel*, 196.
[61] See Turner, "*Mission,*" 138-166.
[62] Brian S. Rosner, "The Glory of God in Paul's Missionary Theology and Practice" in Brian S. Rosner (ed), *Paul as Missionary: Identity, Activity and Practice* (London: T&T Clark, 2011), 158-168. Rosner finds a pattern of ethical teaching related to the glory of God in 1 Thessalonians, Ephesians, Colossians, and Titus, shared with the principal letters.

body will engage itself in the performance[63] and proclamation of truth, exercising discernment of all types and variations of error and deception. It is intricately wired and linked to remain united to the head with every part and cell contributing to the growth of the body.

The metaphor of a growing body points to both the transformation of those already incorporated as well as the ingathering of those who are outside the body. When read in the light of what was already said about the body in 1:22-23, the notion of Christ as the one who fills all things in all places with the ever expanding gospel community, the church, as his body cannot be discounted. Further, within the rhetorical flow, the challenges of the passages such as maintaining the unity of the body, its protection against deceptive philosophies, engagement in truth, and the release of all gifts for the facilitation of every part to be active point to a missional exercise of love—the propagation of truth. The apostles, prophets, evangelists, and pastor teachers are all ministers of the word and witnesses to the truth of the gospel.[64] They proclaim and teach the truth.

The *sitz-im-leben* of the gifts of ministry is the missional existence of the church in the world. Christian synagogues and basilicas will need to wait for the dawn of the first quarter of the fourth century.[65] Prior to Constantine's patronage, gatherings for corporate worship refers to house fellowships, where relatives, friends and inquisitive seekers may walk-in-at-will. Both Paul (1 Cor 14:23-24) and James (James 2:1-9) point to casual visitors in a Christian gathering, just as the several meal settings in the gospels point to a walk-in-at-will to hear the discourses. The tenement workshop space would have been the evangelistic, pastoral,

---

[63] Gombis, *Drama of Ephesians*, 133-153, discusses this role of gifted ministers as directors and coaches, who empower the church for the performance of truth that is subversive. This is missional existence.

[64] See Marshall, "*Who were the Evangelists*," 251-263.

[65] "Unless claims for recent discoveries of early Christian meeting places are confirmed, the earliest building certainly devoted to Christian use is at Dura Europos on the Euphrates River in eastern Roman Syria. It was a house that came into Christian possession and was remodelled in the 240s. Two rooms were combined to form the assembly room, and another room became a baptistery—the only room decorated with pictures. Dura was destroyed by the Sassanian Persians in 256, so the house's use as a church was short-lived". E. Fergusson, "Why and when did Christians start building special buildings for worship," *Christian History* (November, 2008). www.christianhistory.net (accessed 5 January, 2017).

and catechetical settings of Paul as an apostle. The saints of Pauline churches engaged in the world did not seek withdrawal into cloistered communities. Therefore, the practice of truth with the discernment of error (4:14) and careful avoidance of human deceptions make sense in the humdrum of daily existence. This witness is possible because the risen Christ has equipped the church through his ministers, and the body of Christ participates in the virtues of the fruit of the Spirit. The ongoing work of the risen Christ is the work of the Spirit as clarified in 1 Corinthians 12-14, and Romans 12 by Paul himself.

Mission as the Witness of a Jesus Shaped Morality

The primary witness of the new creation is through the unity of the church as argued above. Further, the new creation humanity in Christ is made known through the construction of moral communities that are countercultural. This is because reconciliation to God leads to a sharing in the life of God (4:17-19). Jesus becomes the moral template of the new creation (4:20). This unique way of referring to the moral education of the church in all likelihood points to something like the imitation of Jesus, the hallmark for Christian morality (4:21). The former ways of thinking are to be renounced (4:22) for a renewal to take place in the way a Christian thinks. It is possible to attribute this renewal to the Holy Spirit (4:23). The new creation beings are to be clothed with the new identity that is patterned after God and created in righteousness, and true holiness (4:24). In a similar treatment of the clothing imagery in Colossians (3:10), the new man according to God is expressly the image of God explained as the virtues of godliness (Col 3:12-15). Bearing the image of God or living lives that are constructed in imitation of Jesus is a missional witness of the new creation. It is enabled by the Spirit and engages the function of the image of God or the royal priesthood of the holy nation of God. Gombis qualifies such missional morality as engagement in divine warfare against the powers that have corrupted and misguided humanity into moral decay (2:1-3; 4:17-19).[66]

The community patterned after the image of the creator God needs to shed off vices such as falsehood, stealing, anger of various shades, destructive speech, slander, and bitterness (4:25-31). These negative

---

[66] Gombis, *Drama of Ephesians*, 160.

patterns of conduct destroy the unity of the community. Persistence in such old patterns grieves the Holy Spirit by whom they are sealed for the day of redemption (4:30). Thus, unlike Israel of old, the renewed people of God should walk in step with the Spirit and not hurt or grieve him (Isa 63:10). The Spirit guaranteed hope of future redemption inspires the renewed people of God to imitate God as his children. God's kindness, forbearance, and forgiveness (see 4:2, 32 cf. 2:4-7) revealed in his covenant with Israel and now supremely manifested in the Christ event ought to be reflected by the image of God. The sealing with the Spirit for future redemption in other words refers to their adoption to the family of God. As God's children, they are to imitate God (5:1) and live their lives as loving sacrifices as shown by Jesus, the Son of God (5:1-2). The messianic shape of community love does not keep those outside away from its reach. The *agape*-love of God shown to both Jews and Gentiles (1:4; 2:4) now becomes the character trait of the community, both to those in and those who are still outside the community. This is both witness and representation of God through a lifestyle that befits the covenant community—the saints, the people of God, the image of God—the royal priesthood.

The covenant community ought not to live like those who worship idols and are led by passions that corrupt (2:1-3; 4:17-19 cf. 5:3-7). Such conduct leads to the wrath of God (2:3; 5:6). Therefore, they ought not to be shareholders in the lifestyle of the children of wrath, since now they are partakers of the promises in the Messiah (3:6; 5:7).[67] They who were once in darkness have now become light in the Lord (5:8). They ought to walk in the light (5:8) bearing fruit in all forms of goodness, righteousness, and truth (5:9) which are virtues that recall the image of God in 4:24. Their transformed minds enable them to discern what pleases God (5:10) and to expose the deeds of darkness (5:11-14). The metaphor of light combines both the conduct and the function of making truth known through being, advocacy, service and apologetic engagement. The appointment of Israel as the light to the nations is appropriated to the messianic family of God. There is a wake-up call (5:14) which summarises the light metaphor with Christ shining on the ones who come out of stupor.

---

[67] These are the only two uses of *summetchos* in the New Testament. Gorman correctly points out that this does not lead to an insulation from the world but a missional engagement similar to 1 Corinthians 5:9-11. Gorman, *Becoming the Gospel*, 196.

MISSION AS LIFE IN THE SPIRIT

The ones on whom Christ shines, they wake up to lead wise conduct (5:15-17). Their lives are controlled by the Spirit and not by other intoxicants (5:18). Spirit controlled people worship God gladly and gratefully, and communicate graciously with each other being submissive to one another. Such influence of the Spirit dominates individual character formation and social formation by regulating the household (5:21-6:9). The transformed household flourishes when Christian virtues such as respect and love for one another and submission to each other determine interpersonal dynamics. The template of family life is the exchange of Christ's love for one another (5:25-30). Children ought to obey their parents and parents should not provoke their children to exasperation (6:1-4). Slave masters likewise need to behave differently from those in darkness (6:5-9).

A family unit built on the love of Christ and controlled by the Spirit is a powerful witness as a miniature of the universal body of Christ (5:31-32). The *paterfamilias* does not rule supreme as if he were an emperor of the tiny kingdom of his family. His life is to be regulated by monogamy,[68] loyalty, respect, and love of the spouse for whose welfare he ought to genuinely imitate the Messiah. The monogamous family is counter cultural to the Roman practice of legal wives, concubines, and keeping pleasure girls. The *paterfamilias* may not treat children the way others do as if they were insignificant or can be exposed. They are to be nourished (*ektrephete*) and brought up as accountable to God (6:4). The slave owning *paterfamilias* is not a supreme master—he himself is a slave to God and will be held accountable. This radical restructuring of the Asian social unit intends to make it a demonstration piece of humanity as shaped by the Messiah and the Spirit. Rather than social acquiescence to existing norms, there is a transformational engagement with culture. The counter-cultural pattern of the messianic household is itself a missional existence.[69] When the family ideology shaped by messianic model and praxis is read in the

---

[68] This is strongly suggested by the following: i) the allusion to Genesis 2:24; ii) the use of one flesh in other places as a prevention against all forms of extra marital sexual engagement (1 Cor 6:16); and iii) the mystery of marriage as denoting the Messiah and his people for there is one Lord and one body (Eph 1:23; 4:4)!

[69] Darko, *No Longer*, 71-108, argues against the theory of cultural acquiescence for social integration to the outside world. He argues for shared values with the rest of society which is regulated by the identity of the people which is unique, as members of the larger *ecclesia*.

light of imperial system of the emperor as the *paterfamilias* of the empire, the counter-cultural stance of the messianic household code shines forth.

Mission as the Eschatological Struggle of the Royal Priesthood (6:10-20)

The corporate witness of the church is now presented as a struggle against evil forces (6:12) from whose dominion they have been delivered as they participate in the reign of Christ (2:4-6).[70] Missional engagement is presented as a conflict that requires the church to be clothed with the gospel as wearing the armour of God (6:13 cf. Isa 11:5; 57:7; 59:17).[71] The various pieces of the armour are—belt of truth, breastplate of righteousness, shield of faith, helmet of salvation, the sword of the Spirit which is the Word of God, and the preparedness to share the gospel as shoes. Each piece points to the gospel. The *messianic* soldier is clothed with the gospel! The struggle takes various postures. The primary challenge is to make a stand (used 3 times in 6:13-14).[72] Covered with the armour of the gospel, the offensive weapon is the Word of God, which is the sword of the Spirit. Prayer in the Spirit also becomes a means of attack (6:18-19). Prayer becomes missional intercession for all the saints and the ministry of the apostles.[73] The readiness to share the gospel, therefore, is a corporate witness of the church not only to those within their local combat area but also far beyond where the apostles are engaged in the same mission.[74]

One engages in the conflict with the power and strength of the Lord (6:10). Power points back to the resurrection and exaltation of the Messiah as the ruler of all (1:18-23) and the formation of the church as sharing in the risen Messiah (2:4-6). It is God's power that causes apostolic ministry to flourish (3:7). The Holy Spirit deposits this power in the believer's heart (3:16). In short, sharing in the kingdom of God

---

[70] For the identity of the enemy as spiritual forces, see Best, *Ephesians*, 593. Several others may see here a reference to political or socio-economic structures. The spiritual nature of the latter should prevent an either/ or reading.

[71] Gombis, *Drama of Ephesians*, 158, refers to Isaiah 59:15-19 and the church becomes the warrior of God.

[72] Best, *Ephesians*, 591.

[73] Best, *Ephesians*, 608, finds a veiled reference to spread the gospel in the use of making known (1:9; 3:4; 6:19).

[74] See Eckhard J. Schnabel, *Paul the Missionary: Realities, Strategies, Methods* (Downers Grove, IL: InterVarsity Press, 2008), 145-149.

by faith and the experience of the Spirit equips the church for missional engagement. It challenges the legitimacy of all meta-narratives that rival the gospel of the Messiah's true kingdom. Mission is not the onus of specialist officers of the church, as it is the mandate of the whole royal priesthood. In the words of Gorman:

> [W]hen we put this passage in conversation with its chief sources, or inter texts, namely Is 11:5; 59:17 and 52:7, we are pressed to conclude that peacemaking is more than obeying or even imitating God. It is in a profound sense, wearing God, putting God on, dressing in God's attributes, all understood Christologically…it is participating in the very life of God who makes peace in and through Christ…when we embody and thus become the gospel of peace. Such embodiment will be proactive and will involve movement…the Gospel must not be *taken to* the world but *walked into* the world, incarnationally, we might say. [75]

In conclusion, the missional role of the eschatological community of God underlines its identity and the ethical life empowered by the Spirit. Paul, in Ephesians, redefines the identity of the people of God as a multiethnic Messiah-Spirit people from the new covenant perspective that itself implies an all-inclusive mission beyond the Jewish ethnic boundaries based on the redemptive historical template. Such a missional engagement of the eschatological people of God is to be realised only by the empowerment of the Spirit. Hence, for Paul, the missional mandate in chapters 1-3 is attached to the very existence or identity of the community. It is nuanced in *berakah*, the prayer report, its existence as a community of resurrection, the *Pax Christi*, and the announcement of the messianic secret. In other words, the *trinitarian missio Dei* works out God's plan to reconcile all things in heaven and earth in the Messiah (1:10), by his faithful fulfilment of the promise to Abraham to bless all the families of the earth (Gen 12:3) in the Messiah-Spirit family of God. The making of this order of humanity as the temple of God and as the royal priesthood, is the refashioning of humanity in the image of God, with direct access to him, filled with his fullness, as the body of Christ and indwelt by the Spirit. These concepts bring together multiple missional nuances, of both *missio Dei* and the mission of the church, of both centripetal and centrifugal dimensions of witness. The unifying activity of the Spirit and

---

[75] Gorman, *Becoming the Gospel*, 206.

the showcasing of the "single family of God" embodied in the multi-racial ecclesial communities lead to an expansion of the church. The moral identity of this family of God develops counter culturally in the Jesus-model, enacted in lives controlled by the Spirit. The multi-faceted walk of the church in the power of God is its missional engagement while participating in authentic humanity shaped by the Messiah and Spirit. The community's firm stance in the truth of the gospel engages all forms of evil, corporate and behavioural, in prayerful resistance along with authentic witness to the plan and purposes of God. Thus, in Ephesians, the re-visioning of God's eschatological community is, through and through, missional in purpose.

3

HOLY SPIRIT AND CHRISTIAN MISSION IN A RELIGIOUS PLURALISTIC CONTEXT

Timothy C. Tennent*

THREE KEY QUESTIONS

There are several questions which this chapter seeks to answer. First, what role does the Holy Spirit play in the life and ministry of the early church? An examination of this question will help to demonstrate the growing prominence of the Holy Spirit in the life and experience of the church after Pentecost. Second, we must explore in what way the apostolic church as portrayed in Acts is intended to be a model for the church today. Does Acts function *descriptively*, giving us an accurate historical record of what happened, without necessarily saying that the practice and experience of the first century is what it should be in the twenty first century? Or, does Acts function *prescriptively*, giving us a positive model for the church of all times, cultures and ages to emulate. If it is the former, then the church in the book of Acts is more like a "seed" out of which the twenty first century church grows and, looking back, it may be difficult to see the

---

* **Timothy C. Tennent**, PhD, is President and Professor of World Christianity, Asbury Theological Seminary, Kentucky, USA. He has authored several important articles and books. His important publications include, *Theology in the Context of World Christianity: How the Global Church is Influencing the Way We Think about and Discuss Theology* (Grand Rapids, MI: Zondervan, 2007), and more recently, *Invitation to World Missions: A Trinitarian Missiology for the Twenty-first Century* (Grand Rapids: Kergel Academic, 2010).

continuity between the "acorn" of the apostolic church and the "oak" of today. If it is the latter, then the church in the book of Acts is more like a "blueprint" which the contemporary church should emulate and follow as closely as possible. Finally, what particular role does the third person of the Trinity play in the unfolding of the *missio Dei* and fulfilling God's promise to Abraham? All of these questions will also be examined within the context of contemporary pluralism.

THE HOLY SPIRIT IN THE LIFE AND EXPERIENCE OF THE EARLY CHURCH

In the contemporary Protestant churches, salvation has often become privatized, which gives the church a mere *instrumental* role, effectively conceding that the gospel story was completed at the cross and resurrection. Pluralism also tends to see the church in instrumental terms. From this perspective, the church's role – and therefore the work of missions – is, at best, merely to look back and tell the world what happened at the cross and resurrection. In a more pluralistic context, it becomes merely a metaphor for secular social engagement. Of course, the cross and resurrection must always remain central to the church's proclamation.[1] However, it is important to recognize that the gospel does not stop at the cross and resurrection, but continues to unfold in God's ongoing initiatives at Pentecost and subsequent ministry of the third person of the Trinity in the life of the church.

Luke portrays the coming of the Holy Spirit on the day of Pentecost as another kind of divine invasion; an extension of the incarnation through the abiding and empowering presence of the Holy Spirit. The Holy Spirit is not merely an impersonal "force," or a *donum superadditum*, (ie, a spiritual "add on"). Rather, the Holy Spirit is the authoritative, empowering presence of the Living God, "another self-revealing extension of his person and vitality into history."[2] God's actions in salvation-history continue to unfold in the world. The Holy Spirit is the ongoing reminder

---

[1] It should be noted that an emphasis on pneumatology should not erode our christology, since the Holy Spirit functions as the chief witness to Jesus Christ.

[2] Max Turner, "The 'Spirit of Prophecy' as the Power of Israel's Restoration and Witness" in I. Howard Marshall and David Peterson (eds), *Witness to the Gospel: The Theology of Acts* (Grand Rapids, MI: William B. Eerdmans, 1998), 329.

that God does not just exercise "imperial authority" *over* the world, but is an "executive authority" to act *in* the world.[3]

There are three major themes which help to summarize the purpose and work of the Holy Spirit in the life of the early church.

First, *the Holy Spirit empowers the church for a global mission.* Just prior to the ascension, Jesus tells his disciples to wait until they have been "baptized with the Holy Spirit" (Acts 1:5). Jesus goes on to say, "you will receive power when the Holy Spirit comes on you; and you will be my witnesses in Jerusalem, and in all Judea, and Samaria, and to the ends of the earth" (Acts 1:8). Ten days later, when the day of Pentecost dawns, we find a small group of Jesus' followers praying in Jerusalem. The Holy Spirit dramatically descends in a violent wind and with fire, two of the central images of the presence of God in the Old Testament. The fire, for example, immediately calls to mind how Yahweh appeared to Moses in "flames of fire" at the burning bush (Exod 3:2), the pillar of fire which protected and guided the Israelites in the wilderness (Exod 13:21, 22), and Yahweh's descent onto Mt. Sinai in fire at the giving of the Law (Exod 19:18). Pentecost was, after all, the time when the Israelites celebrated the giving of the Law. The wind recalls the breath of God which gave life at creation (Gen 1:7) or the manifest presence of God to the prophets (1 Kgs 19:11, 12, Ezek 1:4; Nah 1:3).

The disciples began to "speak in other tongues" as the Spirit enabled them (Acts 2:4). This manifestation should be understood as more than a mere *sociological* event, enabling foreign visitors who were in Jerusalem for the feasts of Passover and Pentecost to hear the gospel in their own language (Acts 2:6-12). Rather, it was a *theological* statement whereby God takes the initiative to overturn the chaos of Babel which symbolized the global rebellion against God (Gen 11:1-9) and, in its place, empowers the church for a global mission of redemption to the ends of the earth. At Pentecost, the birthday of the church, a small group of Jewish followers of Jesus are baptized into the reality of the infinite translatability of the

---

[3] John A. Studebaker Jr., *The Lord is the Spirit: The Authority of the Holy Spirit in Contemporary Theology and Church Practice* (Eugene, Oregon: Pickwick Publications, 2008), 7.

gospel for every language and culture.[4] In the theology of Luke, it is important that the empowerment of the Holy Spirit for global mission is linked to the infinite translatability of the Christian gospel.

Second, *the Holy Spirit endues the church with God's authority.* In responding to some Pentecostal exegetes who only emphasize the role of the Holy Spirit in empowering believers for witness, Max Turner makes the observation that several of the key manifestations of the Holy Spirit in the book of Acts are not linked to an empowerment for witness theme.[5] In several texts people are filled with the Holy Spirit to give service or direction to the church. For example, in Acts 6:1-7, the seven deacons are filled with the Holy Spirit to serve the church. Similarly, in Paul's farewell to the elders at Ephesus, he acknowledges that it was the Holy Spirit who had appointed them as overseers of the church (Acts 20:27). In Acts 11, Agabus is filled with the Holy Spirit to inform the church that a severe famine will spread over the entire Roman world. In Acts 15:28, the Holy Spirit directs the church in their decision regarding the terms through which Gentile believers were to be admitted into the church. The Holy Spirit extends the judgment of God on both the church and on the unbelieving world (Acts 5:3, 9; 13:9). Thus, the Holy Spirit serves not only to empower the church to witness, but also as the "teacher of the church" and the "executor of Christ's will in the world" (John 15:26; 16:14, 15).[6] The Holy Spirit conveys revelation to the church by communicating to the church the will of God, thereby, helping to bring the church under the authority of Christ. The early church regularly confesses that it is the Holy Spirit who inspired the biblical authors and, thereby, delivered to the church the Word of God (Acts 1:16; 4:25).

Third, the Holy Spirit extends the in-breaking of the new creation through the powerful manifestation of signs and wonders and holiness of life. On the day of Pentecost, Peter declares that the coming of the Holy Spirit was in fulfilment of Joel's prophecy whereby God would "show wonders in the heavens above and signs on the earth below" (Acts 2:19). The ministry of the early church reflected the ministry of Jesus Christ

---

[4] I am indebted to Kwame Bediao for pointing out that language is not merely a vehicle of communication, but the central way we give expression to our culture.

[5] Turner, *"The 'Spirit of Prophecy,'"* 341.

[6] Studebaker Jr., *The Lord is the Spirit*, 12, 19.

in the emphasis on the proclamation of the Word through preaching and teaching, and in the ongoing ways in which the realities of the new creation continued to break into the present order through signs and wonders and holy living. Luke records that "[e]veryone was filled with awe at the many wonders and signs performed by the apostles" (Acts 2:43). The manifestation of signs and wonders was not limited to the apostles, but was also evidenced in the ministry of Stephen (Acts 6:8) and Philip (Acts 8:6,13).

The manifestation of signs and wonders was understood to accompany the preaching of the Word to provide divine confirmation of God's presence working through the church, bringing a unity of word and deed. For example, in Acts 4:30-31, the church prayed: "'Stretch out your hand to heal and perform signs and wonders through the name of your holy servant Jesus.' After they prayed, the place where they were meeting was shaken. And they were all filled with the Holy Spirit and spoke the word of God boldly." Later, in the ministry of Paul and Barnabas in Iconium, Luke records that they "spent considerable time there, speaking boldly for the Lord, who confirmed the message of his grace by enabling them to perform signs and wonders" (14:3).

The Spirit's role in extending the in-breaking of the new creation is not limited to an evangelistic or missional context. Joel Green points out that in Luke's writings the reception of the Spirit in the life of the believer is an integral aspect of his understanding of salvation.[7] It is not an extra, an "add on" for a dedicated few. When Peter preaches, he declares to the entire assembly that if they believe, they "will receive the gift of the Holy Spirit" (2:38). Peter goes on to assure them that this promise includes not only those who heard it, but their children and "for all who are far off—for all whom the Lord our God will call" (Acts 2:39). The same Spirit who empowers us for witness, is the one who empowers us for holy living. The same Spirit who transforms the unbelieving nations of the world is

---

[7] Green argues that there are four aspects of Luke's understanding of salvation: 1. Incorporation and participation in the christocentric community of God's people. 2. Rescue from our enemies. 3. Forgiveness of sins. 4. Reception of the Holy Spirit. See Joel Green, "Salvation to the End of the Earth (Acts 13:47): God as Saviour in the Acts of the Apostles" in I. Howard Marshall and David Peterson (eds), *Witness to the Gospel: The Theology of Acts*, 90-95.

the one who transforms our hearts, teaching us to say "no" to sin, and to embrace the righteousness of Jesus Christ.[8]

ACTS AS DESCRIPTIVE HISTORY OR PRESCRIPTIVE MODEL?

Three key themes were explored in our overview of the person and role of the Holy Spirit in Acts: The Spirit empowers the church for global mission, endues the church with divine authority, and extends the in-breaking of the new creation through signs and wonders and the manifestation of holiness in the life of the church. We now come to our second key question. Is the evidence concerning the work of the Holy Spirit in Acts intended to be historically *descriptive* or missiologically *prescriptive*? To put it plainly, is it appropriate for the twenty first century church to expect visions from God in the ongoing direction of his mission? Should those who preach across new cultural and social boundaries pray that the Holy Spirit confirm their preaching through the in-breaking of signs and wonders? If so, then why is this supernatural dimension seemingly absent from so many churches? Now that the church has the scriptures, do we still need the kind of supernatural intervention which is characterized by the Holy Spirit's interaction with the early church in Acts? Another way of getting at the question is to ask in what way does Acts serve as a *history* of the early church and in what way is it a *theological treatise* reflecting the early church's missiology? If Acts is primarily an historical work, can missiology, pneumatology, theology, and ecclesiology be drawn out in ways analogous to how doctrine is derived from the apostolic letters or John's apocalypse?

Since none of these questions are new, it is important that we begin with a historical overview of the development of pneumatology in the West which has shaped the context of how we in the West have approached these questions. Second, we will explore how the emergence of Pentecostalism and the rise of the majority world church in the twentieth century have influenced the church's understanding of the Holy

---

[8] The twin roles of the Holy Spirit as an agent of holiness and the One who empowers for witness is seen in the Methodist and the Keswick roots of Pentecostalism. Wesley emphasized the role of the Spirit as the sanctifier. In contrast, Keswick pneumatology emphasized that the Holy Spirit empowered the believer for witness, service and evangelism. In the New Testament, the Holy Spirit transforms both the inner life *and* our external witness.

Spirit and the interpretation of Acts. Finally, we will explore how this might impact contemporary missiological thinking, strategy, and praxis.

HISTORICAL DEVELOPMENT OF PNEUMATOLOGY

Jaraslav Pelikan, in his survey of the development of Christian doctrine, points out that the doctrine of the Trinity represents the apex of doctrinal development in the early church. Pelikan writes, "[i]n this dogma the church vindicated the monotheism that had been at issue in its conflicts with Judaism." Jesus Christ, the redeemer, did "not belong to some lower order of divine reality, but was God himself."[9] Jesus fully shared in the essence of the Father (*homoousios*, not *homoiousios*). Likewise, the Holy Spirit shares fully in the divine essence, since the scriptures give him both the titles as well as the prerogatives of deity. The church affirmed one God (one *ousia*), in three eternal personal distinctions (three *hypostases*).

However, the relative paucity of biblical references to the deity of the Holy Spirit as compared with the deity of Jesus Christ meant that it took quite some time for a full orbed trinitarian theology to develop. In fact, for some time, there was a fairly strong Spirit christology which did not acknowledge the Holy Spirit as a third person of the Trinity, and even as late as AD 380, Gregory of Nazianzus conceded that, "of the wise men among ourselves, some have conceived of him (the Holy Spirit) as an activity, some as a creature, some as God; and some have been uncertain what to call him...and therefore they neither worship him nor treat him with dishonor, but take up a neutral position."[10] This ambiguity and neutrality is reflected in the Apostles' Creed, (which is probably based on the earlier 2nd century Roman Creed) and the original Nicene Creed of AD 325, which simply states that "[w]e believe in the Holy Spirit" without further commentary. In AD 381, a second ecumenical council met in Constantinople. The further deliberations on the Holy Spirit led the council to amplify and to clarify the faith of the Nicene Creed so

---

[9] Jaraslav Pelikan, *The Christian Tradition: A History of the Development of Doctrine*, vol. 1 of The Emergence of the Catholic Tradition, 100-600 A.D. (Chicago: University of Chicago Press, 1971), 172, 173.

[10] Pelikan, *The Christian Tradition*, 213.

that it unequivocally declared the deity of the Holy Spirit.[11] The Niceno-Constantinopolitan Creed declares, "[w]e believe in the Holy Spirit, the Lord and Giver of Life, who proceedeth from the Father, who with the Father and the Son together is worshipped and glorified, who spoke by the prophets."[12]

Even though the deity of the Holy Spirit was resolved by AD 381, discussions about the exact nature and relations of the Trinity continued for almost a century.[13] All of this had a profound, cumulative effect on theological discourse in the western tradition concerning the Holy Spirit. Because the ecumenical discussions about the Holy Spirit were focused primarily on the deity of the Holy Spirit and his relationship within the Trinity, there was a serious neglect of a full development of his work. Indeed, William Menzies points out that "the ancient church from the second century through the ninth century was almost totally preoccupied with questions pertaining to the identity of Jesus Christ, so that what was said of the Holy Spirit was largely an appendage to theology, and was limited largely to ontology, the Being of God within his inter-trinitarian relationships."[14] That remained largely unchanged during medieval scholarship.

The Reformation's emphasis on the authority of Scripture, ecclesiology, and christology are clearly reflected in the post-Reformation attempt to systematize the theological deposit of the Reformers. However,

---

[11] The first ecumenical council (Nicea, AD 325) had been pre-occupied with responding to various challenges to the deity of Jesus Christ and therefore was not in a position to consider the deity of the Holy Spirit. The deity of the Father, Son and Holy Spirit which was affirmed in AD 381 implies the Trinity, although the full doctrine of the Trinity was not officially reaffirmed until the fifth ecumenical council in Constantinople in AD 553.

[12] Philip Schaff and Henry Wace (eds), *Nicene and Post-Nicene Fathers*, vol. 14 of The Seven Ecumenical Councils (Peabody, MA: Hendrickson Publishers), 163. It should be noted that the phrase "and the Son" (*filioque*) was not inserted after the phrase, "who proceedeth from the father" until the year 447 at the Synod of Toledo in Spain. The Eastern church does not accept the addition of this phrase.

[13] Acknowledgement of the deity of the Holy Spirit must not be confused with a full affirmation of the Trinity. The Trinity was officially reaffirmed in the fifth ecumenical council in Constantinople in AD 553. As late as AD 380, Gregory of Nazianzus conceded that "to be only slightly in error (about the Holy Spirit) was to be orthodox." See Pelikan, *The Christian Tradition*, 213.

[14] William W. Menzies, "The Holy Spirit in Christian Theology" in Kenneth Kantzer and Stanley Gundry (eds), *Perspectives on Evangelical Theology* (Grand Rapids, MI: Baker Books, 1979), 67.

this meant that, as was the case during the patristic period, a full development of the doctrine of the Holy Spirit was delayed and several vital aspects of the person and work of the Holy Spirit were neglected in post-Reformation Protestant theology in the West.

Over time, several major theological traditions developed which either denied completely or extremely limited the active role of the Holy Spirit in performing miracles, divine healing, demonic deliverance, prophecy, tongue speaking, and other elements which later would become central features of the Pentecostal doctrine of the Holy Spirit. This tendency is evident in many expressions of Reformed theology as well as the later nineteenth century emergence of dispensationalism, although the precise lines of their argumentation against the exercise of the gifts of the Holy Spirit today are quite different from one another.

Space does not permit an analysis and evaluation of each of the systems of thought and how they argue the cessationist position. Indeed, there are many different forms and degrees of cessationism. Some would go so far as to deny all subjective forms of guidance such as someone claiming that the Lord was leading them to do something or that the Holy Spirit had helped them in understanding a particular passage of Scripture. Others are, practically speaking, partial cessationists, opposing the exercise of certain gifts such as prophecy and tongue-speaking, but functioning as continuationists when it comes to praying for the sick or believing that the Holy Spirit can directly speak to someone.

There are also different ideas as to the original purpose of these supernatural gifts. Some argue that the apostolic miracles served to grant authority to the ministers in the church, whereas others claim they were given only to attest to his Word. There are also different ideas as to exactly when and why these gifts stopped. For example, some argue that the gifts ceased after the canon of Scripture was completed, while others say it was when the last apostle died. Still others insist that the exercise of spiritual gifts died out gradually over the first four centuries until the official persecution ceased and Christianity was granted full legal status in the Roman Empire. Some argue that while the gifts are not a normal part of the life of the church, they might still be manifested by God in extraordinary situations. But regardless of which of these schemes are followed, the point is that theological reflection in the West gradually became dominated by a range of theological systems which denied that the full exercise of the supernatural gifts of the Holy Spirit was a normative, much less essential, part of the church's *ongoing* life and witness in the world.

B.B. Warfield, the great nineteenth century Princeton theologian, is one of the most well-known and influential writers representing the cessationist viewpoint. In his book, *Counterfeit Miracles*, Warfield argued that the diffusion of miraculous gifts by the Holy Spirit was confined to the apostolic church and "they necessarily passed away with it." He insisted that "the theologians of the post-Reformation era, a very clear-headed body of men, taught with great distinctiveness that the charismata ceased with the Apostolic age."[15] This Princeton theological tradition[16] influenced a large part of the Reformed tradition and subsequent systematic theologies in the West. A typical example can be found in Louis Berkhof's *Systematic Theology*, a classic text in Reformed theology, still in use today. Berkhof devotes significant attention in Part 1 (Doctrine of God) of his theology to defending the deity, personality and prerogatives of the Holy Spirit within the larger setting of his defense of the doctrine of the Trinity. Later, in part four (Doctrine of the Application of the Work of Redemption), Berkhof discusses the work of the Holy Spirit in applying the work of Christ into our lives (e.g., regeneration) and in personal holiness (e.g., sanctification).

---

[15] B.B. Warfield, *Counterfeit Miracles* (New York: Charles Scribner's Sons, 1918), 6. Warfield's view is that the miracles ceased with the last person upon whom the apostles conferred the working of miracles through the imposition of their hands, explaining the gradual decline of miracles (23). It should be noted that B.B. Warfield specifically uses A.J. Gordon's *The Ministry of Healing, or Miracles of Cure in All Ages* as the best book representing his opponent's position. See 159-160. A.J. Gordon taught, for example, that "it is still the duty and privilege of believers to receive the Holy Spirit by a conscious, definite act of appropriating faith, just as they received Jesus Christ.... To say that in receiving Christ we necessarily received in the same act the gift of the Spirit, seems to confound what the Scriptures make distinct. For it is as sinners that we accept Christ for our justification, but it is as sons that we accept the Spirit for our sanctification... logically and chronologically the gift of the Spirit is subsequent to repentance." See A.J. Gordon, *The Ministry of the Spirit* (Philadelphia: American Baptist Publication Society, 1894), 76, 77. A century earlier, Jonathan Edwards taught that the gifts of prophecy, tongues and revelations would cease and "vanish away" when the church reached maturity. Edwards did not accept the supernatural gifts as valid for today and he explicitly states that he did not expect, or desire, a restoration of these miraculous gifts in the latter days prior to the inauguration of the millennium. See C.C. Goen (ed), *Works of Jonathan Edwards*, vol. 4 of The Distinguishing Marks (New Haven: Yale University Press, 1972), 280, 281.

[16] The Princeton theology refers to the period when great theologians such as Archibald Alexander, Charles Hodge, A.A. Hodge and B.B. Warfield taught at Princeton Theological Seminary.

In part five (Doctrine of the Church), Berkhof is silent about the role of the Holy Spirit in empowering the church for witness and global missions.

In summary, traditional western understanding of pneumatology is adequate in its treatment of the Spirit's place in the Trinity and his role in soteriology, but is often silent about many of the key elements present in the book of Acts, including the baptism of the Holy Spirit, divine healing, speaking in tongues, the role of the Holy Spirit in the mission of the church, and so forth. In fact, many of the older western systematic theologies did not even develop the person and work of the Holy Spirit as a separate category of study, but rather developed their theology of the Holy Spirit as subsets under the doctrine of God and the doctrine of soteriology.[17] The pluralistic agenda seeks to downplay any objective reference point to God's sovereign power being extended into the life and witness of the church. However, in the closing decades of the twentieth century, the renewed emphasis on the Trinity and the rise of Pentecostalism resulted in an increasing interest in the work of the Holy Spirit. We will now explore how the emergence of Pentecostalism and the rise of the majority world churches have influenced western pneumatology and missions practice.

Pentecostalism and the Rise of the Majority World Church

The twenty first century mission is shaped by seven megatrends. Two of the trends, global Christianity and the increasing numbers of Christians who are not identified with the traditional tri-partite identification of Roman Catholic, Eastern Orthodox, and Protestant branches of Christianity, are seen in the rise of Pentecostalism which now comprises a global force of half a billion adherents, making it one of the most dramatic shifts in Christian alignment in history.

Pentecostalism traces its origins to a series of revival movements which simultaneously emerged in the first decade of the twentieth century. In the United States, Pentecostalism traces its origin to a black preacher named William Seymour from Louisiana who came to Los Angeles,

---

[17] See, for example, Henry C. Thiessen, *Lectures in Systematic Theology*, rev. (Grand Rapids, MI: William B. Eerdmans, 1979).

teaching that God was restoring the first century apostolic church which included a fresh visitation of Pentecost whereby believers could be baptized in the Holy Spirit, speak in unknown tongues, be empowered for witness, and live a holy life.

Seymour had first learned this message from the former Methodist preacher, and now healing evangelist from Kansas, Charles Parham (1873-1929). Seymour fervently believed that the time of God's visitation had come to Los Angeles. What is now known as the Azusa street revivals began on Sunday, April 15, 1906, when Jenny Evans Moore spoke in tongues at the conclusion of the service at the Azusa street mission. News about this move of the Holy Spirit spread throughout Los Angeles. A few days later, the front page of the *Los Angeles Daily Times* contained the extended headline: "Weird Babble of Tongues, New Sect of Fanatics Breaking Loose, Wild Scene Last Night on Azusa Street, Gurgle of Wordless Talk by a Sister."[18] This was the first public announcement that something dramatic was happening on Azusa street.

The revival lasted from April 1906 through the early months of 1909 and drew tens of thousands of people from all over the world, who came to witness the outpouring of the Holy Spirit during one of the three daily services. Over the three year period, the Azusa street mission could hardly contain the crowds as thousands found redemption in Jesus Christ and experienced what was known as a "second Pentecost." It is not surprising that when Seymour began to publish a newspaper to help spread his teachings in September 1906, his lead article in the inaugural edition was entitled, "Pentecost Has Come!"

Similar revivals, independent of the Azusa street meetings, included the famous Welsh revival that lasted from September 1904 to June 1905 and witnessed over ten thousand people coming to Christ. A few years later, revivals broke out in Korea, several of which occurred in what is today North Korea, including Wonsan and Pyongyang. These Korean revivals became known as the "Korean Pentecost."[19]

---

[18] [n.a.], "Weird Babble of Tongues," *Los Angeles Daily Times*, 18 April, 1906, 1.

[19] Allan Anderson, *An Introduction to Pentecostalism* (Cambridge: Cambridge University Press, 2004), 37.

The evangelistic and missionary fervor that burst forth from these revivals, in turn, helped to spark new waves of Pentecostalism around the world. For example, Welsh missionaries working in India, fresh from the revivals in Wales, witnessed dramatic Pentecostal revivals in the Khasi Hills of northeast India. In 1906, another revival broke out near Pune, India, at the Mukti Mission of the famous Brahmin convert to Christianity, Pandita Ramabai. Similar revival movements occurred in China as well as several countries of Africa, including the Ivory Coast, Ghana, and Nigeria.

Pentecostal scholar Allan Anderson points out that the Azusa street revival "turned a fairly localized and insignificant new Christian sect into an international movement that sent workers to more than twenty-five nations in only two years."[20] Similar evangelistic and cross-cultural initiatives occurred out of the other revivals. If Pentecostalism is, as the title of Harvey Cox's landmark book declares, a "fire from heaven," then it is a fire that has spread around the world.[21]

One of the affirmations which unite all Pentecostals is the belief that the practice and exercise of spiritual gifts as exhibited in the Book of Acts should be *normative* for the church today. Pentecostalism is fundamentally a renewal movement, seeking to challenge blind spots in the western development of pneumatology which focused on the person of the Holy Spirit and neglected a proper understanding of his work. We will first explore three ways in which Pentecostalism has influenced Christianity in general and then examine the specific ways it has impacted missions practice.

First, Pentecostals believe that the full range of gifts and miraculous manifestations of the Spirit present in the New Testament are available for believers today. Pentecostals reject any notion that Acts is merely descriptive and no longer applicable to believers today. They reject the idea that the gifts of the Holy Spirit are either limited to the first century,

---

[20] Allan Anderson, "To All Points of the Compass: The Azusa Street Revival and Global Pentecostalism," *Enrichment Journal*, online journal of the General Council of the Assemblies of God (http://enrichmentjournal.ag.org/200602/200602_164_AllPoints.cfm) (accessed 30 June, 2008).

[21] Harvey Cox, *Fire from Heaven: The Rise of Pentecostal Spirituality and the Reshaping of Religion in the 21st Century* (Reading, MA: Addison Wesley, 1995).

or passed away with the apostles. This view is, perhaps, summed up best by one of the early pioneers of Pentecostalism, the itinerant evangelist Aimee Semple McPherson, who once asked, "Is Jesus Christ the Great I Am? or is He the Great I Was?"[22] Pentecostals believe that the Holy Spirit continues to make available to the church the full range of Jesus' miraculous ministry as well as the apostolic "signs and wonders" explored earlier. Pentecostals understand that if someone is demon possessed, then having the demon cast out in the name of Jesus is still part of the good news and the practical extension of Christ's triumphant victory over the principalities and powers (Col 2:14, 15; Eph 6:12). In other words, if the Holy Spirit is alive and real, then he must have the power and the means to extend his dynamic life in real and concrete ways into the lives of those who are suffering. If God raised the dead in the first century, why can't he do it in the twenty first century?

Second, Pentecostalism has unleashed a renewed emphasis on the practice of worship. Pentecostals are known for less formalized and expressive forms of worship, including lifting hands, dancing, shouting, and clapping. While this should not eclipse the rich heritage of theologically sound hymnology or liturgical worship, one cannot help but observe that many of the forms of worship around the world have dramatically changed since the advent of Pentecostalism which has stimulated deep reflection about the nature and practice of worship.

Third, because Pentecostals believe that they are living in the last days before the return of Christ, they are marked by a special urgency to evangelize the world. The effective evangelism exhibited by Pentecostals can also be attributed to their distinctive peumatology which was not encumbered by the truncated pneumatology which was so prevalent in North American theologies. The Holy Spirit is not only a full person of the Godhead, a member of the Trinity; he not only inspired the Holy Scripture and regenerates us; but he also empowers us for effective evangelism. Pentecostals were convinced that the Holy Spirit confirms the preaching of the gospel and the declaration of the resurrection of Jesus

---

[22] Aimee Semple McPherson, from her Divine Healing Sermons, as quoted in Cecil Robeck Jr., "Pentecostals and Apostolic Faith: Implications for Ecumenism," *Pneuma: The Journal of the Society for Pentecostal Studies* 8 (1986), 64.

through giving signs and wonders, just as he did through those unlearned fishermen and tax collectors who were his first apostles.

Influence on Missions Practice

These new emphases within Pentecostalism, coupled with the extraordinary growth of the movement around the world, have had a profound effect on Christianity as a global force, including the practice of missions in several key ways.

1. Birth of "Global Christianity"

First, Pentecostalism had led the way in the rise of what is now known as "global Christianity." The Pentecostals were among the first to understand the global implications of transcending the traditional denominational divides which have characterized Protestant identity for centuries. Because Pentecostalism did not have its origin in a single church tradition or geographic region, it was birthed in diversity. Modern day Pentecostalism can be traced to classical Pentecostal denominations as well as to indigenous revivals erupting on five different continents. A second wave of Pentecostalism has swept through mainline Protestant, Roman Catholic, and Eastern Orthodox churches. This diverse background forced Pentecostals to embrace unity in spiritual terms, rather than in structural or doctrinal terms. This is why the word "Pentecostal" is frequently used both as an adjective as well as a noun in a way which is not generally found with terms such as Lutheran or Methodist. One can consider themselves to be a pentecostal Roman Catholic or a pentecostal Methodist without fear of contradiction. In fact, one of the most dynamic Pentecostal movements in Chile emerged within the Methodist church under the leadership of an American Methodist missionary named Willis Hoover.[23] This spiritual basis for unity means that a Pentecostal can "have true ecumenism or genuine *koinōnia* with all Christians who have a personal relationship with God."[24] Discovering this "common

---

[23] See Willis C. Hoover, *History of the Pentecostal Revival in Chile* (Santiago, Chile: Imprenta Eben-Ezer, 2000).
[24] Cecil M. Robeck Jr., "Pentecostals and the Apostolic Faith: Implications for Ecumenism," *Pneuma: The Journal of the Society for Pentecostal Studies* 9/1 (1987), 65.

spiritual center" is, according to Karl-Wilhelm Westmeir, the reason that Pentecostalism has been able to work across denominational lines.[25]

Because Pentecostals saw themselves as reviving the Apostolic Faith rather than breaking off from or emerging out of any existing movements, it allowed them, even if naïvely, to provide a basis for ecumenism around their common commitment to the biblical witness in Scripture and their shared experience of the Holy Spirit. Though most Pentecostals deride the word ecumenical and, quite frankly, have exhibited as much sectarianism and theological controversy as any other Christian group, it is nevertheless remarkable to see how Pentecostalism has actually contributed positively to ecumenism. The Pentecostals learned the principle of *sola scriptura* from the Reformation, but then used it as a basis for celebrating a supernatural, Apostolic Faith which predated the historical divisiveness of denominationalism. The result was a new basis for cooperation and collaboration in missions which facilitated the rapid spread of Christianity around the world. The growth of the global church in the wake of Pentecostal witness was so profound that Henry Van Dusen coined the expression "Third Force" to describe it.[26]

2. EMPHASIS ON THEO*PRAXIS* OVER FORMAL THEOLOGY

Second, Pentecostals tend to focus outward on evangelism and missions rather than inward on either defending themselves against their critics or expending a lot of energy on defining their own identity. In the formative stages of the emergence of Pentecostalism, the movement held a distrust of academic scholarship which they called a "tragedy, whose fruit is empty churches... the result of our 'theologizing to death.'"[27] Pentecostals were, of course, unconsciously recipients of centuries of serious theological

---

[25] Karl-Wilhelm Westmeier, *Protestant Pentecostalism in Latin America* (London: Associated University Presses, 1999), 19. This is also celebrated in Matthew Marostica's chapter entitled, "The Defeat of Denominational Culture in the Argentine Evangelical Movement" in Christian Smith and Joshua Prokopy (eds), *Latin American Religion in Motion* (New York and London: Routledge, 1999), 148-172.

[26] Henry P. Van Dusen, "The Third Force in Christendom," *Life* (9 June, 1958), 113-124. The first wave refers to Roman Catholic missions and the second wave refers to Protestant missions. It is interesting to note that Eastern Orthodoxy is overlooked by Van Dusen, despite their vigorous and inspiring missionary work in the nineteenth century.

[27] Walter Hollenweger, *Pentecostalism: Origins and Developments Worldwide* (Peabody, MA: Hendrickson, 1997), 194.

reflection in the church upon which their faith depended. Nevertheless, this has not been sufficiently acknowledged because Pentecostals see themselves as a return to the first century and the original Apostolic Faith and practice. Although this anti-intellectualism among Pentecostals has changed significantly in recent years, it is still true that Pentecostals are more interested in theo*praxis* than theology in the formal sense. Pentecostalism is, at its root, an evangelistic-missions movement.

Because of the emphasis on evangelism and missions within Pentecostalism, the movement continues to provide an important check against the tendency for theology to lose its missiological focus and become too rationalistic and theoretical. Our tendency towards a cerebral-oriented scholasticism must learn to appreciate and benefit from the counterbalance of the Pentecostal orientation towards a heart-oriented praxis which fully embraces a supernatural, not a naturalistic, worldview.

In the past, when missionaries arrived with their modified Enlightenment worldview and their restricted, truncated pneumatology, they did not know what to say when someone claimed that a drought was caused by God's judgment, or when concerned parents came and asked the missionary to cast out the demon tormenting their daughter, or when someone claimed they had received a vision to preach the gospel in a new region. Sadly, the missionary often had no training or comprehensive knowledge of categories to respond to their worldview. They had inhabited a Christianized version of a two-tiered universe, whereas they were working among people who lived in what Paul Hiebert insightfully calls the world of the "excluded middle."[28] The only category the missionaries had was a term like "superstition," which they frequently resorted to in order to explain these "spiritualized" explanations of what surely had its basis, they reasoned, in naturalistic explanations. These missionaries were evangelical in their theology, but when it came to pneumatology applied to real life praxis, they were functional deists. This is why Lesslie Newbigin argued that "western missionaries were one of the greatest forces of secularization in history."[29]

---

[28] Paul G. Hiebert, *Anthropological Reflections on Missiological Issues* (Grand Rapids, MI: Baker Academic, 1994), 189-201.

[29] Lesslie Newbigin, *Honest Religion for Secular Man* (Philadelphia: Westminster, 1966), cited by Hiebert, *Anthropological Reflections*, 197.

In contrast, Pentecostalism emerged among uneducated peoples who were the least influenced by the Enlightenment world-view. Furthermore, their personal experience with the Holy Spirit gave them reason to believe that the same Holy Spirit who acted supernaturally in the lives and witness of the apostles is active today in similar ways. The result of this conviction has been the emergence of a global Pentecostal pneumatology that *anticipated* God's ongoing intervention in the world through miraculous healings, prophetic guidance to the church, demonic deliverance from evil, and an empowered witness to the world. In short, the Holy Spirit continues to usher in the first fruits of the new creation into the fallen world. All the future realities of the kingdom are now fully available to all believers through the person and work of the Holy Spirit.

God used the seventeenth century pietistic movement to balance out the tendency towards an overly cerebral scholasticism in post-Reformation Protestant theology in Europe. Pietism became unconsciously ecumenical as it quietly spread its influence through most of European protestantism. Today, there is no formal denomination which has emerged from pietism, but there is hardly a Protestant movement in the world which has not in some way been influenced by pietism.

Today, God is using the Pentecostals in the same way. Indeed, one of the neglected stories of global Pentecostalism is not so much how they have grown as distinct, identifiable Pentecostal groups, but how deeply they have influenced so much of the faith and practice of non-Pentecostals around the world. It is the Pentecostal sense of the immediacy of God's presence and power which has struck a responsive chord in Christians everywhere, and helped to stimulate fresh evangelistic and missional activity.[30] It is also a wonderful reminder how crucial it is that the *noetic* principle in theology (reflection, reason, propositional statements, etc) must always be balanced by the *ontic* principle (immediacy of God's

---

[30] Roman Catholic missiologist John Gorski has noted that "evangelization in the specific sense of announcing the gospel to enable a personal encounter with the living Christ, leading to conversion and discipleship, became a conscious concern of the Catholic church only within the past half century." This was stimulated by the presence of Pentecostals in Latin America. See John Gorski, "How the Catholic Church in Latin America Became Missionary," *International Bulletin of Missionary Research* 27/2 (2003), 60.

presence, personal experience with God, etc).[31] If either of these tendencies is allowed to run unchecked, the church falls into error.

3. BEYOND THE HOMOGENEOUS UNIT PRINCIPLE (HUP) IN MISSIONS STRATEGY

Finally, Pentecostals have provided an important counter-balance to the strong emphasis on reaching unreached people groups on the basis of Donald McGavran's Homogeneous Unit Principle (HUP) which has dominated both the church growth movement and evangelical missions since 1974.[32] According to McGavran, a homogeneous unit refers to "a section of society in which all the members have some characteristics in common."[33] The Homogeneous Unit Principle focused on identifying particular peoples who shared a common cultural, linguistic and social identity and stimulating a "people-movement" within this particular ethnic group. The whole basis for the Homogeneous Unit Principle was the proven sociological fact that people prefer to not cross social and ethnic barriers when becoming a Christian.

Furthermore, people prefer to worship with people who are culturally like themselves.[34] This is the principle which drives the church-growth movement to focus, for example, on young, middle-class unchurched professionals in building mega-churches. This is the same principle used by mission organizations when they, for example, target a particular caste group in India to evangelize. Over the last thirty years, the focus on people groups has become the "holy grail" of evangelical missions and, undoubtedly, there are tens of millions of new Christians in the world today because of the effective application of this principle. But the Pentecostals, by and large, have been reluctant to embrace this principle in their evangelism and mission work. The Azusa street mission was, from the start, a multi-racial event which transcended the normal

---

[31] Paul A. Pommerville, *The Third Force in Missions* (Peabody, MA: Hendrickson, 1985), 68.

[32] As highlighted in chapter twelve, 1974 is the year when Ralph Winter delivered his now famous paper at the first Lausanne Congress on World Evangelization entitled, "The Highest Priority: Cross-Cultural Evangelism." This date is used to mark the shift in mission practice from a focus on places to a focus on peoples.

[33] Donald McGavran, *Understanding Church Growth*, rev. ed. (Grand Rapids, MI: William B. Eerdmans, 1990), 69.

[34] This is the basis for the well known saying that 11:00 a.m. is the most segregated hour in America.

social and ethnic barriers. Pentecostalism and neo-Pentecostalism demonstrated over and over again the power of the Pentecostal message to penetrate high church Anglicans as well as poor, uneducated laborers and then bring them together in a way which confounds the dynamics of proven sociological expectations.

Pentecostals have modeled on a global scale what happened to Peter and Cornelius in Acts 10, which I alluded to in the third part of the chapter. The two men were completely separated, both theologically and culturally. One was an uncircumcized Gentile, the other a law-abiding Jew. In short, they were certainly not part of the same "homogeneous unit." They were not even able to share table fellowship and certainly could not stand in the presence of God together. However, once the Holy Spirit came on the whole household, (Acts 10:44) everything was changed. Peter and Cornelius had a new basis for unity through the power of the Holy Spirit who sovereignly yoked them to one another and to Christ. We normally read Acts 10 as the story of Cornelius' conversion, but a more reflective reading reveals that both men went away transformed. Cornelius was now a full member of the body of Christ and Peter now had his own truncated view of God enlarged and transformed. He now understood that God was a missionary God with a heart for the whole world. The Pentecostals may make evangelicals uncomfortable with their comparative disinterest in formal theology, but they also have the capacity to transform our understanding of God in many positive ways.

In conclusion, the growth of Pentecostalism, neo-Pentecostalism, Charismatic and neo-Charismatic movements globally now exceeds 600 million Christians. This has had a dramatic shape on our understanding of pneumatology and missions practice. Increasingly, missions practice around the world understands the book of Acts not only as an accurate *description* of the Holy Spirit's work through the early church, but also as a *prescriptive* paradigm which should guide the church's practice today.

THE ROLE OF THE HOLY SPIRIT IN DIRECTING AND UNFOLDING THE *MISSIO DEI*

The third and final key question which this chapter seeks to address is how the person and work of the Holy Spirit relates to the *missio Dei*. The ethnic and geographic movement of the book of Acts from Jerusalem to Judea,

Samaria, and to the "ends of the earth" provides an important testimony to the larger global mission to which the church has been called. It reminds us of God's promise and initiative in Genesis 12 to bless all the nations on earth. The witness and growth of the church, therefore, must be seen through the larger frame of God's initiative and action in the *missio Dei*.

Many of the key missiological turning points in Acts are precipitated by supernatural visions, including the conversion of Saul of Tarsus (Acts 9:3-4), Ananias' obedience (Acts 9:19), Cornelius' conversion (Acts 10:3), Peter's obedience (Acts 10:9-10), and shaping the direction of Paul's missionary journeys (Acts 16:9), giving testimony to the Holy Spirit's role as the director of God's mission in and through the life and witness of the church.

Through visions, words of revelation, and signs and wonders, the Holy Spirit leads the church, not only in effective evangelism and witness, but into a deeper understanding of the *missio Dei*, often in ways which surprised the early Jewish Christians by challenging many of their attitudes and pre-existing ideas about God's work. Because of the reputation of Saul of Tarsus as an enemy of the church, Ananias was reluctant to go to him. But he did so in direct response to a vision (Acts 9:10-19). Later, a God-fearing Gentile named Cornelius sent for Peter in response to another vision (Acts 10:1-8). As an observant Jew, Peter was clearly uncomfortable going into Cornelius' home and only went in response to a vision (Acts 10:9-16) and the direct action of the Holy Spirit speaking to him. Luke records that "[w]hile Peter was still thinking about the vision, the Spirit said to him, 'Simon, three men are looking for you. So get up and go downstairs. Do not hesitate to go with them, for I have sent them'" (Acts 10:19). The Holy Spirit took the initiative in the Gentile mission and is portrayed as the central actor in both speaking and sending.

Acts 13 records the sending out of Paul and his companions on the first of several church planting initiatives, widely known today as the missionary journeys of Paul.[35] Paul and Barnabas were senior leaders in the church at Antioch. Barnabas had been sent from the Jerusalem church to Antioch in order to help strengthen the young church. Barnabas had recruited Paul to help him in the work (Acts 11:25, 26). During the next year, Paul and Barnabas devoted themselves fully to teaching and discipling the new believers. Later, while the church was worshiping and fasting, "the Holy Spirit said, 'Set apart for me Barnabas and Saul for the work to which I have called them'" (Acts 13:2). The church obeyed and became the sending church for the apostle Paul, evidenced not only through the laying on of hands to commission them (Acts 13:3), but the eventual return of the missionaries to Antioch whereby they "gathered the church together and reported all that God had done through them" (Acts 14:27).[36] However, seen through the lens of the *missio Dei*, it is clear that Antioch's role as the sending church is clearly subordinate to the prior sending agency of the Holy Spirit.[37]

The Holy Spirit not only initiated, called, and sent the missionaries into the Gentile mission, he continued to direct the mission on the field. For example, during the second missionary journey, Paul's missionary band was "kept by the Holy Spirit from preaching the word in the province of Asia" (Acts 16:6). When they came to the border of Mysia and tried to enter Bithynia, the "Spirit of Jesus would not allow them to" (Acts 16:7). The text does not tell us precisely *how* the Holy Spirit prevented their northward journey, nor are we told *why* turning to the west (towards Europe) was given priority. Nevertheless, the band turned to the west and travelled to Troas on the coast when, once again, the Holy Spirit intervened by giving Paul a vision of a "man of Macedonia" who stood

---

[35] I prefer to call them "church planting initiatives" rather than missionary journeys to clarify the common misconception that Paul is rapidly traveling from town to town on an extended evangelistic campaign. Paul's ministry of church planting takes place over a thirteen year period. It is beyond the scope of this work to explore each of Paul's journeys. Acts records three major church planting initiatives (13:1-14:28; 15:36-18:22; 18:23-21:17). Some scholars argue that other textual and historical evidence supports that Paul went on a fourth mission, perhaps to Spain, between his first and second imprisonments in Rome.

[36] See also Acts 18:22 when Paul returned to Antioch after the second journey. His third journey, however, ended in Jerusalem, not Antioch. Acts records that Paul reported about his ministry among the Gentiles to the "pillars" of the church in Jerusalem.

[37] This is not to diminish the doctrine of ecclesiology in mission sending, but, rather, to emphasize the importance of conceptualizing the church's role within the larger context of the *missio Dei*.

before Paul and begged him to "'come over to Macedonia and help us'" (Acts 16:9). It is this vision which precipitated Paul and his companions to cross the Aegean Sea into Europe. A woman named Lydia, a dealer in purple cloth, was the first to respond to the gospel in Europe, when "the Lord opened her heart to respond to Paul's message" (Acts 16:14). Lydia represented the first-fruit of a great spiritual harvest in Europe.

The unfolding story of Acts is certainly about the obedience of the early church to the great commission of Christ. However, it is also the story of the ongoing initiatives of God the Father through the Holy Spirit to direct and guide his church to extend the *missio Dei* and fulfil his promise to Abraham. The Holy Spirit is still the agent of initiating, calling, sending, and directing the unfolding of the *missio Dei* as he was in the life of the early church.

In conclusion, this chapter began by examining the role of the Holy Spirit in the life and witness of the early church, as recorded in Acts. We then demonstrated how the slow development of a full and robust pneumatology caused the church to neglect a proper emphasis on the work of the Holy Spirit in the church and in our global witness in the world. An embarrassing gap developed between the church in Acts and the life and practice of many churches around the world. During the twentieth century, the Pentecostal movement served to reawaken the church to the normative aspect of the Holy Spirit's activity in the church, and in our witness in the world. Ultimately, the Spirit is the central agent in the ongoing unfolding of the *missio Dei* enabling the church to experience the realities of the new creation in the present. There have been, of course, glaring inconsistencies and theological problems within Pentecostalism, as with any Christian movement. If, in this chapter, I have neglected the "mote" in the Pentecostal eye, it is only because I am so painfully aware of the "beam" in my own eye. In other words, I maintain that despite the problems, Pentecostalism remains an important corrective to the blind spots in the pneumatological theory and practice which has dominated the West for centuries. As Samuel Escobar has wisely stated, evangelical protestantism emphasized the "continuity in truth by the Word," whereas

Pentecostalism has emphasized the "continuity in life by the Spirit."[38] To be faithful to Christ in the twenty-first century, the church desperately needs the dynamic union of both.

---

[38] Samuel Escobar, "A Missiological Approach to Latin American Protestantism," *International Review of Mission* 87/345 (1998), 172.

4

HOLY SPIRIT IN PENTECOSTAL MISSION PRAXIS IN INDIA: A PARADIGM FOR MISSION IN PLURALISTIC CONTEXT

*Shaibu Abraham**

Pentecostalism is one of the major Christian denominations that is rapidly growing in India today. According to the *World Christian Encyclopaedia*, in the year 2000, over half of India's Christians were Pentecostals/Charismatics.[1] By 2016, the proportion has increased even further among the tribal groups, *dalits* and lower castes in rural areas, and the middle class population in urban centres. Anyone who travels across the cities and villages of India can see ample evidences of the growth of Pentecostalism among the common masses. My own exposure and research over the past twenty years has shown that many are joining this movement. Such a rapid growth in the midst of other religions and ideological groups is noticed by researchers, academicians, and sociologists and they are probing into the reasons behind it. Pentecostals credit the incredible growth of the movement to the work of the Holy Spirit and their untiring mission

---

* **Shaibu Abraham**, PhD, is Assistant Professor in Christian Theology at India Bible College and Seminary, Kerala. He completed his doctoral studies in Pentecostal Studies at the University of Birmingham, UK.

[1] See David B. Barrett, George T. Kurian and Todd M. Johnson, *World Christian Encyclopedia*, 2nd ed (New York: Oxford University Press, 2001), 360.

activities. Here, we shall explore the significance of the work of the Holy Spirit in the Pentecostal mission praxis in India and suggest a theology of mission in a pluralistic context. However, at first, we shall study the rapid growth of the movement and, then, the Pentecostal mission that is augmented by the activities of the Spirit.

INDIAN PENTECOSTALISM: A MISSIONARY MOVE IN THE INDIAN CONTEXT

From its inception in the beginning of the last century with the revival movements,[2] Indian Pentecostalism has grown into a stream of important religious and missionary force in the Indian society. The visible manifestations of the Holy Spirit in the beginning of the last century and the subsequent years have resulted in the proliferation of the movement into a reckoning force. Several Indian cities, towns, and villages have come under the grip of the strong wind of the Holy Spirit. As a result, many people groups have been experiencing the ever-empowering and liberating power of the Holy Spirit. Today, some of the largest Christian congregations in India are Pentecostal such as those in Chennai, Kolkata, Mumbai, and New Delhi.[3]

In South India, the movement has considerable influence among the middle class and the urban population. The South Indian states like Kerala, Tamil Nadu, and Andhra Pradesh have witnessed a major growth of varied indigenous Pentecostal movements.[4] In Kerala, many

---

[2] G.B. McGee, "Pentecostal and Pentecostal-like Movements (1860-1910)" in Stanley M. Burgess (ed), *New International Dictionary of Pentecostal and Charismatic Movements* (Grand Rapids, MI: Zondervan, 2002), 118-119. Also see G.B. McGee, "Pentecostal Phenomena and Revivals in India: Implication for Indigenous Church Leadership," *International Bulletin of Missionary Research* 20/3 (1996), 112-114.

[3] Chief Editor, "Editorial – Pentecostalism," *Dharma Deepika* 6/2 (2002), 2.

[4] Michael Bergunder, *The South Indian Pentecostal Movement in the Twentieth Century* (Cambridge: Eerdmans, 2008); Roger E. Hedlund, "Indigenous Pentecostalism in India" in Allan Anderson and Edmond Tang (eds), *Asian and Pentecostal: The Charismatic Face of Christianity in Asia* (Carlisle: Regnum Books International, 2005); Roger E. Hedlund, *Christianity is Indian: The Emergence of an Indigenous Community,* rev. ed. (Delhi: ISPCK, 2004). For example, in Chennai city itself, two Pentecostal churches claim a membership of 25,000 to 30,000 each, who meet in multiple services, and include people from all walks of life; New Life Assembly of God (AoG) Anna Salai Little Mount, Chennai; for more details see website: http://www.nlag.org.in/about_us.htm (accessed 22 December, 2009). Another church, Apostolic Christian Assembly (ACA), Purasavakkam, Chennai, claims 30,000 members and it also claims to have 250 branches in Chennai city.

adherents of the mainline denominations have moved away from their respective churches to join the Pentecostal churches, a fact that is noticed by the secular press too. Shaji reports that "[t]he Pentecostal movement's growing clout has alarmed the Syrian Christian church, which commands the largest following. Several of its denominations – like the Jacobites and Marthomites – have witnessed a sharp erosion in their ranks."[5]

In North India, Pentecostal growth has taken place, primarily, among the poor, tribals, *dalits*, and the people of low castes in rural areas. The tribal belt of North India, comprising of states like Rajasthan, Gujarat, Maharashtra, Madhya Pradesh, Bihar, Jharkhand, Chhattisgarh, and Orissa, has experienced remarkable growth. Most of these Pentecostals are poor and illiterate. They live in small hamlets in remote villages, where facilities like transportation, medical help, and schooling are limited. Arun Jones, who has undertaken some research in North India, says that the middle-class mainline Protestants are generally not interested to welcome low caste and poor people into their churches. However, Pentecostals welcome everyone, beyond their caste and class differences. Furthermore, Pentecostalism is attracting people from lower castes, *dalits*, and tribals because it provides them with a sense of dignity and hope that are usually denied to them in other sections of the Indian society. Thus, Pentecostal fellowships tend to have more appeal to lower class and caste population.[6]

Also, the Indian Pentecostal movement is highly contextual and indigenous in nature; the worship, practices, and lifestyle of its members reflect the culture and practices of their respective locality. Roger Hedlund underlines that while the traditional Roman Catholic, Orthodox, and Protestant denominations debate the questions of contextualisation, adaptation, accommodation, and the cultural transformation of the Christian faith, in Pentecostal churches cultural incarnation of the faith is a normal phenomenon.[7] In addition, Pentecostals in their mission activities are persistent in their presentation of Jesus as the unique Savior. These elements have enabled them to develop a form of Pentecostalism

---

[5] K.A. Shaji, "Holy Ghost on Malabar Coast," *Tehelka* 4/42(2007), http://www.tehelka.com/ story_main34.asp?filename=Ne271007holyghost.asp (accessed 22 December, 2009).

[6] Arun W. Jones, "Faces of Pentecostalism in North India Today" sent by the author through e-mail on 22 December 2009. It is also published in *Society* 46/6 (2009), 504-509.

[7] Roger E. Hedlund, *Quest for Identity: India's Churches of Indigenous Origin, The "Little Tradition" in Indian Christianity* (Delhi: ISPCK, 2000), 3.

true to its cultural context and, thus, attract thousands of ordinary people to its fold.

BAPTISM OF THE HOLY SPIRIT: THE POWER FOR MISSION

As we turn to analyze the rapid growth of Pentecostal churches in India, though we can count many factors, the one that stands distinct is the reliance of the Pentecostal mission on the power of the Holy Spirit. In general terms, the central tenet for mission, evangelism, and church growth of Pentecostal mission in India has been the empowerment received through the baptism of the Holy Spirit. The Pentecostals internalise and apply the paradigmatic missionary text in the book of Acts to their lives: "you will receive power when the Holy Spirit has come upon you; and you will be my witnesses in Jerusalem, in all Judea and Samaria, and to the ends of the earth" (Acts 1:8). The dependence on the power of the Spirit and biblical mandate imparts internal strength and outward thrust to the movement in the difficult terrains of the Indian mission. Most Pentecostal scholars forcefully argue that the baptism of the Spirit is to empower us for mission. Luke portrays the Spirit in prophetic terms and as the source of power for effective witness.[8] Pentecostals take it literally and emulate it in their mission praxis.

How does the Spirit baptism provide impetus for mission? When a person is baptized in the Spirit, the Spirit experience enables one to envision realities around him/her in a new light. This radical change facilitates an ordinary person to plunge into the deeper dimension of God's tasks that would have been impossible without the power of the Spirit. Leonard Lovett brings out this phenomenon vividly saying, "[b]aptism in the Holy Spirit is perceived as being the spiritual baptism where Jesus the baptizer exercises his sovereign will, control, and possession of us through the person of the Holy Spirit.... Experientially then, Spirit-baptism in this context is a radical encounter of the divine with the human

---

[8] From the beginning, the Pentecostal movement considered the baptism of the Holy Spirit as a post-conversion experience which brings empowerment for mission in the world that featured in Acts 2 on the day of Pentecost, especially evidenced by unknown tongues "subsequent" to conversion experience. See Robert P. Menzies, *Empowered for Witness* (Sheffield: Sheffield Academic Press, 2001), 232-243; Roger Stronstad, *The Prophethood of All Believers - A Study in Luke's Charismatic Theology* (Sheffield: Sheffield Academic Press, 1999).

spirit. God infuses it with *dunamis,* thus opening the way for transforming vertical discipleship into horizontal responsibility."[9] He continues saying,

> [f]or 'Where the Spirit of the Lord is, there is liberty' is a claim long attested to and affirmed by Pentecostal-charismatic believers.... The Spirit is God and God is expressed in community, shattering and renewing, rending and healing, revealing and transforming, lifting and liberating a people unto God. When the human spirit is grasped and energised by the Holy Spirit, it is given the necessary power to go beyond itself enabling it to perform tasks beyond our normally anticipated human ability and comprehension.[10]

Hence, the baptism of the Holy Spirit brings a better understanding of the realities of the society and individuals, and directs believers for mission because the Holy Spirit is the missionary Spirit. The Holy Spirit is the agent of sanctification and also gives power for service with a concept of mission being grounded in historical experience but with consequences which go beyond present history. The Holy Spirit enables a person to experience the paradox of suffering and the power of renunciation. One is enabled to side with the oppressed and to become a servant of the poor by becoming poor in the spirit (humility).[11] Richard Shaull studying the Pentecostalism in Latin America says that, "among the Pentecostals today it is the experience of the presence and power of God in the baptism of the Holy Spirit that changes everything and gives life a new direction and a call to mission in the world."[12] Bridges Johns explains the inner dynamics of this experience of common believers in a theological category:

> The experience of sanctification has created utopian visions among people who do not employ critical-reflective, principled, formal operational thought processes. They have experienced...'imaginal transformation'. By experiencing the holy, there is a creative reorganisation of the imagination (self) and the emergence of a new

---

[9] Leonard Lovett, "Liberation: A Dual-Edged Sword," *Pneuma: Journal of the Society for Pentecostal Studies* 9/2 (1987), 166.

[10] Lovett, "Liberation: A Dual-Edged Sword," 165.

[11] Cheryl Bridges Johns, *Pentecostal Formation - A Pedagogy among the Oppressed* (Sheffield: Sheffield Academic Press, 1998), 100.

[12] Richard Shaull and Waldo Cesar, *Pentecostalism and the Future of the Christian Churches* (Grand Rapids, MI: William B. Eerdmans, 2000), 195.

gestalt. The corresponding action, therefore, is directed by this altered perception of the world.[13]

Further, the Spirit baptism provides an angular vision for a social ethic designed to promote social justice in a divided world. Murray Dempster, a Pentecostal ethicist, asserts that the coming of the Spirit at Pentecost has profound implications for integrating the Old Testament conception of social justice into a distinctively Pentecostal social ethic. The Pentecost narrative is the story of the transfer of the charismatic Spirit from Jesus to the disciples. By this transfer of the Spirit, disciples become the heirs and successors to the earthly ministry of Jesus and they would continue to do and teach those things which Jesus began to do and teach. Now, the ministry of Jesus placed him directly in the tradition of the law and the prophets. Jesus' proclamation of the gospel as good news to the poor, the captives and the hungry, demonstrates his continuity with the ethical message of the Old Testament. Hence, "a Pentecostal social ethic grounded exegetically in Luke-Acts is a kingdom ethic made operational within the charismatic community by the empowerment of the Spirit."[14] Thus, a Spirit-filled person becomes an instrument of the Spirit to carry out a prophetic ministry that leads to liberation and transformation in the pattern of Jesus' earthly ministry.

THE GIFTS OF THE SPIRIT: THE MEANS OF PENTECOSTAL MISSION

If the baptism in the Spirit empowers the believers for mission, the gifts of the Spirit act as instruments of mission activities. As we have seen, the Pentecostals believe that being filled with the Spirit means to equip an individual in such a way that one becomes an instrument for the ongoing process of the Spirit in the church and in the world. Here, the gifts of the Spirit play unique roles. They enable the believers to act in the world as Jesus acted. "Social values embedded in 'the fruits of the Spirit and the gifts of the Spirit' have implications for the way in which the church

---

[13] Bridges Johns, *Pentecostal Formation*, 94. Bridges Johns uses the term "utopian visions" in a positive sense to denote the Spirit-given insight to a sanctified believer, resulting in an "altered perception" of the world and an alternative consciousness.

[14] Murray W. Dempster, "Pentecostal Social Concern and the Biblical Mandate for Social Justice," *Pneuma: Journal of the Society for Pentecostal Studies* 9/2 (1987), 146-147.

functions in the society," says Young-Gi Hong.[15] The *charismata* equip the believers to move beyond their ability in this world of spiritual as well as physical bondages, rescuing people through healing their body and mind and bringing them to the kingdom of God. There are many charismatic gifts in operation, such as healing, exorcism, prophecy, word of wisdom, word of knowledge, discerning the spirits, and so on. These gifts are widely used by missionaries, pastors and ordinary believers to bring changes in the lives of suffering people and they join Pentecostal churches.

Now as we turn to the Indian context, most of the evangelists and pastors engaged in mission activities are either semi-literate, illiterate, or have no theological education. However, the new strength and vigour they receive through the infilling of the Spirit and the ability to use the gifts of the Spirit propel them to go out into the world to alleviate suffering of the people, even though they themselves go through such situations. They carry out tasks beyond their capacity and bring great changes in the life of the suffering people. This account of the spiritual gifts gives us the clues to understand the reasons behind the large influx of people into the Pentecostal churches in India.

THE PENTECOSTAL MISSION: THE MEANS OF CHURCH GROWTH

For Pentecostals, the missionary endeavours are not an end in themselves but they are a means to church growth. From the beginning of the movement itself missionaries focused on bringing people to the churches. Even social and charitable ministries were also targeted to add new members. Moreover, every member of a church acts as a missionary wherever one is situated and makes it a divine commission to bring people to congregation. Allan Anderson correctly recognises that Pentecostal evangelism is geared towards church planting, a central feature of all Pentecostal mission activities. Unlike several other churches, Pentecostal churches are missionary by nature among whom the dichotomy between "church" and "mission" do not exist. This "central missiological thrust"

---

[15] Young-Gi Hong, "Church and Mission: A Pentecostal Perspective," *International Review of Mission* 90/358 (2001), 300.

is clearly a "strong point in Pentecostalism" and central to its existence.[16] Church growth studies have repeatedly shown that the Pentecostal and Charismatic churches experience explosive growth where the power of God is manifested through enthusiastic worship and signs and wonders. In Pentecostal congregations, people practically experience the presence of God through the Holy Spirit and the exercise of gifts of the Spirit. This plays a dominant role in the expansion of the church. Here, we shall explore some of the charismatic gifts and some mission activities that are greatly used in Pentecostal churches, which attract people to their fold.

"Healing" in the Context of Illness and Lack of Health Care

One of the prominent aspects of the Indian Pentecostal mission is its emphasis on bodily healing. Health care facilities are scant, as well as in disarray, in remote villages while a large majority suffer from various illnesses causing hundreds of deaths every year. It is a well-known scandal that India has not fared well in terms of the proportion of total health expenditure that is financed by the government.[17] In 2009, it was reported that about two hundred fifty million of the Indian population do not have access to basic medical care.[18] Moreover, nearly half of the total number of children under the age of five were under-nourished which extended to adults, as well. Over half the women population and nearly one-fourth of the Indian men were anaemic. This is a direct consequence of the

---

[16] Allan Anderson, "Towards a Pentecostal Theology for Majority World," *Asian Journal of Pentecostal Studies* 8/1 (2005), 29-47, 37.

[17] Venkatesh Athreya, "Far from Healthy," *Frontline* 27/01 (2-15 January, 2010). http://www.Frontlineonnet. com/stories/20100115270108400.htm (accessed 4 January 2010).

[18] N.R. Narayana Murthy, *A Better India, A Better World* (New Delhi: Penguin Books India Pvt. Ltd, 2009), xiii; The findings of NFHS-3 shows that the infant mortality rate (IMR) before one year of age, is 57, which means more than one in 18 infants die before they are one year old.

continued lack of balanced nutrition from childhood into adulthood, especially, among women.[19]

Besides, lack of financial resources, widespread poverty, and inadequate transportation facilities have adversely affected the chances of healing of even ordinary diseases. Many of the Pentecostal believers in North India testify that they had experienced divine healing and so they joined Pentecostal churches.[20] We need to remember that even when they seek medical help from physicians available in villages, in many cases, this results in mere wastage of their hard-earned resources because, in practice, they do not get the desired result.[21] For example, a mission report from the state of Orissa states,

> Evangelist Elias Digal from Lakoti church informed of the healing testimony of a lady who was suffering from a blood condition for a long time. She was fed up with medications and tried traditional religious practices, which in turn also proved futile. She spent lot [sic] of money and was totally disappointed. Three months back, one of her neighbours, who is a believer, guided her to church and there she came to know Jesus the healer. She requested prayer from the pastor and believers of the church for her healing. On that day the saints prayed earnestly for that expectant lady that she could receive her miraculous healing. Now she is the happiest one to attend the church with all her dear ones in her

---

[19] R. Ramachandran and T.K. Rajalakshmi, "Unhealthy Trend," *Frontline* 26/07 (28 March–10 April, 2009).http://www. frontlineonnet.com/fl2607/stories/20090410260702100.htm (accessed 14 November 2009). Women are the worst hit in terms of access to health services. According to the NFHS-3 data, only 17.3 per cent of women have ever received any service from a health care worker. Only 17.9 per cent of the public health centres have a woman doctor. As a direct consequence, 56.2 per cent of women (aged 15-49) are anaemic, which actually represents an increase from the NFHS-2 data of 51.8 per cent. The percentage of pregnant women who are anaemic has also increased from 49.7 to 57.9 per cent. This condition has greatly affected the health of the poor and was clearly testified to in the interviews.

[20] Interview by author (Udaipur, India, 15 September 2009). A research was conducted in 2009, in the North Indian states of Rajasthan, Gujarat, Maharashtra, Madhya Pradesh and the South Indian states of Kerala and Tamil Nadu choosing a number of Pentecostal churches to know why people are joining the Pentecostal movement.

[21] Abhijit Banerjee, Angus Deaton, and Esther Duflo, "Health Care Delivery in Rural Rajasthan," *Economic and Political Weekly* (28 February 2004), 944. http://epw.in.ezproxye.bham.ac.uk/epw/uploads/articles/7389.pdf (accessed 25 November 2009). Akash Acharya and M. Kent Ranson, "Health Care Financing for the Poor: Community-based Health Insurance Schemes in Gujarat," *Economic and Political Weekly* (17 September 2005), 4141. http://epw.in.ezproxye.bham.ac.uk/epw/uploads/ articles/1133.pdf (accessed 25 November 2009).

family as they all repented, believed and were baptised in the water to join the body of Christ.[22]

Such healing miracles are noted even by secular academicians. Ghanshyam Shah, Professor of Social Science at Jawaharlal Nehru University, New Delhi, accounts for healing as the main reason for tribals to accept Christianity. He writes that:

> [t]here are various reasons, as given by them, for accepting Christianity. The most common reasons are curing of diseases, relief from tension related to day-to-day problems, faith in prayer which helped them in their personal crises, particularly recovery from illness.[23]

Then, he quotes a testimony:

> I was sick and tried "Bhuva-Bhagat" [traditional healers] but could not get relief. My neighbour, who is a Christian, suggested to me to meet the "Padari" [priest] and ask him to offer a prayer for my recovery. I knew the Padari as he used to visit us. I told him about my illness. He asked me to join him for the prayer and I began to feel better. From that day I attended prayers regularly and later became "Cristi" [Christian].[24]

Similarly, David Hardiman of the University of Warwick, U.K., who conducted a study on healing among the tribals in Gujarat, claims that he too collected testimonies of Pentecostal "faith healing." He says, "we managed to meet some of them [the Pentecostals] and attend their meetings for worship in the Dangs, in 2005, that incorporated healing testimonies (*sakshi*)."[25] He further mentions that the "[f]aith healing by bodies such as the Pentecostalists has come to the fore in recent years, as much in the rich countries of the West, as in the poor and underdeveloped tribal belts of India."[26] There are many such testimonies of healing taking place through the work of evangelists and even ordinary members, which

---

[22] Editor, "From our Mission Field: Report from Orissa," *Cross & Crown* (September-October 2001), 13.

[23] Ghanshyam Shah, "Conversion, Reconversion and the State: Recent Events in the Dangs," *Economic and Political Weekly* (6 February 1999), 315. http://epw.in/epw/uploads/articles/8620.pdf (accessed 2 May 2010).

[24] Shah, "Conversion, Reconversion and the State," 315.

[25] David Hardiman and Gauri Raje, "Practices of Healing in Tribal Gujarat," *Economic and Political Weekly* (1 March, 2008), 49. Also see David Hardiman, "Healing, Medical Power and the Poor: Contests in Tribal India," *Economic and Political Weekly* (21 April, 2007), 1405-1406.

[26] Hardiman, "Healing, Medical Power and the Poor," 1406.

change the lives of the people. Once a pastor said, "Church is like a hospital; many people come and get the healing and go back."[27]

This is true in the South Indian states too, including Kerala. Having conducted a field research among Syrian and *dalit* Pentecostals in Kerala, P.G. Abraham shows that the participants testified that the majority of them had "physical problems in their life" and joined the Pentecostal churches because of their deliverance from varied troubles and healing from diseases.[28] Similarly, Siga Arles, a distinguished Indian missiologist, speaking about the Pentecostal churches in Karnataka (Kolar Gold Field) highlights the "power of healing" that attracts both Christians and non-Christians to the Pentecostal churches.[29] Thus, it is obvious that the gift of healing enables the Pentecostal churches to alleviate the suffering of the people and adds new members to the churches.

"Exorcism" in the Context of Demonic Oppression

Another dominant missionary practice, especially in the Indian villages, is the casting out of evil spirits that liberates people from the clutches of demonic oppression. There are plenty of testimonies related to people being delivered from demonic possessions and attack of malevolent spirits. According to villagers, many diseases are caused by the evil spirit attacks or are perpetuated by evil practices. They believe that any attack from the wicked spirits can have severe repercussions and can be even life-threatening. Tribals and *dalits* believe in a number of spirits, both benevolent and malevolent. Their whole social and religious life is

---

[27] Focus Group Interview (Tabor Church, Gujarat, 6 September 2009).

[28] He conducted the study to understand the caste discrimination among various Pentecostal denominations; P.G. Abraham, *Caste and Christianity: A Pentecostal Perspective* (Kumbhaza, Kerala: Crown Books, 2003), 116-118. He notes the response of the people: "1. I have experienced God's deliverance in my trouble. 2. I have experienced God's healing power in my sickness. 3. God had delivered me from devilish attack."

[29] Siga Arles, "Indigenous Pentecostal Church Growth at KGF (Kolar Gold Field), Karnataka" in Roger E. Hedlund (ed), *Christianity is Indian: The Emergence of an Indigenous Community*, rev. edn. (Delhi: ISPCK, 2004), 392-393, 395.

intricately related to the spirit world.[30] Various categories of spirits such as the village spirits, the clan spirits, and the spirits of the ancestors, etc, are identified.[31] The fear of these spirits motivates people to worship and offer sacrifices to them.[32] While exploring the religion of *dalits* in Chhattisgarh, Bauman also portrays a similar picture.

> The religion of rural Chhattisgarh in the nineteenth and early twentieth centuries was (and in many ways still is) about power and control, about survival, protection and order. It was about the concerns of everyday, about diagnosing illness, interpreting omens and signs and about performing rituals intended to smooth one's path in this life and the next.[33]

Traditional healers claim that they can deliver the villagers from the spirits.[34] When poor villagers fail to get any result through traditional religious practices, they approach pastors for their rescue as a last resort. The *Economic and Political Weekly*, for instance, undergirds this fact. Commenting on the reasons why Oraons, a group in Orissa, accept Christianity, Pati says, "[i]n a context of uncertainties and insecurities the Oraons, for example, felt that Christianity protected them from the

---

[30] For a comprehensive understanding of the names of spirits worshipped by various tribal groups in different states of India see, H.H. Risley and E.A. Gait, *Census of India 1921, Religion* (Calcutta: Superintendent Government Printing, India, 1923). Also see http://www.archive.org/stream/cu31924014522746#page/n179/mode/2up (accessed 11 July 2010). Paul G. Hiebert, "Spiritual Warfare and World View" in Roger E. Hedlund and Paul Joshua Bhakiaraj (eds), *Missiology for the 21st Century: South Asian Perspective* (Delhi: ISPCK, 2004), 472.

[31] Ghanshyam Shah, "Conversion, Reconversion and the State: Recent Events in the Dangs," *Economic and Political Weekly* (6 February, 1999): 315. http://epw.in/epw/uploads/articles/8620. pdf (accessed 2 May 2010). Abraham M. Ayrookhuziel, "Distinctive Characteristics of Folk Traditions" in Gnana Robinson (ed), *Religions of the Marginalised: Towards a Phenomenology and Methodology of Study* (Delhi: ISPCK, 1998), 2-4.

[32] Daniel Katapali, "Indigenous Missions and the Savara Tribal Church of Srikakulam" in Roger E. Hedlund (ed), *Christianity is Indian: The Emergence of an Indigenous Community*, 270; Sathianathan Clarke, *Dalits and Christianity: Subaltern Religion and Liberation Theology in India* (New Delhi: Oxford University Press, 1999), 71-75; Chad M. Bauman, *Christian Identity and Dalit Religion in Hindu India, 1868-1947* (Grand Rapids, MI: William B. Eerdmans, 2008),40-41; Ayrookhuziel, "Distinctive Characteristics of Folk Traditions," 2-3; Kancha Ilaiah, *Why I am not a Hindu: A Sudra Critique of Hindutva Philosophy, Culture and Political Economy*, 2nd ed. (Calcutta: Samya, 2005), 91-96.

[33] Bauman, *Christian Identity and Dalit Religion*, 40.

[34] Traditional healers first ask for a cockerel to sacrifice; if there is no relief, after seven days a goat is sacrificed. They also use alcohol, incense-sticks and other materials to either please the spirits or ward them off. A cockerel, even in the village will cost Rs.250-300 and a goat more than Rs.3000-5000. Moreover, *bhopa* (traditional healer) also may demand big amounts like Rs.1,000-5,000.

witches and 'bhoots', who were powerless against this system."[35] Many of the members who attend the churches share such incidents. They also hand down their testimonies to the suffering people.

Further, the Pentecostal pastors and evangelists become instrumental in rescuing people from the grip of evil powers. Parsing Baria, an evangelist of the Filadelfia church in the Panchmahal district in Gujarat, speaks about the miraculous recovery of a family whose children fell prey to the curse and attack from the wicked spirits. He says that:

> The Lord told me to go to a family that was being tormented with sickness and consistent deaths. Four children in that family had died following which even the cattle began to fall prey. The entire household moved to another locality to escape the curse, but the curse followed. Much prayer was done and the Lord through a miracle restored to them what they had lost over the years.[36]

Such incidents result in the rapid growth of Pentecostalism among the poor villagers.[37] Undoubtedly, here, we also find many functional parallels between Pentecostalism and animism. For example, the Pentecostal worldview is closer to animistic view, except that there is no longer a need to appease a whole pantheon of spirits through magical means. The major difference between Pentecostals and people in animistic cultures is that the former affirm that there is only *one* spirit, the Holy Spirit.[38]

"Transformation" in the Context of Poverty

Another area in which Pentecostal spirituality and mission in the Spirit transform the life of the poor masses in India is their economic situation. Even though India is the third largest economy in the world and has an expanding market economy, it is fast earning the dubious distinction of

---

[35] Biswamoy Pati, "Identity, Hegemony, Resistance: Conversions in Orissa, 1800-2000," *Economic and Political Weekly* (3 November, 2001), 4204.

[36] [n.a.], "Field News," *Cross & Crown* 26/6 (August-September, 1996), 21.

[37] Focus Group Interview, Hebron Church, Rajasthan, 9 August, 2009.

[38] Donald E. Miller and Tetsunao Yamamori, *Global Pentecostalism: The New Face of Christian Social Engagement* (Berkeley, California: University of California Press, 2007), 24-25.

being "the hunger capital of the world."[39] The nutritional status of children has not improved over the past five years.[40] India has forty per cent of the malnourished children in the world. Rural unemployment is rampant and this leads to poverty and affects the poor badly. It was reported in 2009 that three hundred eighteen million Indians did not have access to safe drinking water.[41] The struggles of the common people, especially farmers, are increasing day by day. Agrarian depression continues as do farmer suicides. Every year, over twenty thousand farmers commit suicide out of despair over failing crops and huge debt, a phenomenon that continues even today.[42]

Importantly, the tribals, *dalits*, and people of other low castes in the Indian society, among whom the Pentecostal movement is fast growing, spend most of their meagre resources either for traditional religious practices or medical treatment. As a result, they come to a stage where they are burdened by debt and poverty. The options before them are either to borrow money from someone, or sell their property or to end their life. Many men in villages end their lives due to financial debt and poverty, leaving behind women and children to mend their own lives.[43] In such a situation, the Pentecostal message of healing, deliverance, and Jesus as one who provides for their life makes a huge impact upon their lives. Such transformations enable them to save their hard-earned resources to provide for their other needs. It has enhanced their living standard. Better food, clothing, and new facilities at home evoke a new sense of empowerment in them as well as in the sight of others.[44]

Additionally, it is found that the Pentecostal believers prosper far better than other people both in financial terms and in educating their

---

[39] R. Ramachandran and T.K. Rajalakshmi, "Unhealthy Trend," *Frontline* 26/07 (28 March–10 April, 2009).http://www.frontlineonnet.com/fl2607/stories/20090410260702100.htm (accessed 14 November 2009).

[40] Ramachandran and Rajalakshmi, "Unhealthy Trend."

41 N.R. Narayana Murthy, *A Better India, A Better World* (New Delhi: Penguin Books India Pvt. Ltd, 2009), xiii.

[42] N.A. Mujumdar, "Rural Development: New Perceptions," *Economic and Political Weekly* (28 September, 2002), 3983. http://epw.in.ezproxyd.bham.ac.uk/epw/uploads/articles/4601.pdf (accessed 16 November, 2009).

[43] Focus Group Interview (Tabor Church, Gujarat, 30 August 2009).

[44] Interview by author (Udaipur, 8 July 2009).

children. McGavran calls it "redemption and lift."[45] They wear better clothes, improve cleanliness, and are healthier. The obvious reason may be that they no longer spend their resources on alcohol, traditional religious practices, or in activities regarded as sexually immoral.[46] Abraham also shows that the same is true in Kerala. He says that "the majority responded that there has been a change in the economic life from their previous stage."[47] This change has happened "when they turned into Pentecostal churches, abolished all malpractices such as smoking, drinking and going for sorcery, etc. This resulted in the saving of huge amounts which could later be used for their family needs."[48] Donald Miller and Tetsunao Yamamori observe this as one of the positive effects of Pentecostalism:

> There is substantial evidence for the 'social uplift' associated with Pentecostalism, in that Pentecostals have a competitive economic advantage over their neighbours because of their moral proscriptions against alcohol, drugs, gambling and womanising. Without these social evils, believers may produce surplus capital that can then be invested in business enterprises or in the education and welfare of their families.[49]

On the other hand, most of the Pentecostal churches are strict in their outlook on holiness. Such a stringent discipline helps keep people away from old bad habits. David Hardiman observes that "[c]onversion was seen as providing a means to transform their lives for the better, in which they abandoned the old wild ways of traditional tribal life, and became sober, hard-working and god-fearing."[50] Thus, the Pentecostal way of life brings a definitive transformation in the life of the poor people.

"Testimony" in the Context of Religious Pluralism

The ordinary believers who received divine healing, freedom from the spirits, and whose economic situation has been improved, make it a rallying point to testify to their compatriots the changes that have happened in their lives. The story they narrate is the story of the power

---

[45] Donald McGavran, *Understanding Church Growth* (Grand Rapids, MI: William B. Eerdmans, 1970), 260-277; C. Peter Wagner, *Look Out! The Pentecostals are Coming* (Illinois: Creation House, 1973), 93-94.
[46] Focus Group Interview (Hebron Church, Rajasthan, 9 August 2009).
[47] Abraham, *Caste and Christianity*, 122.
[48] Abraham, *Caste and Christianity*, 112-123.
[49] Miller and Yamamori, *Global Pentecostalism*, 33.
[50] Hardiman and Raje, "Practices of Healing in Tribal Gujarat," 49.

of Jesus bringing changes to their lives and their improved conditions. Such sharing of personal experiences touches the lives of the suffering individuals for they originate from people whom they already knew, who were once like them and have undergone similar predicaments. However, now, they see that they have been liberated and transformed. Therefore, the listeners are convinced of what is testified and in many cases it is readily accepted.[51]

Consequently, the idea of Jesus as the Saviour and the Lord is a deep-rooted understanding among the believers. Knowingly or unknowingly, they extrapolate the idea that Jesus is the only Saviour to their family, community, and larger society. Pentecostal believers engage in the sharing of the uniqueness of Jesus in their surrounding and the Spirit enables them to witness Christ with courage. It is firmly believed that only with the help of the Spirit can one achieve it.[52] Besides this, their new found joy as well as the confidence in the efficacy of Jesus to change the predicament of their fellow humans propels them to testify to his uniqueness with urgency. Thus, for the Pentecostal believers, evangelism is, by default, a lifestyle. It is not anything carried out by special agencies or highly trained experts. Rather, evangelism is deeply ingrained in the psyche and daily life of the believers and Jesus as the only Saviour is testified without any hesitation. Moreover, they do not engage in any debate or dialogue in formal sense. The ordinary believers invite people who are in despair to "come and taste what they have been experiencing."[53] They pray for the needs of the people and miracles take place. Then, they boldly proclaim that Jesus is the greatest of all.[54] This way of communicating and sharing of life experiences explain rapid proliferation of the Pentecostal churches in India.

Nevertheless, in the midst of rapid growth, Pentecostals became a frequent target of violent communal forces. Their mission or evangelistic endeavours attract the ire of religious fundamentalists and lead to violent attacks. The Pentecostal practices of divine healing, exorcism, or use of other charismatic gifts for people who are in dire need are considered

---

[51] Interview (Maharashtra, 2 September, 2009).
[52] Interview (Maharashtra, 2 September 2009).
[53] Focus Group Interview (Tabor Church, Gujarat, 6 September 2009).
[54] Interview (Hebron Church, Rajasthan, 5 August 2009).

as influencing people for forcible conversion. Even without the slightest provocation, pastors and missionaries are attacked, churches are vandalised, Bibles are burned, and believers are terrorised and brutalised. When such incidents take place, very often the authorities and police either look away or abet the perpetrators of violence and register court cases against the Pentecostal believers and preachers in the name of forcible conversions. Carrying out these sorts of attack is not unique to the Hindutva proponents. Even members of other religious groups resort to similar actions when a person joins a Pentecostal church leaving their flock.

Such a context warrants a mission strategy which avoids violence and also nurtures a harmonious relationship in society. At the same time, those who are in dire need of deliverance from evil spiritual forces or seek salvation through Christ are to be reached out to. According to Anderson, there is an urgent need to ponder upon the relationship between the Christian gospel and the ancient pre-Christian religions that continue to give meaning to people's understanding of their lives. Demonising these religions will not help the cause of evangelism and the healthy growth of the church today.[55] Therefore, it is significant to have a valid, vibrant Pentecostal theology of religions, or what I want to call "pneumato-centric mission theology for pluralistic context." Such a Spirit-centred mission theology "does not compromise biblical, historic Christianity or act condescendingly or contemptuously towards other world religions, that is also desirable for Pentecostals and for our friends of other faiths."[56]

PNEUMATO-CENTRIC PENTECOSTAL MISSION FOR PLURALISTIC CONTEXT

Although Pentecostals are generally hesitant to discuss the issue of religious pluralism and related questions, recently Pentecostal scholars

---

[55] Allan Anderson, "Towards a Pentecostal Missiology for the Majority World," *Asian Journal of Pentecostal Studies* 8/1 (2005), 38.

[56] Tony Richie, "Neither Naïve nor Narrow: A Balanced Pentecostal Approach to Christian Theology of Religions," *Presented to the Annual Meeting of the American Academy of Religion*, Philadelphia, PA, 19-22 November 2005, 2. http://www.ncccusa.org/pdfs/naive.pdf (accessed 2 November 2010). Also see Tony Richie, "Speaking by the Spirit: A Wesleyan-Pentecostal Theology of Testimony as a Model for Interreligious Encounter and Dialogue in the USA with Global Implications" (PhD Thesis, University of Middlesex, 2010).

are beginning to appreciate the need for dialogue with other religions and have a developed theology of religions. Now more pastors and evangelists encounter people of other faiths. Taking this reality into consideration, Kärkkäinen argues that it is vital to include theology of religions in the Christian educational curriculum.[57] Similarly, Richie contends that it is not appropriate to relegate all religious experiences beyond the border of the institutional church to the demonic realm. Although there is no salvation outside Christ, this does not mean that there is no possibility of salvation outside the church.[58]

Amos Yong argues that the stress of Charismatic-Pentecostal pneumatology on the universality of experience of God through the Spirit may contribute to a contemporary Christian theology of religions.[59] He sees the presence of the Spirit active in creation and in all cultures, which includes religions because the Spirit has been poured out on all flesh.[60] The emphasis of pneumatic elements enables Pentecostals to be open to other religious traditions. According to him, a Pentecostal-Charismatic theology of religions should free human beings for participation in interreligious dialogue. The goal of such dialogues is not merely to agree on similarities, rather even the "activity of apologetics needs to be included in acknowledging such conversations to be in the service of the righteousness, peace and truth that characterise the Kingdom of God."[61] He articulates "pneumatological imagination" as an experience of and orientation to the Holy Spirit through which one may determine the presence of the Holy Spirit. He also stresses that it is vital to discern

---

[57] Veli-Matti Kärkkäinen, *An Introduction to the Theology of Religions: Biblical, Historical, & Contemporary Perspectives* (Illinois: InterVarsity Press, 2003), 20; Veli-Matti Kärkkäinen, *Trinity and Religious Pluralism: The Doctrine of the Trinity in Christian Theology of Religions* (Hants: Ashgate, 2004); Samuel Solivan, "Interreligious Dialogue: An Hispanic American Pentecostal Perspective" in S. Mark Heim (ed), *Grounds for Understanding: Ecumenical Responses to Religious Pluralism* (Grand Rapids, MI: William B. Eerdmans, 1998), 37-45.

[58] Tony Richie, "'The Unity of Spirit': Are Pentecostals Inherently Ecumenists and Inclusivists?," *Journal of the European Pentecostal Theological Association* 26/1 (2006), 31-33.

[59] Amos Yong, *Discerning the Spirit(s): A Pentecostal-Charismatic Theology of Religions*, Journal of Pentecostal Theology Supplement Series (Sheffield: Sheffield Academic Press, 2000), 29-30.

[60] Amos Yong, *The Spirit Poured Out on All Flesh: Pentecostalism and the Possibility of Global Theology* (Grand Rapids, MI: Baker Academic, 2005).

[61] Yong, *Discerning the Spirit(s)*, 313.

the absence of the divine or presence of the demonic in other religious traditions.[62]

Yong proposes a theological framework for interfaith encounter. First, God is universally present by his Spirit. Therefore, he sustains religions for his divine purposes. Second, the Spirit ushers in the kingdom of God. Hence, the signs of the kingdom are made manifest through the Spirit's presence. Third, when there are signs of resistance to and activity against the kingdom of God, the Spirit can be said to be absent from religions.[63] Nonetheless, he emphasises that the possibility of the presence of the Spirit in other religions should not de-emphasise the centrality of Christ to salvation, nor should it undermine the importance of evangelism.[64]

Similarly, Richie draws on the narrative of Acts 2 and the day of Pentecost to offer a Pentecostal perspective of dialogue.[65] The outpouring of the Spirit enabled a diversity of tongues; the many tongues retain their particularity even as they point to the unity of the one Spirit. These tongues represent, at least potentially, many religions, which in turn point to the redemption of religions (eschatologically) as well as of languages and cultures. The tongues or testimonies of the religious other must first be heard in their own terms before a theology of religion can be constructed. This will involve a critical analysis of religious beliefs and practices using a "hermeneutic of charity."[66] With this background, Richie proposes a model of Pentecostal engagement based on the notion of testimony, telling others of what God has done in one's life in order to encourage them. It can be transformative for the testifier and hearer, alike. It contains significant autobiographical elements and doxological content. Use of testimony as a way of interreligious dialogue benefits Pentecostals

---

[62] Amos Yong, "'Not Knowing Where the Wind Blows...': On Envisioning a Pentecostal-Charismatic Theology of Religions," *Journal of Pentecostal Theology* 14 (1999), 81-83.

[63] Mark J. Cartledge, *Testimony in the Spirit* (Farnham: Ashgate, 2010), 144. Also see Yong, *The Spirit Poured Out on All Flesh*, 250–253.

[64] Amos Yong, *Beyond the Impasse: Toward a Pneumatological Theology of Religion* (Grand Rapids, MI: Willian B. Eerdmans, 2003), 52-53.

[65] Richie, "Speaking by the Spirit," 89-90; Cartledge, *Testimony in the Spirit*, 147-148.

[66] Richie, "Speaking by the Spirit," 113-115; Richie, "God's Fairness to People of All Faiths: A Respectful Proposal to Pentecostals for Discussion Regarding World Religions," *Pneuma* 28/1 (2006), 105-119.

as it is integral to the Pentecostal spirituality. It helps them to retain their original energy and vitality.[67]

Hollenweger, however, develops a theology of "dialogical evangelism" that is less rigid and more respectful to mutual sharing of divine experience between members of different religions. It decries a sharp demarcation between Christian mission and interfaith dialogue. This is based on the encounter of Peter and Cornelius (Acts 10) and is used as a biblical model for the contemporary Pentecostals. Significantly, both participants learn from each other as the Holy Spirit is poured out afresh.[68]

It seems that emphasis on pneumatological elements in Pentecostal spirituality makes it possible to interact with other religious traditions. Added to that, for the Indian Pentecostals, the centrality of Christ is a point of contact with other religionists. This point of contact is actualised through their testimonies and activities of signs and wonders which happen through the agency of the Spirit. Richie, rightly, endorses a typical Pentecostal position saying, "[i]nclusivism by no means necessitates even a nascent compromise of Christian integrity or of Pentecostal theology and spirituality; rather, it enables Pentecostals to witness with respect to every one of the limitless love of God in his Son by the power of the Spirit."[69] Since ordinary Pentecostals constantly interact with people of other faiths and also come under the attack of extremist social elements, this notion can be useful for context.

Concluding our discussion, it is obvious that the primary reason behind the rapid growth of the Pentecostal churches in India is the enthusiastic mission and the evangelistic activities of missionaries, pastors, and ordinary believers. Besides their experience of the Spirit baptism that propels them to act in unlikely places and situations, the use of *charismata* enables them to set free many people from their predicaments. The charismatic gifts like healing and exorcism attract

---

[67] Richie, "Speaking by the Spirit," 165-166.
[68] Walter J. Hollenweger, "Critical Issues for Pentecostals" in Allan H. Anderson and Walter J. Hollenweger (eds), *Pentecostals after a Century: Global Perspectives on a Movement in Transition* (Sheffield: Sheffield Academic Press, 1999), 176-191; Walter J. Hollenweger, "Evangelism: A Non-Colonial Model," *Journal of Pentecostal Theology* 7 (1995), 116-121.
[69] Richie, "'The Unity of Spirit'," 34.

suffering people to the Pentecostal churches and bring transformation to their lives. Nonetheless, the Pentecostal message is not always welcomed. Rather, it attracts the ire of the religious fanatic elements and invites persecution. In such a context, a pneumato-centric mission theology which acknowledges other religious traditions without compromising the Pentecostal mission practices can greatly benefit and avoid confrontation with co-religionists.

5

PROPHETIC SPEECH AND ACTION AS WITNESS TO CHRIST'S RESURRECTION

Gary Tyra[*]

In the year 2011 two books were published, both of which encouraged their readers to adopt a prophetic approach to missional engagement. In *The Holy Spirit in Mission: Prophetic Speech and Action in Christian Witness*,[1] I issued a call for evangelical Christians living in the non-majority world to humbly open themselves to a *pneumatologically real* version of prophetic speech and action, suggesting that the same kind of missional fruitfulness evident in the book of Acts and currently being experienced by Pentecostal-Charismatic disciples living and ministering in the urban centres of the Global South can be experienced in the industrial West as well. Aimed as it was at an evangelical readership, it presumed a hopeful

---

[*] **Gary Tyra**, DMin, is Professor of Biblical and Practical Theology at Vanguard University (Southern California). He has completed his doctoral studies at Fuller Theological Seminary, USA. He has also served as the senior pastor for three churches over a twenty seven years period, one of which was a church plant. His most recently published works include: *A Missional Orthodoxy: Theology and Ministry in a Post-Christian Context* (Downers Grove, Ill.: InterVarsity Press Academic, 2013); and *Pursuing Moral Faithfulness: Ethics and Christian Discipleship* (Downers Grove, Ill.: InterVarsity Press Academic, 2015).

[1] Gary Tyra, *The Holy Spirit in Mission: Prophetic Speech and Action in Christian Witness* (Downers Grove, Ill.: InterVarsity Press Academic, 2011).

yet biblically constrained exclusivist understanding of salvation,[2] and a strong commitment to the fulfilling of the Great Commission.

That same year witnessed the release of *Prophetic Dialogue: Reflections on Christian Mission Today* co-authored by Roman Catholic missiologists Stephen B. Bevans and Roger P. Schroeder.[3] This volume seems to have presumed a more international audience, an inclusivist (if not pluralist) understanding of salvation,[4] and a robust commitment to interreligious dialogue.[5]

Despite the differences which exist between the intended audiences of these two volumes and the manner in which each work understands the nature of prophetic speech and action, I am convinced that the two proposals are, ironically, quite complementary. That said, I want to write this essay by posing a couple of potentially provocative questions. *First, differing cultural contexts notwithstanding, what if there was a Spirit-empowered approach to Christian mission that made it possible for rank-and-file Christian disciples (cultural insiders) to interact with family members, neighbors, friends, co-workers, and even strangers in the marketplace in such a way as to bear a strong, salient, and compelling witness to the resurrection of Jesus Christ? Second, would not such a pneumatologically real approach to prophetic dialogue prove to be a "game changer" even in ministry settings which, religiously speaking, are highly pluralistic?*

---

[2] Soteriological exclusivism holds that, while God is free to save anyone he wants, the Bible seems to emphasize the importance of a confession of faith in the resurrection and, hence, lordship of Jesus Christ (e.g., see Rom 10:9; 1 Cor 15:1–5). Along with Timothy Tennent, I prefer a descriptor such as revelatory particularism over the term "exclusivism." See Timothy C. Tennent, *Invitation to World Missions: A Trinitarian Missiology for the Twenty-first Century* (Grand Rapids: Kregel Academic, 2010), 220–21.

[3] Stephen B. Bevans and Roger P. Schroeder, *Prophetic Dialogue: Reflections on Christian Mission Today* (Maryknoll, NY: Orbis Books, 2011).

[4] Bevans and Schroeder, *Prophetic Dialogue*, 22.

[5] At the risk of oversimplifying things, while soteriological pluralism insists that all religions can be salvific, most forms of soteriological inclusivism hold that even though it is the cross work of Christ which underwrites the experience of salvation, an explicit confession of Christ as Lord is not necessary. Christ can "anonymously" save people who have never heard of him, or are incapable of a thoughtful commitment to him, or who, for a variety of reasons are reticent to confess him as Lord. Instead of a conscious and public commitment to Christ, the criterion for (or earmark of) salvation in both pluralism and inclusivism is a commitment to making the world a better place through personal morality, peacemaking, pursuing social justice, and engaging in creation care.

While I very much believe that mission in today's world needs to be dialogical rather than demagogic in nature,[6] it is my conviction that the phenomenon of prophetic (Spirit-prompted) speech and action—Christian disciples speaking and acting into the lives of hurting people at the behest of the risen Jesus—has what it takes to cause many people, regardless of the nature of their religiosity, to take a second look at what the Christian scriptures have to say about Jesus. Where an approach to Christian mission that is grounded in a realist rather than non-realist understanding and experience of the Spirit of Christ is at work, huge numbers of Christian disciples are being made, even in cultural settings where many religious paths are on offer. A premise with which Bevans, Schroeder, and I heartily concur is that Christians living in even highly pluralistic settings need not feel the need to choose between a dialogic and prophetic engagement in Christian witness. In this chapter I provide a cursory summary of three salient aspects of my own missiological proposal, and then reflect a bit on how it compares with the one proffered by Bevans and Schroeder. The effect, I trust, will be inspirational as well as informational. And rightly so since we have good reason to believe that the same Spirit of mission who enabled the first-century followers of the risen Jesus to impact their religiously pluralistic world with tangible representations of God's kingdom is eager to do so in the twenty-first century as well.

THE MISSIONAL PNEUMATOLOGY PROFFERED IN *THE HOLY SPIRIT IN MISSION*

In the introduction to *The Holy Spirit in Mission*, I cite one of the articles of faith included in the "Cape Town Commitment" created at Cape Town 2010: Third Lausanne Congress on World Evangelization. The particular article of faith is one which emphasizes the importance of the Holy Spirit to the mission of the church. This article says,

> We love the Holy Spirit within the unity of the Trinity, along with God the Father and God the Son. He is the missionary Spirit sent by the missionary Father and the missionary Son, breathing life and power into God's missionary Church. We love and pray for the presence of the Holy Spirit because without the witness of the Spirit to Christ, our

---

[6] See Tyra, *A Missional Orthodoxy*, 210.

own witness is futile. Without the convicting work of the Spirit, our preaching is in vain. Without the gifts, guidance and power of the Spirit, our mission is mere human effort. And without the fruit of the Spirit, our unattractive lives cannot reflect the beauty of the gospel.[7]

I am struck by the assertion that the Holy Spirit is "the missionary Spirit of the missionary Father and the missionary Son, breathing life and power into God's missionary church." Indeed, my purpose in writing *The Holy Spirit in Mission* was to produce a work that might serve as a practical biblical theology of the Spirit that can aid in the formation of biblically informed, Spirit-empowered, missionally faithful Christians and churches.

In a nutshell, the overarching themes of the book are as follows:

- The Holy Spirit is a missionary Spirit committed to fulfilling God's mission (*missio Dei*) in the world.
- The Holy Spirit has a penchant for using God's people to accomplish God's missional purposes.
- There's a connection (in the Bible as a whole) between the coming of the Spirit and the phenomenon of Spirit-enabled speech and action.
- There's a connection (in the Book of Acts in particular) between Spirit-enabled speech and action and a missional faithfulness/fruitfulness.
- The same kind of missional faithfulness/fruitfulness we see at work in the Christianity that is currently "blowing up" in the Global South can also occur in the West as well.
- What is needed in the West is a biblically-informed missional pneumatology that can unite all evangelicals around the goal of forming more missionally faithful churches!

What follows in the first half of this essay is a cursory overview of three salient components of the proposal put forward in *The Holy Spirit in Mission*. Becoming at least a bit familiar with the missional pneumatology

---

[7] "The Cape Town Commitment," http://www.lausanne.org/ctcommitment (accessed 30 September, 2016).

proffered in my own work is crucial to the reader's ability to understand the manner in which I subsequently interact with the "prophetic dialogue" proposal put forward by Bevans and Schroeder.

The Biblical Case for Prophetic Capacity

It is my contention that scattered throughout the Bible are passages which seem to connect the coming of the Spirit upon God's people with the phenomenon of prophetic speech and action. In chapter one of *The Holy Spirit in Mission*, I provide a survey of many of these passages. However, this survey is much more than a simple listing of multiple proof texts. Instead, what we find spread across both testaments is a coherent, extremely meaningful *pneumatological* story/drama comprised of three main chapters/acts, each filled with much illustrative material/story-advancing scenes.

In the first chapter/act of this story, we discover how, at a pivotal moment near the beginning of the Old Testament era, Moses, himself a prophet (Deut 34:10), expressed a wish that all of God's people would be filled with God's Spirit and become involved in prophetic activity (Num 11:29 cf. 11:25–28). Then, as if to illustrate this connection between the Spirit and the prophetic phenomenon Moses had in mind, throughout the rest of the Old Testament are many passages which seem to indicate that prophetic activity—both prophetic speech and action—routinely occurs when God's Spirit comes upon people who belong to him (e.g., 1 Sam 10:6, 9–10; 19:19–20, 23; Num 24:2-3; 1 Chr 12:18; 2 Chr 15:1-2; 20:14–15; 24:20; Isa 61:1; Ezek 11:5).

In the second chapter/act of the story, the setting of which is near the end of the Old Testament era, we find God inspiring the prophet Joel to announce that Moses' wish (that all of God's people might be filled with God's Spirit and become involved in prophetic activity) will someday come true! Because of the importance of this passage, I will cite it here:

> And afterward, I will pour out my Spirit on all people. Your sons and daughters will prophesy, your old men will dream dreams, your young men will see visions. Even on my servants, both men and women, I will pour out my Spirit in those days. (Joel 2:28–29)

There is a sense in which this is how the Old Testament ends with respect to its pneumatology—with this promise of a future outpouring of the Spirit upon all of God's people regardless of traditional gender and socio-economic distinctions.

However, this second chapter/act of the pneumatological story continues as, moving forward in biblical history, we discover in the New Testament as well many passages which seem to evidence a connection between the Holy Spirit and prophetic speech and action. For example, moving us closer to the third act in the pneumatological drama there are several sections in the Gospel of Luke which seem to emphasize such a "connection":

- The prophetic activity in the infancy narratives of Luke (Luke 1:41–45, 67; 2:25-28).

- The prophetic activity in the inauguration narrative of Luke (Luke 3:21–22; 4:1–13; 4:14–30; 4:31–44; cf. Isa 61:1).

- The prophetic activity alluded to in Jesus' preparation of his disciples (Luke 12:11–12; cf. Matt 10:18–20).

And yet, it is in the book of Acts that we witness the formal unveiling of the third chapter/act of the story as an inspired apostle Peter boldly announces to a curious crowd that, with the coming of the Holy Spirit on the day of Pentecost, both Moses' wish and Joel's promise have finally been fulfilled! Again, because of its importance, I will cite this passage here:

> Then Peter stood up with the Eleven, raised his voice and addressed the crowd: 'Fellow Jews and all of you who live in Jerusalem, let me explain this to you; listen carefully to what I say. These men are not drunk, as you suppose. It's only nine in the morning! No, this is what was spoken by the prophet Joel: 'In the last days, God says, I will pour out my Spirit on all people. Your sons and daughters will prophesy, your young men will see visions, your old men will dream dreams. Even on my servants, both men and women, I will pour out my Spirit in those days, and they will prophesy.' (Acts 2:14–18)

Please note how Peter seems to be underscoring the connection between what was happening to the one hundred and twenty on the day of Pentecost and the phenomenon of prophecy! According to Peter, the immediate result of the outpouring of the Holy Spirit on the day of Pentecost was to impart to *all* of Christ's followers a new prophetic capacity to speak and act on God's behalf.

But this is not the end of the pneumatological story *per se*. Many more passages supportive of the "connection" are provided in the remainder of the New Testament. For example, the rest of the book of Acts is replete with stories of Christ-followers being empowered by the Holy Spirit to engage in prophetic speech and action. Indeed, in no less than twenty one of the twenty eight chapters which make up the book of Acts, I can identify an explicit reference to some form of prophetic activity. Over and over again in Acts we find people being filled or re-filled with the Holy Spirit and, as a result:

- *praising God with prophetic speech;*
- *hearing personal words of encouragement;*
- *receiving special ministry assignments;*
- *speaking and acting into the lives of others in Christ's name;*
- *making a difference in people's lives; and (in the process)*
- *being used by the Holy Spirit to achieve God's missional purposes in the world!*

Moreover, we should also take note of how the "connection" we see presented in the rest of the Bible shows up in some of Paul's letters as well. Despite the fact that Paul's pneumatology seems to be more soteriological in nature (oriented toward the experience of salvation) than the "vocational," "charismatic," or "missional" pneumatology apparent in Luke-Acts,[8] I believe that it is possible to identify passages in Paul's writings which seem to connect the phenomenon of prophetic activity with the coming of the Spirit,[9] and which suggest that the activity of the Spirit in the lives of believers can and should exercise a missional effect.[10] For the sake of space, I will simply list these passages here: Romans

---

[8] See Tyra, *The Holy Spirit in Mission*, 68–69.
[9] For more on this, see Tyra, *The Holy Spirit in Mission*, 68–74.
[10] Certainly, this was the case with Paul himself as Acts 13:9-12 makes clear..

8:15–16 (cf. Gal 4:6); Romans 8:26–27; 1 Corinthians 12–14; Ephesians 5:15–20.

In sum, the Bible as a whole seems to evidence a dynamic connection between empowering encounters with the Holy Spirit—the Spirit of mission—and the phenomenon of prophetic activity (Spirit-prompted and enabled speech and action). Fully recognizing the limitations inherent in a summary of a survey, it is nevertheless my hope that this attempt at one will enable the reader to understand a critical contention that lies at the heart of my missiological proposal.

THE *CHARISMATIC* NATURE OF PROPHETIC SPEECH AND ACTION

Earlier in this chapter I referred to a *"pneumatologically real* version of prophetic speech and action" and a "realist rather than non-realist understanding and experience of the Spirit of Christ." In a nutshell, the "pneumatological realism" I have in mind[11] insists that, given the radical importance of the Holy Spirit to every aspect of the economy of God (from creation to redemption to consummation), and to the nature of reality itself, Christ's followers should *expect* to experience God's Spirit in ways that are real (ie, personal, interactive, and phenomenal) rather than merely theoretical, conceptual, or ritualistic. Moreover, the sincere Christian disciple should expect that these interactions with the Spirit possess the potential to be both *epistemologically helpful*—ie, revelatory in terms of God's love, will, and purposes (Eph 1:17; 3:16–19; Col 1:9; 1 Cor

---

[11] See Gary Tyra, *A Missional Orthodoxy*, 220–227; Tyra, *Pursuing Moral Faithfulness*, 20, 22–23, 29, 52–53, 124, 150, 158, 199, 206, 236, 272, 275, 286.

2:6–16)—and *existentially impactful*—ie, transformative, life-shaping, and ministry-engendering (Gal 5:22-23; Col 1:10–12)—in their effect.[12]

Please keep this definition in mind as I press on to indicate that chapter two of *The Holy Spirit in Mission* provides its readers with a nuanced discussion of the three main ways I see the first followers of Jesus engaging in ministry in a Spirit-prompted, Spirit-enabled, *ad hoc* manner. These three main categories of Spirit-empowered ministry are: prophetic evangelism, prophetic edification, *and* prophetic equipping. While pointing out the numerous places in the book of Acts where these three types of Spirit-empowered ministry activity are evidenced, I present the story of Ananias being sent by God in a *charismatic* manner to minister to a blinded and confused Saul of Tarsus (Acts 9:10–22) as a paradigm of sorts for what I have in mind when I speak of a missional engagement in prophetic speech and action. I suggest that this passage, understood in the context of the book of Acts as a whole, can serve as an indication of what the impartation of prophetic capacity involves: *a Spirit-empowered ability to hear God's voice, receive ministry assignments from him, speak and act into the lives of hurting people on Christ's behalf, making disciples and fulfilling God's missional purposes in the world as a result.*

What is more, I go on in this chapter to relate several real-life, extra-biblical stories which serve to indicate the ability and eagerness

---

[12] One should note that my advocacy for a "pneumatological realism" does not equate with a commitment to the "turn to pneumatology" which, in an attempt to forge an inclusive (if not pluralistic) theology of religions, has been advocated by not a few theologians, both Catholic and Protestant, liberal and evangelical, Pentecostal-Charismatic and non-Pentecostal-Charismatic. Put simply, the idea here is that if the work of the Spirit in the world at large (the *Creator Spiritus*) can be untethered from the work of Christ (and the church), it may be possible to see the Holy Spirit working in other religions in a manner that is actually salvific rather than as simply preparing people to hear/receive the Christian gospel. For more on the pneumatological turn, see C.H. Pinnock, *A Wideness in God's Mercy: The Finality of Jesus Christ in a World of Religions* (Grand Rapids, MI: Zondervan, 1992); Amos Yong, *Discerning the Spirit(s): A Pentecostal-Charismatic Contribution to Christian Theology of Religions* (Sheffield: Sheffield Academic Press, 2000). See also Amos Yong, "Christological Constraints in Shifting Contexts: Jesus Christ, Prophetic Dialogue and the Missio Spiritus in a Pluralistic World" in Stephen B. Bevans and Cathy Ross (eds), *Mission on the Road to Emmaus: Constants, Contexts, and Prophetic Dialogue* (London: SCM Press/ Maryknoll: Orbis Books, 2015), 19-33. For a critique of this pneumatological turn from a Pentecostal perspective, see Simon Chan, *Grassroots Asian Theology: Thinking the Faith from the Ground Up* (Downers Grove, Ill.: InterVarsity Press Academic, 2014), 129–142. For an evangelical critique, see Todd Miles, *A God of Many Understandings?: The Gospel and a Theology of Religions* (Nashville, TN: B&H Publishing, 2010), 150–161, 212–239.

of the Spirit of mission to effect the same type of prophetic evangelism, edification, and equipping in the contemporary era through rank-and-file followers of Jesus.

Prophetic Speech and Action and the Growth of Global Pentecostalism

Then, moving forward, the argument presented in chapter three of *The Holy Spirit in Mission* is that the same kind of missional faithfulness/fruitfulness we see in the book of Acts should be recognized as one of the primary reasons for the prolific growth of Pentecostal-Charismatic Christianity around the world,[13] even in areas earmarked by a tremendous degree of religious pluralism.

Traditionally, the proposed explanations for the phenomenal growth of Pentecostalism worldwide emphasize the ease with which the Pentecostal version of the Christian faith is contextualized in various Majority World cultures,[14] and/or the numerous *benefits*—physical, spiritual, and psychological/sociological—which this version of the Christian faith tends to produce in the lives of those who embrace it.[15] In the quote presented below we seem to find a synthesis of these two traditionally popular explanations:

> Pentecostals responded to what they experienced as a void left by rationalistic western forms of Christianity that had unwittingly initiated what amounted to the destruction of traditional spiritual values. Pentecostals declared a message that reclaimed the biblical traditions of healing and protection from evil, they demonstrated the practical effects of these traditions and by so doing became heralds of a Christianity that was really meaningful. Thus, Pentecostalism went a long way towards meeting physical, emotional and spiritual needs of people in the Majority World, offering solutions to life's problems and ways to cope in what was often a threatening and hostile world.[16]

---

[13] See Mark Noll, *The New Shape of World Christianity* (Downers Grove, IL: InterVarsity Press Academic, 2009), 42-43; David Barrett, et al., *World Christian Encyclopedia* (New York: Oxford University Press, 2001), 4; Allan Anderson, *An Introduction to Pentecostalism* (New York: Cambridge University Press, 2004), 123, 279; Jenkins, Phillip, *The Next Christendom: The Coming of Global Christianity* (New York: Oxford University Press, 2007), 8–9.

[14] Anderson, *An Introduction to Pentecostalism*, 201-202, 212-213, 215-216, 223-224, 283-284.

[15] For more on this, see Tyra, *The Holy Spirit in Mission*, 107–112.

[16] Anderson, *An Introduction to Pentecostalism*, 212.

At the same time, there are other scholars who contend that the traditional explanations, by themselves, cannot fully explain Pentecostalism's amazing ability to see remarkable numbers of rank-and-file church members move past a consumeristic preoccupation with the gospel's benefits toward an enthusiastic and fruitful missional engagement in their homes, neighborhoods, workplace, marketplace, and so on.[17] The question is how to explain this unique ability Pentecostal and Charismatic churches possess to motivate their members toward a vigorous missional ministry engagement with their cultural peers.

It is my contention that yet another reason why Pentecostalism is growing so rapidly around the world is that, because of their embrace of a pneumatological realism, multitudes of rank-and-file Pentecostal believers have been willing to follow the personal leading of the Spirit of mission to speak and act prophetically (in an Ananias-like manner) into the lives of hurting people living in their communities. In addition to some demographic evidence,[18] and evidence from the literature devoted to global Pentecostalism,[19] I also cite some anecdotes from the field which indicate how common it is for rank-and-file church members to feel prompted by the Spirit of mission to go to certain people, humbly yet boldly speaking and acting into their lives on behalf of the risen Christ.[20] According to these anecdotes, this pneumatologically real version of prophetic speech and action often creates opportunities for *ministry conversations* that end up resulting in *ministry conversions* as well—people joyously coming to faith in Christ, undergoing water baptism, and then commencing a life of Christian discipleship.[21] It appears to be true that when hurting people sense that *the risen Jesus* has sent someone to them, speaking and acting into their lives in a grace-imbued manner, it is hard for the recipients of these mercy-saturated words and deeds to continue

---

[17] For example, see Grant McClung, "Truth on Fire: Pentecostals and an Urgent Missiology" in Grant McClung (ed), *Azusa Street and Beyond; 100 Years of Commentary on the Global Pentecostal/Charismatic Movement* (Gainesville, FL: Bridge-Logos, 2006), 78, 81. See also Paul A. Pomerville, *Introduction to Missions: An Independent-study Textbook* (Irving, TX: ICI University Press, 1987), 95–97.

[18] See Tyra, *The Holy Spirit in Mission*, 118–119.

[19] See Tyra, *The Holy Spirit in Mission*, 119–121.

[20] The importance of a "humble boldness" or "bold humility" in missional ministry is something Bevans and Schroeder, following David Bosch, stress repeatedly. See Bevans and Schroeder, *Prophetic Dialogue*, 2, 38, 61–62, 112, 145.

[21] See Bevans and Schroeder, *Prophetic Dialogue*, 122–126.

to ignore or relativize the Jesus of the Christian scriptures. Thus, the phenomenon of a pneumatologically real version of prophetic speech and action has to be considered at least one of the most plausible explanations for the growth of Pentecostalism around the world.

I realize that just referring to the evidence available for an idea is not by itself a compelling argument for it. And yet, because of limitations of space, this will have to suffice. I am hopeful, however, that the way in which I've summarized some significant components of the missional pneumatology presented in *The Holy Spirit in Mission* will enable the reader of this essay to understand the observations I make in the discussion presented below.

PROPHETIC SPEECH AND ACTION *VIS-À-VIS* "PROPHETIC DIALOGUE"

In the final section of this chapter my intention is to do two things: (1) briefly indicate just a few of the things about the proposal put forward by Bevans and Schroeder that I very much resonate with; and (2) pose three critical questions I believe merit some further attention.

SOME THINGS I APPRECIATE ABOUT THE PROPOSAL PRESENTED IN PROPHETIC DIALOGUE

First, as someone who has devoted an entire work to the dialectical nature of missional theology and the corresponding need to not fall prey to the false antitheses often associated with it,[22] I very much appreciate the way Bevans and Schroeder have sought to find a synthesis between three potentially disparate understandings of mission: "(1) mission as participation in the mission of the Triune God (*missio Dei*), (2) mission as liberating service of the Reign of God, and (3) mission as proclamation of Jesus Christ as universal savior."[23] Bevans elaborates a bit on this proposed synthesis in a paper titled "Mission as Prophetic Dialogue." In that paper he provides this very balanced understanding of the mission of God:

---

[22] See Tyra, *A Missional Orthodoxy*.
[23] Bevans and Schroeder, *Prophetic Dialogue*, 2.

> It is not simply about the expansion of the church, but about the transformation of the world, hoping for the day when God will establish God's Reign within the whole of creation. But nor is mission simply working for justice, or cooperating with the other great faiths of humanity, or committing oneself to human solidarity. Mission is the witness and proclamation of God's love and action revealed in the concrete history of Jesus of Nazareth, and is an invitation to relationship and partnership with God through relationship with him, in the power of his Holy Spirit.[24]

While I could wish that in *Prophetic Dialogue* Bevans and Schroeder would have referred in an explicit manner to the making of Christian disciples—a missional ministry dynamic specifically prescribed by Jesus (see Matt 28:18-20)—the language utilized in the quotes presented above suggest a commitment on their part to the notion that mission is more than an interreligious dialogue aimed at making the world a better place. Bevans and Schroeder are very careful to disavow a proclamation of the gospel that is imperious in nature.[25] While affirming this conviction, I would like to think that they maintain the hope that a proclamation of the gospel in "bold humility" might result in the making of Christian disciples as per the great commission.

Second, as someone who has written of the need for those engaged in missional ministry to live in genuine humility as *servants* of both reality and their neighbors, always alert to the role which *hospitality* and *reciprocity* play in missional conversations,[26] I deeply value the way Bevans and Schroeder emphasize the need for a contemporary engagement in mission to be dialogical in nature.[27]

Third, at the same time, I am also very pleased to find an emphasis upon the prophetic in the missiology of Bevans and Schroeder. Having pointed out that, biblically speaking, prophecy is not just predictive (*speaking before*) but also declarative (*speaking forth*),[28] these authors go on to explain that mission as prophecy involves: "speaking forth" without words (witness); "speaking forth" with words (proclamation); "speaking

---

[24] Bevans, "*Mission as Prophetic Dialogue.*"
[25] Bevans, "*Mission as Prophetic Dialogue,*" 22.
[26] Tyra, *A Missional Orthodoxy*, 42–47.
[27] Bevans and Schroeder, *Prophetic Dialogue*, 22–29.
[28] Bevans and Schroeder, *Prophetic Dialogue*, 42.

against" without words (being a contrast community); and "speaking against" in words (speaking truth to power).[29]

Moreover, not only do Bevans and Schroeder emphasize the need for Christian mission to involve both dialogue and prophecy, they also affirm how very important it is for the missionary to be sensitive to the ministry promptings provided by the Holy Spirit.[30] As the previous section of this essay indicated, this missional sensitivity to the Spirit is a prominent theme in *The Holy Spirit in Mission*. While my understanding of the role which the Spirit of mission intends prophetic speech and action to play in Christian witness differs in some respects from that of Bevans and Schroeder, I am nevertheless grateful for their commitment to the notions that: (1) "the Holy Spirit is the principal agent in evangelization,"[31] and (2) Christian mission can and should be conducted in a prophetic as well as dialogical manner.

THREE THINGS TO THINK ABOUT GOING FORWARD

And yet, as appreciative as I am of these aspects of *Prophetic Dialogue,* I do want to pose at least three questions that I feel need to be addressed. These critical queries are born of the way in which my understanding of how the Bible characterizes the prophetic component of Christian mission differs from the way Bevans and Schroeder seem to conceive of it.

- First, is the "prophetic dialogue" described by Bevans and Schroeder actually the "synthesis" they refer to it as?

On the one hand, Bevans and Schroeder speak of the need to maintain a *balance* between the dynamics of dialogue and prophecy when engaging in mission and ministry.[32] But, on the other hand, they also seem to suggest that there are times when one must privilege the dialogic over the prophetic.[33] Ultimately, their position seems to be that the norm is for the dialogic to take precedence over the prophetic, never vice-versa.[34] If

---

[29] Bevans and Schroeder, *Prophetic Dialogue*, 43–48.
[30] Bevans and Schroeder, *Prophetic Dialogue*, 55.
[31] Paul VI, *Evangelization in the Modern World* (*Evangelii Nutiandi*), 75, cited by Bevans and Schroeder, *Prophetic Dialogue*, 137.
[32] Bevans and Schroeder, *Prophetic Dialogue*, 112.
[33] Bevans and Schroeder, *Prophetic Dialogue*, 55.
[34] Bevans and Schroeder, *Prophetic Dialogue*, 49, 90, 99, 154–155.

this observation holds true, it raises in my mind the question: How can the concept of "prophetic dialogue" represent a true synthesis between "mission as dialogue" and "mission as prophetic" if one ministry dynamic ends up qualifying not just the "when" and "how" of the other, but the "if" as well?

- Second, could it be that it is because of the essentially non-charismatic manner in which Bevans and Schroeder seem to conceive of prophetic speech and action that they feel justified in prioritizing dialogical concerns over it?

Another observation I will put forward is that Bevans and Schroeder seem to reduce the prophetic to: a non-verbal representation of God's loving character, a verbal rehearsal of the church's historic teaching concerning Christ, and a denunciation (verbal or non-verbal) of some form of injustice at work in the culture. Given this understanding of the prophetic, it is understandable that they might argue that it can and should be normed by dialogical concerns.[35] But what if there is a more nuanced way of understanding the prophetic phenomenon,[36] and, therefore, another way of understanding the role of prophetic speech and action in Christian witness? What if there is such a thing as a missional engagement with the "other" that takes the form of a Spirit-prompted word or deed that is delivered *ad hoc* in a Christ-honouring, grace-imbued and grace-redolent manner?[37] If it is possible that the Spirit of mission is still in the business of prompting and enabling Christ's followers to speak and act into the lives of their cultural peers in mercy-saturated ways at the behest of the risen Christ, how appropriate would it be for the ministry agent to suppress this prophetic activity out of some perceived dialogical concerns? It seems to me that the very definition of "prophetic" is at issue here. How biblically informed will our understanding of this dynamic be?

- Finally, would not a truly incarnational approach to missional ministry contextualization require a very carefully balanced

---

[35] Bevans and Schroeder, *Prophetic Dialogue*, 3, 20, 47–52, 60, 63.

[36] For more on this, see my discussion of the nature of the prophetic phenomenon—how it includes both a discernment (charismatic) and deployment (confrontational) dynamic—in Tyra, *Pursuing Moral Faithfulness*, 166–167.

[37] To be true to Scripture, I suppose one would have to also allow for the possibility of a confrontational interaction as well (see Acts 13:4–12).

engagement in prophetic dialogue in general, and the prophetic component of it in particular?

Bevans and Schroeder appear eager to endorse an "incarnational" approach to missional ministry.[38] In my book, *A Missional Orthodoxy: Theology and Ministry in a Post-Christian Context*, I suggested that a conceptual analogy might exist between the nature of Christ's incarnation and an *incarnational* approach to ministry contextualization. Put simply, in the same way that the Chalcedonian definition hammered out by the church fathers in AD 451 insisted that we avoid any unevenness in our appraisal of the divine and human natures in the incarnate Christ, a truly *incarnational* approach to ministry contextualization will require *a balanced sensitivity* to both the *divine* element inherent in the gospel—the Christological verities which "underwrite the Christian gospel"[39]—and the *human* element inherent in the conditions "on the ground" within any given ministry context. In other words, I suggested that just as a hypostatic union of the two natures of Christ is necessary for a theologically coherent conception of the revelatory and redemptive ministries accomplished by him, a carefully balanced sensitivity is crucial if we are to avoid an insufficient contextualisation of the gospel (contra 1 Cor 9:20-22) on the one hand, or an over-contextualization of the gospel (contra Jude 1:3) on the other.[40]

Could it be that a similar commitment to balancing the human and divine is required of a truly "incarnational" understanding of prophetic dialogue in general, and the prophetic component of it in particular? If so, would it not be inappropriate, in an incarnational approach, to privilege one missional dynamic over the other? And with respect to the prophetic component in particular, does not 2 Peter 1:21 imply that a truly prophetic word (or deed) will derive from some sort of charismatic interaction with God that is earmarked by an *inspirational immediacy*? Is there no room in the prophetic component of "prophetic dialogue" for the Spirit of mission to prompt a cultural insider to speak and act into the life of the "other" in

---

[38] Bevans and Schroeder, *Prophetic Dialogue*, 46, 71.
[39] Tyra, *A Missional Orthodoxy*, 15, 49–51, 72–79, 80, 85 n. 67, 86, 95–96, 102–109, 114, 121–122, 168, 184, 196, 208, 211, 249–250, 349, 356–357, 368.
[40] Tyra, *A Missional Orthodoxy*, 95–110.

a charismatic, Ananias-like manner intended by the risen Christ to take the ministry conversation (dialogue) to the next level?

While there are other questions which might be posed here, these three will have to suffice. In sum, I can honestly say that despite some ways in which the proposal for a prophetic dialogue proffered by Bevans and Schroeder differs from the missional pneumatology I presented in *The Holy Spirit in Mission*, I really do view them as complementary. If I had had *Prophetic Dialogue* in front of me when I wrote *The Holy Spirit in Mission* and *A Missional Orthodoxy*, it would have enhanced what I had to say in those works about the dialogical rather than demagogical manner Christians can and should engage in missional ministry. Likewise, I would like to think that this essay might provide the practitioners of prophetic dialogue something to think and pray about. *Perhaps there is a Spirit-empowered way to speak and act into the lives of our cultural peers which, while gracious, sensitive, and respectful, also provides a powerful witness to the resurrection of Jesus Christ.* For the sake of God's kingdom come and coming, may the conversation regarding the nature of a truly prophetic prophetic dialogue continue!

6

HAS THE CATHOLIC CHARISMATIC RENEWAL MOVEMENT HELPED IN BUILDING A MORE JUST SOCIETY?

*Reginald Alva SVD**

In this paper, we shall examine the characteristic features of the Catholic Charismatic Renewal Movement (CCRM), which could be instrumental in building a more just society. The resources for this paper will be the various church documents, documents on the CCRM, and views of some prominent theologians on the CCRM.

BRIEF HISTORY OF THE CATHOLIC CHARISMATIC RENEWAL MOVEMENT

The CCRM began in 1967 in the US at Duquesne University, Pennsylvania.[1] The teachings of the Second Vatican Council and Protestant Pentecostalism

---

* **Reginald Alva SVD**, PhD, is a Catholic priest, who teaches at Nanzan University, Japan. He is also involved in pastoral and renewal work in the Roman Catholic church of Japan. He has licentiate in Biblical Theology and he took his doctorate in Theology (Spirituality) from Pontificia Università San Tommaso D'Aquino, Angelicum, Rome. His major publications include, *Mary and the Catholic Charismatic Renewal Movement* (2012), *The Spirituality of the Catholic Charismatic Renewal Movement* (2014), *Spiritual Renewal in Japan: The Journey of the Catholic Charismatic Renewal Movement* (2015).

[1] See Paul Thigpen, "Catholic Charismatic Movement" in Stanley M. Burgess and Eduard M. Van Der Maas (eds), *The New International Dictionary of Pentecostal and Charismatic Movements* (Grand Rapids, MI: Zondervan, 2003), 460.

greatly influenced the CCRM. The Second Vatican Council stressed on the overall renewal and reform of the Roman Catholic church. Catholic Charismatics claim their movement to be the fruit of the teachings of the Second Vatican Council.[2]

The CCRM initially had a phenomenal growth in the US and later in other parts of the world. According to the statistics published by David Barrett, there were around two million Roman Catholic Charismatics in the 1970s.[3] This number swelled to forty million in 1980s. It further increased to one hundred nineteen million in the year 2000. The CCRM registered an impressive growth rate of 14.6 per cent within a span of thirty years. In that year, the global Catholic population was around 1,057,447,000.[4] Out of these, 11,991,000 (11.3 per cent) people claimed to be Charismatics. The thirty year growth rate varied in the seven continents of the world. The growth rate was 32.2 per cent in Africa, 16.6 per cent in Antarctica, 25.1 per cent in Asia, 20.6 per cent in Europe, 7.2 per cent in North America, 16.1 per cent in South America, and 18.8 per cent in Oceania.[5] Interestingly, Africa had the highest growth rate among the seven continents whereas North America, where the Charismatic movement was born had the least growth rate. The CCRM is growing in Africa, Asia, and South America whereas it has already peaked in North America and Europe. Thus, it is clear from the above analysis that the CCRM is largely active in countries, which were former colonies of the European nations.

THE THEOLOGICAL BASIS OF THE CCRM

The CCRM is strongly rooted in trinitarian theology. Even though the CCRM gives importance to the phenomenon of baptism in the Holy Spirit, it is deeply trinitarian.[6] This is because faith in the triune God is

---

[2] Thigpen, "Catholic Charismatic Movement," 460.
[3] See David Barrett and Todd Johnson, "The Catholic Charismatic Renewal, 1959-2025" in *Then Peter Stood Up* (Vatican: International Catholic Charismatic Renewal Services, 2000), 124.
[4] Barrett and Johnson, "The Catholic Charismatic Renewal," 124.
[5] Barrett and Johnson, "The Catholic Charismatic Renewal," 124.
[6] See Reginald Alva, *The Spirituality of the Catholic Charismatic Renewal Movement* (New Delhi: Christian World Imprints, 2014), 27-33.

the foundation of the Roman Catholic faith. The *Catechism of the Catholic Church* notes the centrality of the Trinity in Christian faith:

> The mystery of the Most Holy Trinity is the central mystery of Christian faith and life. It is the mystery of God in himself. It is therefore the source of all the other mysteries of faith, the light that enlightens them. It is the most fundamental and essential teaching in the 'hierarchy of the truths of faith.' The whole history of salvation is identical with the history of the way and the means by which the one true God, Father, Son and Holy Spirit, reveals himself to men 'and reconciles and unites with himself those who turn away from sin.'[7]

Charismatics emphasize on the vital role of the three persons of the Holy Trinity in the life of a person. They maintain that the events of creation, salvation, and Pentecost have intrinsic unity, which forms the basis of Christian faith. Charismatics maintain that it is the baptismal identity, which impels a Christian to share his or her faith with others. They further believe that the Holy Spirit bestows gifts and charisms to all Christians (see 1 Cor 12:4-11). These graces of the Holy Spirit are for the good of all. Thus, the Charismatics stress on the use of spiritual charisms in the church as an essential tool for evangelization. They encourage people to become aware of the tremendous power of the Holy Spirit within them and channelize it for building the kingdom of God (see Luke 17:20-21).

There were two divergent opinions about the existence and exercise of spiritual charisms among the council fathers of the Second Vatican Council. Cardinal Ruffini and his supporters claimed that God gave spiritual charisms to the early church for evangelizing the nations. However, as the church spread to all the nations, the spiritual charisms became very rare and the manifestations of the Holy Spirit became extraordinary. He held that spiritual charisms no longer exist ordinarily in the life of the church. He relegated the active use of spiritual charisms as a practice of the past and discouraged the stress on the charismatic dimension of the church.[8] On the other hand, Cardinal Suenens and his supporters held that the charismatic dimension was very important in the life of the church. Cardinal Suenens noted, "[w]hat would become

---

[7] *Catechism of the Catholic Church*, 234. http://www.vatican.va/archive/ccc_css/archive/catechism/p1s2c1p2.htm (accessed 16 July 2016).

[8] Léon Joseph Suenens, *A New Pentecost?* Francis Martin (trans.) (New York: Seabury Press, 1975), 30-32.

of our Church without the charisms of the doctors, the theologians, the prophets?"[9] He strongly encouraged the use of spiritual charisms by all people of God. The council fathers supported the view of Cardinal Suenens and thus they voted to incorporate a paragraph on the spiritual charisms in the Dogmatic Constitution on the church *Lumen Gentium*.

> It is not only through the sacraments and the ministries of the Church that the Holy Spirit sanctifies and leads the people of God and enriches it with virtues, but allotting his gifts to everyone according as He wills, He distributes special graces among the faithful of every rank. By these gifts He makes them fit and ready to undertake the various tasks and offices which contribute toward the renewal and building up of the Church, according to the words of the Apostle: 'The manifestation of the Spirit is given to everyone for profit.' These charisms, whether they be the more outstanding or the more simple and widely diffused, are to be received with thanksgiving and consolation for they are perfectly suited to and useful for the needs of the Church. Extraordinary gifts are not to be sought after, nor are the fruits of apostolic labor to be presumptuously expected from their use; but judgment as to their genuinity and proper use belongs to those who are appointed leaders in the Church, to whose special competence it belongs, not indeed to extinguish the Spirit, but to test all things and hold fast to that which is good.[10]

The above teaching of the Roman Catholic church on spiritual charisms helped the Charismatics, both women and men to take seriously their baptismal vocation of being a Christian and using their spiritual charisms for the good of all. Thus, Roman Catholic Charismatics emphasize on the active role of the Holy Spirit in the lives of Christians.

THE CCRM AND SOCIAL COMMITMENT

The CCRM unlike Pentecostal churches is strongly rooted in the tradition of the Roman Catholic church.[11] However, the CCRM has some common features with Protestant Pentecostals. Both the Roman Catholic Charismatics as well as the Pentecostals give importance to the phenomenon of baptism in the Holy Spirit, charisms, and fellowship.

---

[9] Suenens, *A New Pentecost?* 30-32.
[10] Dogmatic Constitution on the Church *Lumen Gentium*, no. 12. http://www.vatican.va/archive/hist_councils/ii_vatican_council/documents/vat-ii_const_19641121_lumen-gentium_en.html (accessed 16 July 2016).
[11] See Thigpen, "Catholic Charismatic Movement," 464-465.

Nevertheless, there are also some differences among them on the doctrinal level. Unlike some Pentecostals, Roman Catholic Charismatics do not consider speaking in tongues as an essential sign of the Spirit-baptism.[12]

The CCRM is an ecclesial movement within the Roman Catholic church. It primarily focuses on spiritual renewal of a person. However, Charismatics also take interest in working for the renewal and reformation of the society. This is because the Roman Catholic church has constantly advocated the need for building a just society. Pope John Paul II in his apostolic exhortation *Christifideles Laici* noted that the ecclesial movements should not hesitate to take up their social responsibilities. He noted the following two temptations, which the ecclesial movements like the CCRM need to avoid:

> In particular, two temptations can be cited which they have not always known how to avoid: the temptation of being so strongly interested in Church services and tasks that some fail to become actively engaged in their responsibilities in the professional, social, cultural and political world; and the temptation of legitimizing the unwarranted separation of faith from life, that is, a separation of the Gospel's acceptance from the actual living of the Gospel in various situations in the world.[13]

Charismatics have a great potential to work for social transformation if they put into action the message of the gospel. Charismatics could contribute to build a more just society especially in post-colonial countries where their numbers are increasing enormously. The following are some of the characteristic features of the charismatic spirituality, which they could use to bring spiritual, social, economical and political transformation in the society.

CONVERSION OF HEART

Charismatics give great importance to the phenomenon of baptism in the Holy Spirit. Genuine conversion of heart is one of the pre-requisites

---

[12] See Walter Hollenweger, *Pentecostalism: Origins and Developments Worldwide* (Peabody: Hendrickson Publishers, 1997), 156-159.

[13] John Paul II, Apostolic Exhortation *Christifideles Laici*, no. 2, *AAS* 88/1 (1989), 443-446. http://w2.vatican.va/content/john-paul-ii/en/apost_exhortations/documents/hf_jp-ii_exh_30121988_christifideles-laici.html (accessed 7 September 2015).

to have a profound experience of the Holy Spirit.[14] Charismatics often emphasize on the need of repentance of sins. Due to the growth of secularization, religious beliefs and values are losing their place in the society. Contemporary people often feel embarrassed to call sin by its name. Pope Pius XII noted in his message to the Catechetical Congress in US that "[p]erhaps the greatest sin in the world today is that men have begun to lose the sense of sin."[15]

Charismatics stress on the need to accept one's personal shortcomings and sins. They are indeed witnessing to their faith life when they choose to challenge the sins in their personal lives. Similarly, they need to gather courage to challenge the corporate sins, the unjust and sinful structures present in the society. They need to use their experience of conversion and call upon the powerful lobbies, which exploit the poor to repent and reform.[16]

There are many faces and forms of corporate sins which are ruining the society. The unjust political, economic, and social structures are exploiting the poor people especially in countries, which were victims of colonialism in the past. In many of the former colonial states a great number of injustices were done to the local people. They were mercilessly subjected to slavery and were deprived of their dignity as human persons. Their perpetrators often associated themselves with Christianity but never set an example of following the virtues and values of Christ. Even though colonialism does not exist directly in very many states, the poison of injustice and hatred which started centuries back refuses to die.[17]

In the contemporary world, the subjects of oppression are not only the poor, the weak, the disabled or the underprivileged but also the environment. The philosophy of dominance, which the powerful nations followed during colonialism, continues even to this day in different forms.

---

[14] See Alva, *The Spirituality of the Catholic Charismatic Renewal Movement*, 62-65.

[15] Pius XII, *"Radio Message to the Participants of the National Catechetical Congress, U.S., 26 October 1946."* http://w2.vatican.va/content/pius-xii/en/speeches/1946/documents/hf_p-xii_spe_19461026_congresso-catechistico-naz.html (accessed 4 September 2015).

[16] See Matthias Wenk, "The Holy Spirit As Transforming Power Within A Society: Pneumatological Spirituality and Its Political/Social Relevance For Western Europe," *Journal of Pentecostal Theology* 11/1(2002), 131.

[17] See Mae Elise Cannon, *Social Justice Handbook: Small Steps to a Better World* (Downers Grove, IL: InterVarsity Press, 2009), 94-95.

The economically powerful nations in their pursuit of gathering more resources are ruthlessly exploiting environmental resources especially in economically weaker nations. This unabated greed is due to the emptiness of heart, which contemporary people are facing in their lives. People feel amassing power and wealth can redeem them from their internal turmoil. However, they fail to recognize that nothing but God alone can satisfy their inner needs. Pope Benedict rightly noted in his homily about the co-relation between the internal deserts in a person's life and the external deserts, which people are creating. He noted that:

> [a]nd there are so many kinds of desert. There is the desert of poverty, the desert of hunger and thirst, the desert of abandonment, of loneliness, of destroyed love. There is the desert of God's darkness, the emptiness of souls no longer aware of their dignity or the goal of human life. The external deserts in the world are growing, because the internal deserts have become so vast. Therefore the earth's treasures no longer serve to build God's garden for all to live in, but they have been made to serve the powers of exploitation and destruction. [18]

Charismatics can greatly help people who are facing angst or ennui to find meaning in their lives. The internal transformation of people could lead to the external transformation of the world.[19] Pope Francis too noted about the need of interior conversion to bring genuine changes in the society. He noted that:

> [f]or this reason, the ecological crisis is also a summons to profound interior conversion. It must be said that some committed and prayerful Christians, with the excuse of realism and pragmatism, tend to ridicule expressions of concern for the environment. Others are passive; they choose not to change their habits and thus become inconsistent. So what they all need is an ecological conversion, whereby the effects of their encounter with Jesus Christ become evident in their relationship with the world around them. Living our vocation to be protectors of

---

[18] Benedict XVI, "Homily for the Solemn Inauguration of the Petrine MinistryApril 24, 2005," *AAS* 97 (2005), 710. http://w2.vatican.va/content/benedict-xvi/en/homilies/2005/documents/hf_ben-xvi_hom_20050424_inizio-pontificato.html (accessed 4 September 2015).

[19] See Gregory Baum, "Structures of Sin" in Gregory Baum and Robert Ellsberg (eds), *The Logic of Solidarity* (New York: Orbis Books, 1989), 110-123.

God's handiwork is essential to a life of virtue; it is not an optional or a secondary aspect of our Christian experience.[20]

Charismatics have a great task to put into action their profound experience of the Holy Spirit. They need to raise their voices for the poor, the weak and the oppressed by challenging the unjust realms of power in the society. Their lives need to be models for others. Personal conversion must precede preaching. Before asking others to repent and convert, one must get rid of their own sinfulness.[21] The early Christians challenged the unjust structures and powers even though at the risk of their lives. The power of the Holy Spirit impelled them to make the right choices no matter what the cost. Charismatics need to remember, "God's agenda for transformation has a personal and social dimension. God not only transforms individuals in society, but he also transforms society through individuals in order to restore his creation."[22] God continues to wait upon all, especially those whom the Holy Spirit empowers, to spread his kingdom here on earth. Charismatics need to use their anointing to make the world aware of the excessive anthropocentrism, which disrespects social and environmental harmony.

USING CHARISMS FOR THE GOOD OF ALL

Use of spiritual charisms is an essential feature of charismatic spirituality.[23] Charismatics usually exercise the charisms during prayer services. However, they would do better if they exercise the charisms of the Holy Spirit during not only prayer services but also out in the society. The Holy Spirit does not give charisms only for the benefit of a particular individual but for the benefit of all.[24]

---

[20] Francis, *Encyclical Laudato Si*, no. 217. http://w2.vatican.va/content/francesco/en/encyclicals/documents/papa-francesco_20150524_enciclica-laudato-si.html (accessed 5 September 2015).

[21] See Léon Joseph Suenens and Helder Camara, *Charismatic Renewal and Social Action: A Dialogue* (London: Darton, Longman and Todd, 1979), 51.

[22] Wynand de Kock, "Pentecostal Power for a Pentecostal Task: Empowerment through Engagement in South African Context," *Journal of Pentecostal Theology* 16 (2000), 110.

[23] See Alva, *The Spirituality of the Catholic Charismatic Renewal Movement*, 91.

[24] Francis Sullivan, *Charisms and Charismatic Renewal: A Biblical and Theological Study* (Eugene: Wipf & Stock, 2004), 30-31.

Charismatics sometimes tend to think that the use of charisms is restricted only to the spiritual realm. The power which the Holy Spirit gives has a universal purpose. This power has the potential to radically transform lives of individuals and the whole society. "A specific sense of call and direction by the Holy Spirit is at the heart of a charismatic approach to social issues."[25] The charisms of healing are not only for physical healing but also for healing the ills of society. Francis Macchia noted that the healing ministry has a wide scope and Charismatics need to think about an inclusive healing ministry. He noted that, "[s]ince poverty is a leading cause of disease and death in the world, should not a healing ministry include a fight against the social causes of poverty?"[26] Further, the Holy Spirit gives the charism of discernment not only for discerning spiritual things but also to respond prudently to the signs of the time.[27]

In the Old Testament times, God raised great prophets not only to work miracles and wonders but also to challenge the tyrant and oppressive rulers. Even though some of them faced death for their actions, they never hesitated to make themselves available to carry out the mission. Prophets used their charisms for a greater purpose. Similarly in the New Testament, Paul in the discourse on charisms clarified to the Corinthian community that the charisms are not for spiritual elation of individuals but for the building of the community (see 1 Cor 13). He stressed on the need for using the charisms to serve others. Francis Sullivan and Robert Faricy noted that apart from prayer meetings, Charismatics do exercise the spiritual charisms in the society for the good of all. They noted that:

> [t]he use of charisms is what characterizes Charismatic renewal. Not that charisms in the Church are restricted to the Charismatic movement, of course....The chief use of many charisms is in communal meetings. At almost any large Charismatic prayer meeting, one can observe the charisms of prophecy, of teaching, of leadership, of exhorting and of tongues, both in spontaneous group praise and in prophecy together with the use of the gift of interpretation. However, the use of charisms

---

[25] Larry Christenson, *A Charismatic Approach to Social Action* (Minneapolis: Bethany Fellowship, 1974), 11.

[26] Frank D. Macchia, "Theology, Pentecostal" in Stanley M. Burgess and Eduard M. Van Der Maas (eds), *The New International Dictionary of Pentecostal and Charismatic Movements*, 1136.

[27] See Suenens and Camara, *Charismatic Renewal and Social Action: A Dialogue*, 38-39.

as characteristic of the Charismatic renewal is also found outside the context of prayer meetings.[28]

Charisms are a sign of God's powerful presence in the world.[29] When Charismatics use charisms, they are witnessing to the presence and power of God. If Charismatics could conscientize the oppressed people that God wills social justice then they could fight against the ills in the society. On the other hand, if Charismatics fail to relate the power of God in them with social justice then they would be indirectly encouraging fatalism. Paulo Freire in *Pedagogy of the Oppressed* expressed his fear about fatalism among the underprivileged as follows:

> Fatalism in the guise of docility is the fruit of an historical and sociological situation, not an essential characteristic of a people's behavior. It almost always is related to the power of destiny or fate or fortune—inevitable forces—or to a distorted view of God. Under the sway of magic and myth, the oppressed (especially the peasants, who are almost submerged in nature) see their suffering, the fruit of exploitation, as the will of God—as if God were the creator of this organized disorder.[30]

Cheryl Bridge noted that, "Pentecostalism had a dual prophetic role: denouncing the dominant patterns of the status quo and announcing the patterns of God's kingdom."[31] Charismatics need to be like the Old Testament prophets who used the spiritual charisms but never failed to relate it to social order of their times.

Charismatics need to use the charisms for the good of all without any fear or reservations. They need not restrict the use of charisms only during the prayer services. They could freely use it as the Holy Spirit leads them without any inhibition or fear.

---

[28] Francis Sullivan and Robert Faricy, *Ignatian Exercises, Charismatic Renewal: Similarities, Differences, Contrasts, Convergences* (Eugene: Wipf and Stock, 2011), 2011.

[29] Walter Hollenweger, "Creator Spiritus: The Challenge of Pentecostal Experience to Pentecostal Theology," *Theology* 81 (1978), 32-40.

[30] Paulo Freire, *Pedagogy of the Oppressed*, Myra Bergman Ramos (trans.) (New York: Continuum, 2005), 61-62.

[31] Cheryl Bridges Johns, *Pentecostal Formation: A Pedagogy among the Oppressed* (Eugene: Wipf and Stock Publishers, 1998), 69.

Reaching-out

Charismatics usually have a very strong bond with other members of their prayer group. They give importance to fellowship and sharing within the group. It would be very difficult for an individual to oppose the tyrant political and social system. However, a group of like-minded people can become a great force to oppose the injustice in the system. Charismatics form well-knitted communities and so they could, as groups of like-minded people become a great force in opposing the evils in the society.[32] They can take up political, economic and social issues not as individuals but as a community. By doing so, they will have greater strength to face the strong and influential in the society. Moreover, they will succeed in creating a greater impact in national and international circles.

Charismatics need not restrict their spirit of fellowship only within their groups. In the past, some Charismatics attempted to form covenant communities.[33] Covenant communities consisted only of people who were willing to follow the set rules of the leader. However, such experiments by the Charismatics did not have much success. This shows that Charismatics need to take interest in social issues and need not insulate themselves from the affairs of the world. They would do a great harm to their identity as Spirit-filled people if they resort to escapism. They cannot make a superficial divide between spiritual and worldly affairs. To choose to take the side of the poor, the oppressed and the marginalized means to invite trouble from the rich and the powerful. However, to be a disciple of Jesus a person has to choose the road less traveled. Jesus asked his disciples to choose the narrow way, which may be difficult but sure to lead to moral uprightness (see Matt 7:14). Pope John Paul (formerly Cardinal Karol Wojtyla) noted the importance of the interhuman community as follows:

> The notion of 'neighbor' refers then to the broadest, commonly shared reality of the human being and also to the broadest foundations of interhuman community. Indeed, it is the community of men, of all men, the community formed by their humanness that is the basis of all

---

[32] See Johns, *Pentecostal Formation*, 85.

[33] See Thomas Csordas, "Ritualization of Life" in Martin Lindhardt (ed), *Practicing the Faith: The Ritual Life of Pentecostal-Charismatic Christians* (New York: Berghahn Books, 2011), 129-148.

other communities. Any community detached from this fundamental community must unavoidably lose its specially human character.[34]

Meredith McGuire a sociologist, who has done research on the CCRM, criticized the attitude of some Charismatics for focusing on their own communities and neglecting the larger human community. She noted that:

> [t]heodicies provided by the Catholic Pentecostal belief system legitimate members' middle-class comforts and allow them to express their concern for less comfortable members of society by prayer. The result of these theodicies is that Catholic Pentecostals are generally not only oblivious to social-structural sources of problems, including their problem of secularization, but they are even inured to thinking about structural issues.[35]

Some Charismatic groups think they need not concern themselves with the mundane matters of the world. Their groups exist only for spiritual purposes.[36] This is a distorted understanding of the gospel. The Holy Spirit, which empowers the group, calls on all the members of the group to unite to work for the good of the society.[37] Charismatics could use their strong sense of fellowship to work for the weak and question every form of injustice, which is present in the society. McGuire did acknowledge that the Charismatics have the great potential to bring social transformation if they use their experiences for the benefit of society. She noted that:

> [m]ost Catholic Pentecostal ministries... do have the potential for such small and middle-scale transformations, because they can promote an experience of community, they can create new middle-level leadership roles for their members, and they generate a sense of power to accomplish things that would not otherwise be attempted.[38]

---

[34] Karol Wojtyla, *The Acting Person*, Anna-Teresa Tymieniecka (ed), vol. 10 of Analecta Husserliana: The Year Book of Phenomenological Research, Andrzej Potocki (trans.) (London: D. Reidel Publishing Company, 1979), 293.

[35] Meredith McGuire, *Pentecostal Catholics: Power, Charisma and Order in a Religious Movement* (Philadelphia: Temple University Press, 1982), 213.

[36] See Dhan Prakash, "Toward a Theology of Social Concern: A Pentecostal Perspective," *Asian Journal of Pentecostal Studies* 13/1 (2010), 80.

[37] See Christenson, *A Charismatic Approach to Social Action*, 15.

[38] McGuire, *Pentecostal Catholics*, 215.

Thus, Catholic Charismatics need to reach out to the least in society and make them feel as members of the society.

INTEGRATING WITH THE PEOPLE

The CCRM gives importance to individual and communitarian prayers. Usually each prayer group allots time for intercessory prayers. It is indeed a wonderful practice to pray for the needy. However, a Christian's responsibility and much more for a Spirit-filled Charismatic's responsibility does not end by merely praying for others. One has to actually work for creating a better society. It would be rather very easy to pray for justice and peace but very difficult to do something concretely to make the society more just and peaceful.

Charismatics need to move out from apathy and reach out to the people. They have to take time to be with the people, to listen to them and to understand their problems and pains.[39] Charismatics need to humble themselves to learn from others who are pioneers in the work of social justice. Instead of building fences it would be better to build bridges with people of different faiths, denominations and opinions. Such a partnership approach can greatly help not only the recipients but also those who work for it.[40]

Sometimes well-intended works can become oppressive in nature if they are forced on the people. Catholic Charismatics need to be very careful not to bulldoze the aspirations and opinions of the people whom they are serving. They need to remember that they are not masters but just stewards in the vineyard of the Lord. The vineyard belongs to the Lord. They need to remember the words of Jesus that the greatest must be the servants (see Matt 23:11). All the work, which they intend to do, needs to involve the people concerned. Thus, it would be inclusive and participatory. Every person whom they serve could actively be involved in the work done and get a sense of belongingness to the group. They need to avoid segregation. They could use their spirituality of fellowship in integrating with all, irrespective of their religious affiliations as fellow human beings.

---

[39] See Cannon, *Social Justice Handbook: Small Steps to a Better World*, 97-98.
[40] See Cannon, *Social Justice Handbook: Small Steps to a Better World*, 97-98.

Pentecostal-Charismatics had a great success in South America because they worked with the poor.[41] Charismatics in other parts of the world too need to integrate with the weakest and the poor. They need to wake up the mammoth structures of political, military and economic powers to have concern for the least in the society. Jesus in his lifetime integrated with the poor and did not hesitate to confront the hypocrisy of the powerful. Charismatics need to show their fervent devotion to Jesus, by following his steps and be a part of the project of conscientizing the people to bring genuine transformation in the human society.

POOLING RESOURCES FOR SOCIAL WELFARE

In the contemporary world, greed and unfazed consumerism by the minority rich is depriving the majority poor of the world of their dignity and rights as a human person.[42] There are abundant resources in the world but they are enjoyed only by the rich. In such a scenario, Catholic Charismatics can contribute greatly for the equitable sharing of resources in the society by sharing their resources with the people.

In the early Christian community, "there were no needy persons among them," (Acts 4:34) as they shared their resources with the needy (Acts 4:32) and did not hesitate to sell their possessions to serve one another (Acts 2:44). In the contemporary world, it would be difficult to have an ideal community like the early Christians. However, one can learn from them the true Christian spirit. Charismatics are generally generous in offering their services and wealth for the growth of the community.[43] They need to devise means to use these resources not only for their own community but also for the good of the society. They could help the organizations, which are working for social equity, environmental concerns and political justice. Pope Benedict noted the following about genuine charity:

> Charity...gives real substance to the personal relationship with God and with neighbour; it is the principle not only of micro-relationships

---

[41] See Bridges, *Pentecostal Formation*, 71-73.
[42] See Bridges, *Pentecostal Formation*, 140-141.
[43] See Pierre Hegy, *Wake Up, Lazarus: On Catholic Renewal* (Bloomington: iUniverse, 2012), 24.

(with friends, with family members or within small groups) but also of macro-relationships (social, economic and political ones).[44]

Charismatics need to remember that true religion demands to take care of the weakest. It also demands that one must be willing to share his or her resources for building a more just society (Jas 1:27; 2:14-17).[45] Leonardo Boff in *Come Holy Spirit: Inner Fire, Giver of Life & Comforter of the Poor* acknowledged that the CCRM has greatly contributed in enhancing the faith life of Christians through its unique spirituality. However, he noted that some Charismatics fail to relate their experience of the Holy Spirit to social issues. He noted that:

> [t]here are reductionist tendencies in the overall tone of the CCR movement. Some important elements of the Christian message are lost: without them Jesus' legacy is diminished and becomes less effective. For example, the movement is not always sensitive to the drama of the world and the tragic fate of the poor. That is, the issue of social and ecological justice at the global level seldom appears as theme of reflection and practice.[46]

Roman Catholic Charismatics have the great potential to work for social change by pooling resources from various fields and using them effectively for social welfare.[47] As the Charismatics are a part of the Roman Catholic church, they have a strong backing of a huge organization. They need not hesitate to take the help of various groups within the church organization who are working for social welfare.

In the contemporary world, the imbalance in the distribution of resources is creating great injustices and breeding more violence. Pope Francis noted that:

> [t]he impact of present imbalances is also seen in the premature death of many of the poor, in conflicts sparked by the shortage of resources, and

---

[44] Benedict XVI, Encyclical *Caritas in Veritate* no.2, *AAS* 101 (2009), 642. http://w2.vatican.va/content/benedict-xvi/en/encyclicals/documents/hf_ben-xvi_enc_20090629_caritas-in-veritate.html (accessed 5 September 2015).

[45] See William O'Neill, "Christian Hospitality and Solidarity with the Stranger" in Donald Kerwin and Jill Marie Gerschutz (eds), *And You Welcomed Me: Migration and Catholic Social Teaching* (Lanham: Rowman & Littlefield Publishers, 2009), 149-153.

[46] Leonardo Boff, *Come Holy Spirit: Inner Fire, Giver of Life & Comforter of the Poor* (Maryknoll: Orbis Books, 2015).

[47] See Bridges, *Pentecostal Formation*, 80-81.

in any number of other problems which are insufficiently represented on global agendas.[48]

If Roman Catholic Charismatics could mobilize and pool their resources then it may have a great impact on the society. It could tremendously help in creating a more just society, where every individual can find his or her rightful place.

To conclude, the CCRM is a great blessing for the church, as it has helped her to renew and prepare herself to face the challenges of the modern world. The CCRM also has a great potential to bring about social changes and build a more just society by challenging the unjust political, economic and social structures. Even though the potential of the CCRM is largely untapped because of the complacency of its members, it can commit itself to bring renewal in society by reforming itself. If Roman Catholic Charismatics use their charisms and zeal for the greater good, then the society in which they live will radically change. In the post-colonial set up, the Roman Catholic Charismatics have an added responsibility to share their resources with the deprived, the underprivileged, the oppressed, the poor, the disabled and the weak. They need to work for social equity. The Spirit of God who called Jesus to work for the liberation of the captives (Luke 4:18-19) also continues to call the Roman Catholic Charismatics to pray for healing of memories of victims of social oppression and conversion of the perpetrators. Charismatics need to be at the service of the oppressed and the needy, which also includes the mother earth. They have the potential to contribute in the process of building a harmonious society where each person feels welcomed, accepted, loved, and a part of the human family.

---

[48] Francis, *Encyclical Laudato Si*, no. 48.

7

CALVIN'S THEOLOGY OF THE HOLY SPIRIT AND CHRISTIAN MISSION IN A PLURALISTIC CONTEXT

Matthew Ebenezer*

In the Reformed tradition, the doctrine of the Holy Spirit receives undivided attention under the rubric of pneumatology. A solid biblical and historical foundation ensures that the Holy Spirit receives the right place as the third person of the Trinity and as God Himself. A large part of the credit goes to John Calvin (1509-1564) one of the foremost theologians of the Reformation period. It is Calvin who gave the doctrine of the Holy Spirit its rightful place. B.B. Warfield of Princeton Seminary called Calvin, "preeminently the theologian of the Holy Spirit."[1] Gaffin states that, according to Warfield, "Calvin's distinctive contribution is not, for instance, the doctrines of God's sovereignty or of election and double

---

* **Matthew Ebenezer**, PhD, is Principal of Presbyterian Theological Seminary, Dehradun, India, where he teaches Church History and Practical Theology. His primary interest is in theological education in majority world contexts. He serves on the International Board of World Reformed Fellowship and has taught in theological institutions in India, Sri Lanka, Nepal, and Indonesia. He holds a PhD in Historical Theology from Westminster Theological Seminary, Philadelphia.

[1] B.B. Warfield, "On the Doctrine of the Holy Spirit" in J.E. Meeter (ed), *Selected Shorter Writings of Benjamin B. Warfield*, vol. 1 (Nutley, NJ: Presbyterian and Reformed, 1970), 213-214, cited by Richard B. Gaffin, Jr., "The Holy Spirit," *Westminster Theological Journal* 43/1 (1980), 58.

predestination. These he simply took over from Augustine and others."[2] Calvin's greatest contribution to theology was his teaching on the Holy Spirit. Gaffin quotes Warfield, "[i]n his [Calvin's] hands for the first time in the history of the Church, the doctrine of the Holy Spirit comes to its rights."[3] Calvin studied the work of the Holy Spirit and saw the Spirit's work playing an important role in the process of salvation: in election, justification and sanctification. Over the years, except for occasional studies, the work of the Spirit was not given enough attention. The advent of Pentecostalism at the turn of the twentieth century and the Charismatic movement towards the latter part of that century fired renewed interest in the doctrine of the Holy Spirit. Historically, however, Calvin has a unique place among theologians for giving teaching of the person and work of the Holy Spirit the prominence it deserves.

This paper will outline Calvin's theology of the Holy Spirit, focusing primarily on its soteriological significance, and its relevance to Christian mission in a pluralistic context. At first, we will attempt to look at the doctrine of the Holy Spirit in Calvin's thought, with regard to his deity, his relationship with Scripture, salvation, faith, Christ, and preaching. Then, the application of Calvin's theology of the Holy Spirit to Christian mission in a pluralistic context in his own time will be considered.

THE THEOLOGY OF THE HOLY SPIRIT IN CALVIN'S THOUGHT

The Deity of the Holy Spirit

For Calvin, the divinity of the Holy Spirit is proved by who he is. Calvin refers to creation and explains Genesis 1:2 with reference to the Spirit's work. He says, "the beauty of the universe (which we now perceive) owes its strength and preservation to the power of the Spirit but that before this adornment was added, even then the Spirit was occupied with tending that confused mass."[4] He argues for the divinity of the Spirit from the process of regeneration and says that since the Spirit is the author of

---

[2] Gaffin, "The Holy Spirit," 58.
[3] Gaffin, "The Holy Spirit," 58, (Parenthesis added).
[4] John Calvin, *Institutes of the Christian Religion*, vol. 1, John T. MacHeill (ed), Ford Lewis Battles (trans.), (Philadelphia: The Westminster Press, 1960), I.xiii.14, (Parenthesis added).

regeneration "by his very own energy," it shows that he holds the marks of divinity.[5]

He continues describing the Spirit saying, "[t]hus through him [the Holy Spirit], we come into communion with God, so that we in a way feel his life-giving power toward us. Our justification is his work; from him is power, sanctification [cf. I Cor 6:11], truth, grace, and every good thing that can be conceived, since there is but one Spirit from whom flows every sort of gift [I Cor 12:11]."[6] He also remarks, taking texts that refer to believers as "God's temple" (1 Cor. 3:16-17; 2 Cor 6:16) and other texts where believers are referred to as the "temples of the Holy Spirit" (1 Cor 6:19), that they show that the Holy Spirit is God. Similarly, he cites Peter's rebuke of Ananias for lying against the Holy Spirit and God (Acts 5:3-4). Thus, for Calvin, emphasizing the biblical proofs for the divinity of the Spirit is important for our understanding of his Person and work. The work of the Spirit is closely connected with the Scripture.

THE HOLY SPIRIT AND SCRIPTURE

After speaking about the evidences we see in nature that do not help to gain an understanding of God, Calvin turns to Scripture as that which gives us a true knowledge of God. To him, it is the Scripture alone that gives us knowledge of God.[7] Scripture, for Calvin, is the Word of God. It is this Word through which we get a firm understanding of faith, he says, "[f]or by his Word, God rendered faith unambiguous forever, a faith that should be superior to all opinion."[8] Scripture is absolutely necessary for the believer and without it he would fall into error. Scripture can communicate to the believer what nature cannot.[9]

How may a believer confirm the authority of Scripture? Contrary to the Roman Catholic claims that the credibility of the Scripture is based on the judgment of the church, Calvin asserts that it is not the church, but God who authenticates Scripture.[10] If the church itself is grounded upon

---

[5] Calvin, *Institutes*, I.xiii.14.
[6] Calvin, *Institutes*, I.xiii.14.
[7] Calvin, *Institutes*, I.vi.1.
[8] Calvin, *Institutes*, I.vi.2.
[9] Calvin, *Institutes*, I.vi.3, 4.
[10] Calvin, *Institutes*, I.vii.1.

Scripture, how can it become the authenticating authority for Scripture? So for Calvin, it is God, specifically the Holy Spirit who bears witness to the truthfulness of Scripture. He writes, "[t]hus, the highest proof of Scripture derives in general from the fact that God in person speaks in it. . . . We ought to seek our conviction in a higher place than human reasons, judgements, or conjectures, that is, in the secret testimony of the Spirit."[11] This testimony of the Spirit is very necessary and it is the primary basis for conviction of the authenticity of the Scripture in the heart of man. He writes, "[f]or as God alone is a fit witness of himself in his Word, so also the Word will not find acceptance in men's hearts before it is sealed by the inward testimony of the Spirit."[12] Calvin argues that even from a human perspective the credibility of Scripture can be established because of its supernatural character, but all these are insufficient for our faith, as he observes, "yet of themselves these [supernatural characteristics] are not strong enough to provide a firm faith, until our Heavenly Father . . . lifts reverence for Scripture beyond the realm of controversy."[13] He adds, "[t]herefore, Scripture will ultimately suffice for a saving knowledge of God only when its certainty is founded upon the inward persuasion of the Holy Spirit."[14] Here, we see that Calvin does not base his arguments for the authenticity of Scripture in the many qualities that Scripture possesses but on God Himself, the author of the Scripture, through the inward testimony of the Holy Spirit.

Calvin was also aware of the danger of some who would reject Scripture and appeal to the Holy Spirit. For Calvin, there is a close connection between the Holy Spirit and Scripture. Calvin observes, "[h]e [the Holy Spirit] ought to be sufficient for us as soon as he penetrates into us. But lest under his sign the spirit of Satan should creep in, he would have us recognize him in his own image, which he has stamped upon the Scripture. He is the author of the Scripture: he cannot vary and differ from himself."[15] By saying this Calvin firmly asserts that the Holy Spirit authenticates the Word and the Word itself bears witness to the Spirit. He takes on those who try to quote 2 Corinthians 3:6 ("the letter kills")

---

[11] Calvin, *Institutes*, I.vii.4.
[12] Calvin, *Institutes*, I.vii.4.
[13] Calvin, *Institutes*, I.viii.13, (Parenthesis added).
[14] Calvin, *Institutes*, I.viii.13.
[15] Calvin, *Institutes*, I.ix.2, (Parenthesis added).

by giving the text a reasonable explanation. He writes, "[w]hat is more, in the very same place the apostle calls his preaching 'the ministration of the Spirit' [II Cor. 3:8] meaning, doubtless, that the Holy Spirit so inheres in His truth . . . that only when its proper reverence and dignity are given to the Word does the Holy Spirit show forth His power."[16] This means that there is a close interrelatedness between the Word and the Spirit. The Holy Spirit authenticates the Word and the Word reveals the Spirit.

A danger ever present in the church is that of interpreting the work of the Holy Spirit in such a manner that he stands independent and autonomous in his person and actions. The all too familiar placing of the Holy Spirit in opposition to the Scripture is a result of this thinking, supported by texts such as 2 Corinthians 3:6 ("the letter kills, but the Spirit gives life"). Calvin, after dismissing claims that this refers to the allegorical interpretation of Scripture, writes, "The meaning of this passage, however, is as follows—that, if the word of God is simply uttered with the mouth, it is an occasion of death, and that it is life giving, only when it is received with the heart. The terms letter and spirit, therefore, do not refer to the exposition of the word, but to its influence and fruit.[17]

THE HOLY SPIRIT AND SALVATION

To Calvin, the titles of the Holy Spirit reveal the role that he plays in salvation. Thus, the title "spirit of adoption" shows the goodness of God in embracing us in Christ (Rom 8:15; Gal 4:6). Again, in order to assure us of our salvation, "he is called 'the guarantee and seal' of our inheritance (II Cor 1:22; cf. Eph 1:14). . .he is also called 'life' because of righteousness."[18] Calvin draws attention to the use of the word "water" in describing the Holy Spirit. He writes, "[b]y his secret watering the Spirit makes us fruitful to bring forth the buds of righteousness."[19] He refers to other verses that communicate the idea of water such as Isaiah 55:1; 44:3; John 7:37, and Ezekiel 36:25 where the added idea of power to cleanse and purify is seen.[20]

---

[16] Calvin, *Institutes*, I.ix.3.
[17] John Calvin, *Commentary on the Second Epistle to the Corinthians* (Albany, OR: Books for the Ages, Ages Software, version 1.0, 1998), 73.
[18] Calvin, *Institutes*, III.i.3.
[19] Calvin, *Institutes*, III.i.3.
[20] Calvin, *Institutes*, III.i..3.

Among the other names that are used for the Holy Spirit is "anointing" (1 John 2:20, 27) that convey the idea of restoration and nourishment. The word "fire" is used to show that the Holy Spirit destroys all the polluting marks of sin and kindles in the believer love and devotion (Luke 3:16).[21] Another word that is used for the Holy Spirit is "spring" (John 4:14) from whom we receive spiritual blessings; so also he refers to the "Lord's hand" (Acts 11:21) showing his might. It is this might or power that infuses "divine life" into us so that we are "ruled by his action and prompting." He goes on to say, "[a]ccordingly, whatever good things are in us are the fruits of his grace; and without him our gifts are darkness of mind and perversity of heart (cf. Gal 5:19-21)."[22]

One recurring theme in Calvin's writing is the utter depravity of man. It is this condition that makes the ministry of the Holy Spirit essential in the life of the believer. Calvin talks about the dependence of the believer on the Holy Spirit. Taking texts that refer to man's depravity such as Genesis 6:5 and 8:21, he writes, "[i]f whatever our nature conceives, instigates, undertakes, and attempts is always evil, how can that which is pleasing to God, to whom holiness and righteousness alone are acceptable, even enter our minds?"[23] This dependence on God is a continual necessity, "[a]lthough he [David] had been reborn and had advanced to no mean extent in true godliness, he still confesses that he needs continual direction at every moment, lest he decline from the knowledge with which he has been endowed."[24]

Calvin's teachings on election and eternal security come through clearly when he talks about believers who come to faith. Expounding Genesis 15:21-22 on the birth of Jacob and Esau, he writes, "[i]n speaking of the stronger, it is to show us, that when God's election is steadfast and undoubted, and that we are upheld by his Holy Spirit, we must no longer

---

[21] Calvin, *Institutes* III.i.3. In referring to Calvin's words here, "[o]n the other hand, persistently boiling away and burning up our vicious and inordinate desire, *he enflames our hearts with the love of God and with zealous devotion,*" the editor draws attention to Calvin's emblem of a flaming heart on an outstretched arm bearing the words, "My heart I give to Thee, promptly and sincerely." (n. 6, Emphasis added).
[22] Calvin, *Institutes*, III.i.3.
[23] Calvin, *Institutes*, II.ii.25.
[24] Calvin, *Institutes*, II.ii.25, (Parenthesis added).

fear."[25] The Holy Spirit does not only bring the sinner to salvation by opening his eyes, he holds him up because he (the believer) is elected.

THE HOLY SPIRIT AND FAITH

For Calvin, "faith is the principal work of the Holy Spirit."[26] Taking texts such as, John 1:12-13 (John's prologue referring to children being born of God), Matthew 16:17 (Peter's confession and the reference to this being revealed by the Father), and Ephesians 1:13 ("you were marked in him with a seal, the promised Holy Spirit") he talks of the Spirit being the person who awakens faith in the believers. Without the Spirit the promise of salvation is of no use. He writes, "[s]imilarly, where he says that the Thessalonians have been chosen by God, 'in sanctification of the Spirit and belief in the truth' (II Thess 2:13), he is briefly warning us that faith itself has no other source than the Spirit."[27] Our knowledge of the indwelling of Christ in us is through the Spirit (1 John 3:24; 4:13). It is this Spirit that Christ promised his disciples, "the Spirit of truth. The world cannot accept him" (John 14:17) through whom they would be able to receive "heavenly wisdom."[28] It is the Spirit who brings to mind what was taught by Christ. Calvin explains, "For light would be given the sightless in vain had that Spirit of discernment (John 20:3) not opened the eyes of the mind. . . . Paul so highly commends the ministry of the Spirit (II Cor 3:6) for the reason that teachers would shout to no effect if Christ himself, inner Schoolmaster, did not by his Spirit draw to himself those given to him by the Father (cf. John 6:44; 12:32; 17:6)."[29] For our discussion on mission, this biblical emphasis of Calvin needs to be considered well.

For Calvin, it is the Triune God who harmoniously orchestrates the process of salvation in which faith plays a key role. Taking texts such as John 6:44 ("No one can come to me unless the Father who sent me draws them, and I will raise them up at the last day.") and John 6:65 ("This is why I told you that no one can come to me unless the Father has enabled them."), Calvin's thoughts follow in the stream of Augustine

---

[25] John Calvin, *Sermons on Election and Reprobation, Eleventh Sermon on Jacob and Esau* (Albany, OR: Books for the Ages, Ages Software, version 1.0, 1998), 65.
[26] Calvin, *Institutes* III.i.4.
[27] Calvin, *Institutes*, III.i.4.
[28] Calvin, *Institutes*, III.i.4.
[29] Calvin, *Institutes*, III.i.4.

and are interrelated with the doctrines of election and predestination. He writes of the necessity of the Spirit in order to receive faith. He talks of Paul referring to faith as the work of the Spirit and then goes on to say, while referring to 1 Corinthians 2:4-5, "[h]e (Paul) is speaking, indeed, of outward miracles; but because the wicked, being blind, cannot see these, he includes also that inner seal which he mentions elsewhere (Eph 1:13; 4:30). And God... does not bestow it (salvation) upon all indiscriminately, but by a singular privilege give it to those whom he will."[30]

In the matter of salvation, faith is not something that we generate. It is the Spirit who reveals faith in our hearts. Even though the Word of God is true and perspicuous, our mind, notes Calvin, "has such an inclination to vanity that it can never cleave fast to the truth of God." Sin makes mankind "blind to the light of God's truth. Accordingly, without the illumination of the Holy Spirit, the Word can do nothing."[31] However, for Calvin, the illumination of the mind alone is insufficient; there should also be a strengthening of the heart.[32] In other words, a mere intellectual assent to the truth of the Scripture without a corresponding empowering of the heart falls short of what is required for salvation. He writes, "[i]n both ways, therefore, faith is a singular gift of God, both in that the mind of man is purged so as to be able to taste the truth of God and in that his heart is established therein. For the Spirit is not only the initiator of faith, but increases it by degrees, until by it he leads us to the Kingdom of Heaven."[33]

The Holy Spirit and Christ

To Calvin, it is the Holy Spirit who leads us to Christ. Just as he teaches about understanding the Scripture, in knowing Christ too we are helpless without the intervention of the Holy Spirit. Citing several texts (Matt 11:25; Luke 10:21; Matt 16:17; 1 Cor 2:14; Rom 11:34; 1 Cor 2:16: John 6:44) he says, "[t]herefore, as we cannot come to Christ unless we be drawn by the Spirit of God, so when we are drawn we are lifted up in mind and heart above our understanding.... For this reason, Christ, in clearly interpreting the mysteries of his Kingdom to the two disciples (Luke

---

[30] Calvin, *Institutes*, III.ii.35, (Parenthesis added).
[31] Calvin, *Institutes*, III.ii.33.
[32] Calvin, *Institutes*, III.ii.33.
[33] Calvin, *Institutes*, III.ii.33.

24:27), still makes no headway until 'he opens their minds to understand the Scriptures (Luke 24:45).'"[34]

The close relationship between the Spirit and Christ is so obvious that often there is considerable overlap when referring to them. Calvin comments, "[a]s has already been clearly explained, until our minds become intent upon the Spirit, Christ, so to speak, lies idle because we contemplate him as outside ourselves - indeed far from us."[35] It is the Spirit, then, who makes Christ real to us. This is an important observation. It can be applied to a theoretical or academic understanding of Christ that is of little value without the work of the Spirit who quickens us to experience life in Christ. Calvin makes his point even stronger by saying, "[w]e know, moreover, that he (Christ) benefits only those whose 'Head' he is (Eph. 4:15), for whom he is 'the first-born among brethren' (Rom 8:29), and who, finally, 'have put on him' (Gal 3:27)."[36] Calvin goes on to describe the "sacred wedlock" through which we are united with Christ (Eph 5:30) and then adds, "[b]ut he unites himself to us by the Spirit alone. By the grace and power of the same Spirit we are made his members, to keep us under himself and in turn to possess him."[37]

The Holy Spirit and Preaching

David Steinmetz rightly observes, "Like Athanasius and the early Fathers and unlike modern interpreters of the Bible, Calvin wanted to emphasize the bond of union which the Holy Spirit forges between the grace of Christ and the activity of preaching. The stakes are very high indeed for Calvin since, as 2 Corinthians 3:6 makes clear, the same gospel may be killing letter or life-giving spirit."[38] Calvin himself says, "[n]ow when he (David) says, *Order my steps according to thy word:* he means, that we can do nothing at all, except God governs us by his holy spirit. . . . For although we have the word of God offered unto us, yet shall we profit nothing thereby until such time as God gives us understanding to see it."[39]

---

[34] Calvin, *Institutes*, III.ii.34.
[35] Calvin, *Institutes*, III.i.3.
[36] Calvin, *Institutes*, III.i.3, (Parenthesis added).
[37] Calvin, *Institutes*, III.i.3.
[38] David Steinmetz, "Calvin and the Irrepressible Spirit," *Ex Auditu* 12 (1996), 100.
[39] John Calvin, *Sermons on Psalm 119*, Seventeenth sermon, Psalm 119:133 (Albany, OR: Books for the Ages, Ages Software, version 1.0, 1998), 249. (Old English spellings changed where necessary, also 'holy spirit' capitalized 'Holy Spirit,' in this and other quotations.)

The impact of preaching, then, is not on the effectiveness of the preacher but on the power of God. Unless God opens the eyes of the sinner to perceive the gospel, nothing significant happens. From first to last it is God alone.

Calvin, in a sense, binds the Word of God to the Holy Spirit. The Word cannot have any meaning or effectiveness to any person unless the Holy Spirit illumines the person. Discussing faith he comments, "[i]t (faith) is an understanding which we have of the goodness and favor of GOD, after that he hath illuminated us by his Holy Spirit and by his word. . . .if GOD illuminate us not within, when he sends his holy word, to show us the way, we should always remain as poor strays, or lost sheep."[40] Again in the same line of thought, he speaks of the Holy Spirit's role in making people understand the Word. Here, it appears that Calvin again is talking about the effectiveness of the Word being bound to the ministry of the Holy Spirit. He says that David prayed that his eyes may be opened to "see wonderful things in your law" (Ps 119:18). He continues, "[b]y this expression he evidently means that the sun rises upon the earth when God's Word shines upon men; but they do not have its benefit until he who is called "Father of lights [James 1:17] either gives eyes or opens them."[41]

Calvin's theology of the Holy Spirit shows the crucial role he plays in soteriological matters. He is the quiet but strong presence in the *ordosalutis* and his influence continues beyond salvation to sanctification. He is the one without whom salvation cannot take place. He works harmoniously with the Father and the Son to redeem mankind from sin and destruction.

THE APPLICATION OF CALVIN'S DOCTRINE OF THE HOLY SPIRIT TO MISSIONS IN A PLURALISTIC CONTEXT

A common criticism levelled at the sixteenth century Reformers is that they did not engage in missions. This is a chronologically misplaced argument that ignores the sixteenth century context. The idea of missions,

---

[40] John Calvin, *Sermons on Election and Reprobation*, Eleventh Sermon on Jacob and Esau (Albany, OR: Books for the Ages, Ages Software, version 1.0, 1998), 65, (Parenthesis added).

[41] Calvin, *Institutes*, II.ii.21.

if understood holistically, was very much present in the activities that the Reformers were engaged in, generally: such as a return to evangelical gospel, the pure preaching of the Word of God, developing and embracing a biblical understanding of the sacraments – though the latter was understood differently by the Reformers.

The sixteenth century Reformers are remembered for both their contributions and their lapses. Calvin is no exception. While his followers try to gloss over some of the excesses in Geneva during his tenure, his detractors point out those actions that seem too glaring. A fair appraisal of Calvin needs to consider his overall contribution to holistic missions during his time in Geneva. He represented the cause of the Reformation and the gospel to the rulers of France, England, Poland, Italy and other nation states of Europe.[42] His letters, encouraging the Reformed cause and strengthening those facing persecution and death are impressive.[43] He also gave leadership to the Genevan church that Kingdon says, "proved to be a model for Protestants in much of Europe and America."[44] His academy, which evolved into the University of Geneva, is called "the crown of Calvin's Genevan work."[45] Calvin also sent a "mission" to establish a Protestant colony in Brazil that unfortunately ended in failure.[46] This probably is the closest event that could be understood as missions in the contemporary understanding of the term.

To apply Calvin's theology of the Holy Spirit to missions in a pluralistic context, the idea of a pluralistic context itself needs to be clarified. During Calvin's own time the religious pluralistic element consisted of Roman Catholic, Protestant, Jew, and Turk (or Moslem).[47]

---

[42] Williston Walker, *John Calvin* (New York: Schocken Books, 1969), 379.

[43] See John Calvin, *Selected Works: Tracts and Letters,* vols. 4-7, Henry Beveridge and Jules Bonnet (eds), David Constable (trans.) (Grand Rapids, MI: Baker Book House, 1983).

[44] Robert M. Kingdon, *Church and Society in Reformation Europe* (London: Valiorum, 1985), 215. The church sent out missionaries as is recorded in *The Register of the Company of Pastors of Geneva in the Time of Calvin,* Philip Edgcumbe Hughes (ed. and trans.) (Grand Rapids, MI: William B. Eerdmans, 1966), 3. This *Register,* started only in late 1546, is only a partial account of the missionary activities but still provides a glimpse of the zeal for the gospel.

[45] Walker, *Calvin,* 367.

[46] For some highlights of this expedition see G. Baez-Camargo, "The Earliest Protestant Missionary Venture in Latin America," *Church History* 21 (1952), 135; R. Pierce Beaver, "The Genevan Mission to Brazil," *The Reformed Journal* 17 (1967), 14-20.

[47] Though the Eastern Orthodox churches were very much a presence in their respective areas, the western church consisted primarily of Roman Catholics.

Today, the context is very different. Religious pluralism is a reality in every urban context globally. The real test of Calvin's doctrine of the Holy Spirit is in the contemporary context with its religious pluralism. Calvin's theology of the Holy Spirit, when examined closely, is not contingent on man's actions in the matter of salvation. It is solidly dependent on God alone. Thus, it rises above religious pluralism and is not hindered by the beliefs and practices of various religions.

Calvin's theology of the Holy Spirit cannot be divorced from his other doctrines that are connected with salvation. Thus, the elements of the *order salutis* that lead in a discernible way through election, predestination, calling, justification, sanctification, and glorification play an important role. For instance Calvin, in discussing election, refers to the continual preaching of God's free call.[48] Further, with reference to Romans 8:30 ("those he predestined, he also called; those he called, he also justified"), Calvin views the call, or the hearing of the gospel, as necessary for the elect. The Holy Spirit teaches the elect and makes effective the preached Word.[49]

Calvin also distinguishes between a general call and a special call. His words appear to suggest the work of evangelism. He says the general call is that by which God "invites all equally to himself through the outward preaching of the Word – even those to whom he holds it out as a savor of death (cf. II Cor 2:16)."[50] In reply to Cardinal Sadolet's letter, Calvin refers to his suggestion that men ought to continue in the religion handed down to them by their forefathers and responds that if this were true then Jews, Turks, and Saracens would escape the judgment of God.[51] This shows that man is responsible for his actions; God's sovereignty and mankind's responsibility go hand in hand.

Preaching plays an important role in Calvin's understanding of the process of conversion. He clarifies the relationship between election and the preaching of the gospel when discussing "predestination." He says that God does not speak to men in order to change the things which once

---

[48] Calvin, *Institutes*, III.xxiv.1.
[49] Calvin, *Institutes*, III.xxiv.1.
[50] Calvin, *Institutes*, III.xxiv.8.
[51] John Calvin, *Tracts and Treatises on the Reformation of the Church*, vol. 1, Henry Beveridge (trans.) (Grand Rapids, MI: William B. Eerdmans, 1958), 64.

were decreed by him, but rather to prove how unchanging they are. He further says that it is impossible for those elected to perish, for which reason the elect are handed over to the "faithful guardianship of Christ." He continues by referring to the necessity of their being brought into the fold of Christ and concludes, "[t]herefore, since the elect obtain salvation by hearing the voice of the Shepherd, their election is brought to its realization *only by the external preaching of the gospel.*"[52] When preaching is viewed as an activity in which the Holy Spirit is greatly involved, its importance even for contemporary missions should be emphasized.

Although Calvin had some solid theological views about the work of the Holy Spirit in salvation, yet his own personal reflections seemed to go contrary to his teachings. For example, both in the case of Roman Catholics and Moslems, he had some extreme ideas about their beliefs. After a thorough study of Calvin and his views of Turks, Slomp concludes that though he viewed Moslems negatively and outside the pale of salvation, yet at least in two texts he holds out the possibility of their conversion.[53] Slomp also points out that "Calvin's intense personal concern for the attacks of the Papists led him to portray them as worse than either the Jews or the Turks and Saracens."[54] This seems to be a setback to Calvin's teaching of the Holy Spirit. What are the criteria that he uses to make this judgment? Did the word "Papist" refer to the hierarchy in the church or all church members? If he meant the latter then how would he explain the large number of religious adherents whose faith depended on the principle of *cuiusregio, eiusreligio* ("whose realm, his religion").[55]

In conclusion, Calvin's theology of the Holy Spirit gives hope for mission in contemporary pluralistic contexts. Since the Holy Spirit, as the third person of the Trinity, is intimately involved in the salvation of mankind, and initiates the process of conversion that has been eternally

---

[52] John Calvin, *Concerning Scandals*, John W. Fraser (trans.) (Grand Rapids, MI: William B. Eerdmans, 1978), 54, (Emphasis added).

[53] Jan Slomp, "Calvin and the Turks," *Studies in Interreligious Dialogue* 19/1 (2009), 50-65, see 62-63.

[54] Slomp, *Calvin and the Turks*, 63.

[55] This principle emerged from the Peace of Augsburg (1555) and applied to Roman Catholic and Lutheran territories. This simply meant that the religion of the state would be the religion of the ruler. In other parts of Europe similar actions emerged. In Switzerland, for example, following a public religious debate between the Protestants and Roman Catholics, a large area would change its religious belief following, in this case, the winners of the debate.

decreed, he is the executor of God's perfect will. Despite Calvin's own negative response to the Turks and Roman Catholics it is evident that his teachings on the Holy Spirit along with his emphasis on the biblical doctrine of election give people in pluralistic society the opportunity to respond to the gospel.

Furthermore, the doctrines of election and predestination that he taught when juxtaposed with the activity of the Holy Spirit in the work of redemption provides an impetus for mission and evangelism in a pluralistic society. The utter depravity of humans and their inability to secure salvation by themselves calls for divine intervention. Therefore, regardless of the spiritual and moral condition of people or their religious persuasions, God takes the initiative to supernaturally provide for the sinner all that is required to respond to the call to repentance and faith. In this process the work of the Holy Spirit is paramount. The church responds to mission in obedience to the command of Christ. It submits itself to the lordship of Christ and engages itself in mission in all its forms trusting God to make his Word bear fruit according to his will.

8

THE SHIFT FROM *MISSIO DEI* TO *MISSIO SPIRITŪS* IN RECENT MISSION THINKING: THE INDIAN CONTRIBUTION

Kirsteen Kim*

"Finding out where the Holy Spirit is at work and joining in" has become a watchword in contemporary mission, as evinced by the 2013 World Council of Churches (WCC) policy statement on "mission and evangelism in changing landscapes" (subtitle): *Together towards Life* (TTL).[1] But this interest in the mission of the Spirit is relatively recent. A century ago at the World Missionary Conference in Edinburgh in 1910, the Holy Spirit was hardly referred to except as "the superhuman factor" that empowered the church in mission through prayer.[2] In the mid-twentieth

---

* **Kristeen Kim** PhD is Professor of Theology and World Christianity at Fuller Theological Seminary, USA. In her capacity as vice-moderator of the World Council of Churches' Commission for World Mission and Evangelism, she chaired the drafting group for the WCC statement *Together towards Life*. She is the author of several books, including *Mission in the Spirit* (New Delhi: ISPCK, 2003), and most recently with Sebastian C.H. Kim, *A History of Korean Christianity* (Cambridge: Cambridge University Press, 2015), and she edits the journal *Mission Studies*.

[1] World Council of Churches, *Together towards Life: Mission and Evangelism in Changing Landscapes* (2013). Available at www.oikoumene.org.

[2] World Missionary Conference, 1910, *Report of Commission I: Carrying the Gospel to All the Non-Christian World* (Edinburgh & London: Oliphant, Anderson and Ferrier, 1910), 359-360.

The Shift from *Missio Dei* to *Missio Spiritūs*

century, what had been the continuation committee from Edinburgh – the International Missionary Council (IMC) – originated the *missio Dei* concept when it located mission in the sending nature and activity of God out of love for the world.[3] This chapter will focus on the shift from *missio Dei* to *missio Spiritūs* today. It will examine particularly the significance of this shift in the context of religious pluralism. It will show how the Indian context of religious plurality is central to this development in theology of mission, especially through the representative work of the Protestant Stanley Samartha on interfaith dialogue and of the Roman Catholic Jacques Dupuis on religious pluralism. It will also go on to observe how such insights from the Indian context are appropriated in TTL in the context of mission.

TOGETHER TOWARDS LIFE

The WCC document *Together towards Life* (TTL) may be regarded as the chief evidence for the shift from *missio Dei* (the mission of God) to *missio Spiritūs* (the mission of the Spirit) in recent mission thinking because it was the result of an ecumenical consensual process of drafting. Of the twenty-five members of the Commission for World Mission and Evangelism (CWME) who worked on the document, 50 per cent represented WCC member churches (Protestant and Orthodox), 25 percent were from mission bodies associated with member churches, and 25 per cent of the commissioners were representatives from non-member churches (including evangelical, Pentecostal and Roman Catholic representatives). They were supported in their work by about five WCC staff. The commission is heir to the International Missionary Council (IMC), which originated the *missio Dei* concept. A corollary of the missionary nature of God is "the missionary nature of the church" and, following this logic, the IMC merged with the WCC in 1961. The discovery of "mission," in the sense of the mission of God, superseded the focus on the "missions" of the (western) churches in the colonial period. In the post-war and post-colonial context of the 1940s and 1950s, the church in every continent

---

[3] David J. Bosch, *Transforming Mission: Paradigm Shifts in Theology of Mission* (Maryknoll, NY: Orbis Books, 1991), 389-393; John G. Flett, *The Witness of God: The Trinity, Missio Dei, Karl Barth, and the Nature of Christian Community* (Grand Rapids, MI: William B. Eerdmans, 2010).

was declared to be missionary in so far as it participated in the mission of Christ to the world.

Considering the significant changes in the global landscape in the thirty years since the only previous WCC statement on mission and evangelism,[4] the CWME commissioners made expressing an ecumenical theology of mission for today the main aim of their work. While both WCC documents upheld the "*missio Dei*" paradigm, the 1982 statement construed missions in terms of the coming kingdom of God. This attention to the kingdom was in keeping with the decree *Ad Gentes* of the Second Vatican Council (1965), which described missions as the "duty to spread everywhere the Kingdom of God" (para. 42).[5] However, uniquely for a WCC policy document, TTL is expressed in a framework of theology of the Holy Spirit (pneumatology). This departure is justified and amplified in the first main section of the document, "Spirit of Mission: Breath of Life" which, as its title suggests, takes as its point of departure the statement of the Nicene Creed that the Holy Spirit is "the Giver of Life."

Despite earlier controversy over pneumatology at the seventh WCC general assembly in Canberra (Australia) in 1991,[6] the CWME pursued this pneumatological approach for multiple theological reasons. These included biblical reflection on the Spirit as "the guiding and driving force of mission;"[7] Orthodox insistence on the need for proper attention to pneumatology in ecumenical theology; the liberating work of the Spirit as noted by liberation theologians who saw that "the Spirit of the Lord is upon me" meant "good news to the poor" (Luke 4:18); the desire to reach out to the rapidly growing Pentecostal churches and address their focus on the power and gifts of the Holy Spirit; the rich resources of

---

[4] World Council of Churches, *Mission and Evangelism: An Ecumenical Affirmation* (1982). Available for download from www.mission2005.org.

[5] Second Vatican Council, *Decree* Ad Gentes *on the Mission Activity of the Church* (1965). Available for download from www.vatican.va.

[6] The Canberra assembly was divided by the question of the relationship of the Holy Spirit with the spirits of this world and of pneumatology with christology, as raised by the plenary presentation of the Korean theologian Chung Hyun Kyung. See Michael Kinnamon (ed), *Signs of the Spirit*. Official Report of the Seventh Assembly of the World Council of Churches, Canberra, 1991 (Geneva: World Council of Churches, 1991); Kirsteen Kim, *The Holy Spirit in the World: A Global Conversation* (Maryknoll, NY: Orbis Books, 2007).

[7] David J. Bosch, *Transforming Mission: Paradigm Shifts in Theology of Mission* (Maryknoll, NY: Orbis Books, 1991), 113.

creation pneumatology for the development of theologies of eco-justice; and the pneumatological approach developed by CWME to healing and reconciliation in preparation for the conference in Athens in 2005.[8]

Arguably, the most pressing reason for the adoption of a pneumatological framework was the development of pneumatology in the context of religious pluralism and the need for theology of missions to get around what has been described as "the Christological impasse."[9] Either one affirmed Christ's lordship, and with it the supremacy of Christianity above other religions, the exclusivity of the church and the restriction of eternal salvation, and was thereby condemned as an exclusivist or inclusivist, or one adopted the politically correct view that all religions were equally valid and along with that rejected the doctrines of the Trinity and christology, took a universalist approach to salvation and denied the necessity of Christian mission.[10] There did not appear to be any way in which to link theologically the reality of God's self-disclosure in the lives of people of other faiths while also maintaining the particular and historic confession of the Bible and the church. The San Antonio conference on world mission and evangelism of the WCC in 1989 stated this starkly: "We cannot point to any other way of salvation than Jesus Christ. At the same time we cannot set limits to God's saving power. ...We appreciate this tension, and do not attempt to solve it."[11]

THE INDIAN CONTRIBUTION: STANLEY J. SAMARTHA AND JACQUES DUPUIS

The development of mission pneumatology in the context of religious pluralism is a particular Indian contribution to the shift from *missio Dei* to *missio Spiritūs* in recent mission thinking. The Indian subcontinent

---

[8] Conference website, www.mission2005.org. For documentation of the Athens conference see Jacques Matthey (ed), *Come, Holy Spirit, Heal and Reconcile*. Report of the World Council of Churches Conference on Mission and Evangelism, Athens, May 2005 (Geneva: World Council of Churches, 2008). For background, see Kim, *The Holy Spirit in the World*.

[9] For background see, for example, Amos Yong, *Beyond the Impasse: Toward a Pneumatological Theology of Religions* (Grand Rapids, MI: Baker Academic, 2003).

[10] Cf. Harold Netland, *Encountering Religious Pluralism: The Challenge to Christian Faith and Mission* (Downers Grove, IL: InterVarsity Press, 2001), 9-20.

[11] "Report from Section I", para. 26, in F.R. Wilson (ed), *The San Antonio Report: Your Will Be Done: Mission in Christ's Way* (Geneva: WCC Publications, 1990), 32.

has been the "laboratory" of most reflection on inter-religious dialogue[12] and almost every theologian of religious pluralism is from the Indian subcontinent or draws heavily on Indian experience.[13] In the ecumenical movement the key figure in the development of pneumatology in inter-religious relations is Stanley Samartha, the Methodist theologian from Karnataka, who moved to Geneva in 1968 and became the first secretary of the dialogue unit of the World Council of Churches (WCC). Jacques Dupuis, a Belgian Jesuit, spent 36 years in India where he made a special study of the Holy Spirit in the Indian context.[14] In retirement, he developed what he learnt in India, a definitive Roman Catholic theology of religious pluralism.[15]

STANLEY SAMARTHA: PNEUMATOLOGICAL FOUNDATION FOR DIALOGUE

Although the tripartite response to the perceived problem of proclaiming Christ's lordship in the context of many religions was not articulated by Allan Race until 1983[16] or by Paul Knitter until 1985,[17] at a conference in 1979,[18] Samartha was already expressing a theology of religious pluralism that he had developed while establishing the WCC *Guidelines on Dialogue*.[19] In 1971, Samartha identified three theological foundations for dialogue, including a pneumatological one.[20] Pneumatology was attractive to Samartha for several reasons.

---

[12] Paul F. Knitter, *One Earth Many Religions: Multifaith Dialogue and Global Responsibility* (Maryknoll, NY: Orbis Books, 1995), 157.

[13] Kirsteen Kim, *Joining in with the Spirit: Connecting World Church and Local Mission* (London: SCM Books, 2012), chapter 6.

[14] Jacques Dupuis, *Jesus Christ and His Spirit: Theological Approaches* (Bangalore: Theological Publications in India, 1977).

[15] Jacques Dupuis, *Toward a Christian Theology of Religious Pluralism* (Maryknoll, NY: Orbis Books, 1999).

[16] Alan Race, *Christians and Religious Pluralism: Patterns in the Christian Theology of Religions* (London: SCM Press, 1983).

[17] Paul F. Knitter, *No Other Name? A Critical Survey of Christian Attitudes toward the World Religions* (Maryknoll, NY: Orbis Books, 1985).

[18] Published as Stanley Samartha, "The Lordship of Jesus Christ and Religious Pluralism" in Gerald H. Anderson and Thomas F. Stransky (eds), *Christ's Lordship and Religious Pluralism* (Maryknoll, NY: Orbis Books, 1981), 19-36.

[19] World Council of Churches, *Guidelines on Dialogue with People of Living Faiths and Ideologies* (Geneva: WCC, 1979).

[20] Stanley J. Samartha, "The Holy Spirit and People of Various Faiths, Cultures and Ideologies" in Dow Kirkpatrick (ed), *The Holy Spirit* (Nashville, TN: Tidings, 1974), 20-39.

First, he was searching above all for a pastoral approach to inter-religious relations which would keep the peace in the Indian context of many communities and build a community-of-communities.[21] The fourth assembly of the WCC at Uppsala in 1968 had begun by discussing "the Holy Spirit and the Catholicity of the Church." Samartha drew his pneumatological foundation for dialogue from the statement in John's Gospel that "when he, the Spirit of truth, comes, he will guide you into all the truth" (John 16:13).[22] He saw it as giving grounds for openness to the other since Samartha understood truth to include the truth of other religions.[23] He insisted that in dialogue any partner may speak the truth and that Christians have no monopoly on the Spirit.

Second, the Holy Spirit, being "spiritual," seemed to circumvent hard-line theological confrontations that were damaging to Christian communities in India. When, at the 1979 conference, Samartha was criticised for a lack of attention to Jesus' outspoken criticism of contemporary religious practices,[24] Samartha responded that love is more important than truth.[25] Samartha stressed the experiential nature of dialogue.[26] He regarded it not so much as a method or technique but as "a mood, a spirit, an attitude of love and respect" for "our neighbours of other faiths."[27] He insisted that relations with other religions should not be impersonal but they should be loving and an expression of our Christian spirituality. Dialogue takes place in the "milieu" of the Spirit[28] and so "Spirit," "spirituality," and "dialogue" are "closely related in Samartha's

---

[21] Stanley J. Samartha, "The Nature and Purpose of the Consultation" in Stanley J. Samartha (ed), *Towards World Community: The Colombo Papers* (Geneva: WCC, 1975), 3-13 (6-11).

[22] Samartha, "The Holy Spirit and People of Various Faiths, Cultures and Ideologies."

[23] Samartha characterised dialogue as "commitment and openness." See Eeuwout Klootwijk, *Commitment and Openness: The Interreligious Dialogue and Theology of Religions in the Work of Stanley J. Samartha* (Zoetermeer: Uitgeverij Boekencentrum B.V., 1992).

[24] Arthur F. Glasser, "Response" in Gerald H. Anderson and Thomas F. Stransky (eds), *Christ's Lordship and Religious Pluralism* (Maryknoll, NY: Orbis Books, 1981), 37-45 (40).

[25] Samartha, "The Lordship of Jesus Christ," 54.

[26] Stanley J. Samartha, "More than an Encounter of Commitments: An Interpretation of the Ajaltoun Consultation on 'Dialogue Between Men of Living Faiths'," *International Review of Mission* 59/236 (1970), 392-403 (96-97, 101).

[27] Samartha, "The Lordship of Jesus Christ," 32.

[28] Stanley Samartha, *Courage for Dialogue: Ecumenical Issues in Inter-religious Relationships* (Geneva: WCC, 1981), 75, 73 n.16.

life and work." Furthermore, in the ecumenical movement the Spirit was presented as unifying: the Spirit of "fellowship," and "communion."[29]

Third, the Spirit is associated primarily with life – all life. Samartha took this link directly from the Nicene Creed and, therefore, regarded the Spirit as what unifies humankind.[30] The theme of the Spirit and life came to the fore at the seventh assembly of the WCC in Canberra in 1991 where the Holy Spirit was called upon to "renew the whole creation."[31] Jürgen Moltmann's contribution showed this most clearly: *Spirit of Life – a Universal Affirmation*.[32] Moltmann developed a trinitarian pneumatology that began with the Spirit moving over the waters at creation and, therefore, laid the doctrinal grounds for environmental and eco-theology. Since the Spirit was seen to be at work in the whole creation, this at the same time strengthened Samartha's pneumatological foundation for dialogue. Neither the Spirit nor life is limited to Christians or Christianity; they are part of our common humanity and common home.

The fourth reason Samartha found a pneumatological approach to inter-faith relations attractive was that he saw it to be in keeping with his Indian heritage. He drew parallels between the Indian philosophy of non-dualism – *advaita* – and the spirit of dialogue. In his contribution to John Hick and Paul Knitter's 1987 edited work, *The Myth of Christian Uniqueness*, which advanced a "pluralistic theology of religions,"[33] Samartha understood the pluralistic theology of religions as another way of stating the *advaitic* tenet that the philosophy of the impersonal mystery or universal ultimate is beyond and superior to any personal religion, which was necessarily specific to a particular community. So that, in Samartha's view, Jesus Christ could be described as distinctive but not

---

[29] Norman Goodall (ed), *The Uppsala 68 Report*. Official Report of the Fourth Assembly of the WCC, Uppsala, 1968 (Geneva: WCC, 1968).

[30] "The Holy Spirit and People of Various Faiths, Cultures and Ideologies."

[31] Michael Kinnamon (ed), *Signs of the Spirit*. Official Report of the Seventh Assembly of the WCC, Canberra, 1991 (Geneva: WCC, 1991).

[32] Jürgen Moltmann, *The Spirit of Life – A Universal Affirmation*, Margaret Kohl (trans.) (London: SCM Press, 1992).

[33] John Hick and Paul F. Knitter (eds), *The Myth of Christian Uniqueness: Toward a Pluralistic Theology of Religions* (Maryknoll, NY: Orbis Books, 1987).

unique, penultimate but not final, authoritative for Christians but not Lord of all.[34]

Fifth, to Samartha, pneumatology appeared as a way to bypass these "exclusive claims." He got the idea of using pneumatology from a paper by Orthodox theologian George Khodr, who referred to Irenaeus' understanding of the Trinity as "the two hands of the Father" – Son and Spirit – and suggested that this gave each person of the Trinity a certain "hypostatic independence" that, if applied to theology of religions, allowed the inclusion of other faiths in the economy of the Spirit.[35] Other Orthodox theologians have refuted this approach[36] but Samartha used it to move towards a "pneumatocentric" theology of religions[37] in which christology was included only as a specifically Christian belief – not a universal one.

A final reason that Samartha found pneumatology attractive was that it appeared to bypass the institutional church, which resisted his agenda of dialogue. He was not the only theologian to be frustrated with the church at the time. At the Uppsala assembly of 1968, Hans Hoekendijk had captured the *Zeitgeist* when he insisted that God related directly to the world and could fulfil his purposes by other means if he chose.[38] This secularisation of the *missio Dei* facilitated mission collaboration with development agencies but at the risk of the distinctive contribution of Christian faith. Samartha had moved around the "Christological impasse" but many faithful Christians were alienated by a religious pluralism that rejected the classical expressions of the Trinity and the incarnation.

---

[34] See Hick & Knitter, *The Myth of Christian Uniqueness*, to which Samartha contributed an article, "The Cross and the Rainbow: Christ in a Multireligious Culture," 69-88.

[35] George Khodr, "Christianity in a Pluralist World: The Economy of the Holy Spirit" in Samartha S.J. (ed), *Living Faiths and the Ecumenical Movement* (Geneva: World Council of Churches, 1971), 131-142.

[36] Notably John Zizioulas, who argues that Son and Spirit should be regarded as cooperating in the one mission of God. See John D. Zizioulas, *Being as Communion: Studies in Personhood and the Church* (Crestwood, NY: St Vladimir's Seminary Press, 1985), 124-129.

[37] Paul Knitter, "Stanley Samartha's *One Christ – Many Religions* – Plaudits and Problems," *Current Dialogue* 21 (1991), 25-30 (28); S.J. Samartha "In Search of a Revised Christology: A Response to Paul Knitter," *Current Dialogue* 21 (1991), 30-37 (34).

[38] J.C. Hans Hoekendijk, see J.C. Hoekendijk, "The Church in Missionary Thinking," *International Review of Missions* 41/3 (1952), 324-336. Cf. World Council of Churches, *The Uppsala Report 1968*.

The Roman Catholic theologian Gavin D'Costa, himself of Indian descent, led the counterblast to Hick and Knitter's problematising of the confession of the lordship of Christ by attacking "the myth of a pluralistic theology of religions."[39] As Mark Heim showed, Hick and his colleagues could not claim any vantage point outside a particular frame of reference in order to claim that all religions should be subsumed under pluralism. It is just as possible that all the religions offer different salvations.[40] Similar criticisms were made in India of *advaitic* philosophy. Jesuit and liberation theologian Samuel Rayan, for instance, rejected Samartha's use of *advaita* as intellectually elitist.[41] In addition, Rayan argued that *advaita* was not "the living religion of the people" and that account must be taken of *dalit*, feminist and tribal criticism of brahminical traditions as oppressive.[42] Although Samartha recognised the criticisms, they did not shake his belief in the ubiquity and utility of *advaitic* thinking in India.[43] Furthermore, he remained convinced of the necessity for Christians to eschew "exclusive claims" of christology or Jesus' uniqueness, which appeared to him to cause offence in a multi-faith context.[44]

JACQUES DUPUIS: SPIRIT CHRISTOLOGY

Jacques Dupuis was involved in many of the same debates as Samartha and in the parallel development of pneumatological approaches to theology of religions and theology of mission as in the Roman Catholic church. Rather than seeing religious plurality as resting on a trinitarian foundation like his fellow Roman Catholic Raimundo Panikkar,[45] Dupuis approached plurality as a fact of life which needed a Christian theological

---

[39] Gavin D'Costa (ed), *Christian Uniqueness Reconsidered* (Maryknoll, NY: Orbis Books, 1990).

[40] S. Mark Heim, *Salvations: Truth and Difference in Religion* (Maryknoll, NY: Orbis Books, 1995).

[41] Samuel Rayan, Review of The Hindu Response to the Unbound Christ, *International Review of Mission* 66/262 (1977), 187-188. See also Duncan B. Forrester, "Review of S.J. Samartha, The Hindu Response to the Unbound Christ," *Scottish Journal of Theology* 30/4 (1977), 394-396.

[42] Samuel Rayan, "Spirituality for Inter-Faith Social Action" in Xavier Irudayaraj (ed), *Liberation and Dialogue* (Bangalore: Claretian Publications, 1989), 64-73 (69).

[43] Kirsteen Kim, *Mission in the Spirit* (Delhi: ISPCK, 2003).

[44] S.J. Samartha, *One Christ – Many Religions: Toward a Revised Christology* (Maryknoll, NY: Orbis Books, 1991), 6.

[45] Raimundo Panikkar, *The Trinity and the Religious Experience of Man* (New York: Orbis Books/London: Darton, Longman & Todd, 1973).

interpretation. Nor did he, like Hick and Knitter, try to develop a universal philosophical pluralism. Instead, recognising the particularity of Christian faith, he advanced a *Christian* theology of religious pluralism.[46] Dupuis insisted that Jesus Christ is uniquely saviour but at the same time that other religions have salvific significance.

Like Samartha, Dupuis started from the common Christian confession of the Nicene Creed, but where Samartha saw the creed as freeing the Spirit from christology as the Spirit of life, Dupuis insisted that its trinitarian framework did not allow any bypassing of christological claims. The Spirit must be linked to Christ. In the late 1980s, some Indian Catholic theologians and their supporters were criticised by the Vatican for their alleged view – not unlike Samartha's – that "the mystery of God is not exhausted in the revelation in Jesus Christ but is also revealed in other religions."[47] In this context, Dupuis and others developed Spirit christology, which understands the event of Jesus Christ from the perspective of the presence and activity of the Holy Spirit of God in the world since creation, while also stressing the sending of the Spirit to the world by the risen Christ.[48] Dupuis argued that, because the Holy Spirit is also the Spirit of Christ, a pneumato-centric perspective is faithful to the christo-centric or inclusivist theology of religions of post-Vatican II catholicism. Nevertheless, he saw it as offering hope for a "Christian theology of religious pluralism" since Spirit christology is another way of saying that there is more to theology than christology.[49] Instead of seeing the doctrine of the Trinity as a hindrance to the church embracing religious plurality, he regarded it as expressing a Christian theology of religions in that it both allows for salvation outside the church through the Spirit and yet necessarily links that salvation with God's unique saving action in Jesus Christ.

Dupuis recognised two types of christology in early Christian theology: Spirit christology, which assumes that the same Spirit is

---

[46] Dupuis, *Toward a Christian Theology of Religious Pluralism*.

[47] See Paul Mojzes and Leonard Swidler (eds), *Christian Mission and Interreligious Dialogue* (Lewiston/Queenston/Lampeter: Edwin Mellen Press, 1990); William R. Burrows, *Redemption and Dialogue: Reading* Redemptoris Missio *and Dialogue and Proclamation* (Maryknoll, NY: Orbis Books, 1993).

[48] Dupuis, *Toward a Christian Theology of Religious Pluralism*, 196-198.

[49] Dupuis, *Toward a Christian Theology of Religious Pluralism*, 198-201.

operative in the whole of human history and in the human history of Jesus Christ, and Logos christology, which emphasises the incarnation in first-century Palestine that Christian faith particularly confesses, and which is the origin of the church. For Dupuis, these two christologies together constitute the doctrine of the Trinity. On the one hand, the validity of Spirit christology shows that God's revelation in Jesus Christ does not exhaust the mystery of God. On the other hand, the church as the continuing incarnation, filled with the Spirit of Christ, which gives life to the world is essential for salvation. The church must continue its faithful witness in order for the world to be saved.

Dupuis' *Christian* theology of religious pluralism allowed for other religions to have their own perspective on proper inter-religious relations. Furthermore, he argued that from a Christian perspective, religious pluralism can be seen not only as a fact but also as part of God's creative plan of love for all humankind. He found that other religions offer both "complementarity" to and "convergence" with Christianity and so Christians can learn from them. For example, the Hindu understanding of non-duality (*advaita*) offers a corrective in trinitarian thought to Christian tendencies towards I-thou dichotomies, and that a proper understanding of the relations of the Godhead stands somewhere between duality and non-duality because "the mystery of God" is a "communion in non-duality."[50]

Dupuis' work pushed the boundaries of Roman Catholic theology of religions and drew the attention of the then Cardinal Josef Ratzinger, prefect of the Congregation for the Doctrine of the Faith (CDF), which investigated his work. Although a notification was appended to it by the CDF (24 Jan 2001), it does not refute its thesis but only cautions about going beyond it. Dupuis had succeeded in his aim to stay within classical christological doctrine while showing what is allowed for a theology of pluralism. In this respect, Dupuis resolved the tension that had been expressed by the CWME at San Antonio: the "way of salvation than Jesus Christ" no longer appeared to be in tension with the wider "saving power" of God.

---

[50] Dupuis, *Toward a Christian Theology of Religious Pluralism*, 276-278.

THE HOLY SPIRIT AND CHRISTIAN MISSION IN A PLURALISTIC CONTEXT

TTL is indebted in several ways to the foregoing pneumatologies of religion developed in India. This is not only in relation to its statements on inter-religious relations specifically but also with reference to the more general social plurality even within the same religion or within secularism.

First, in their emphasis on love and the right attitude or spirit, these pneumatologies encourage Christians not to see others as a threat but to take a positive and constructive approach and to look for areas of collaboration. Both Samartha and Dupuis value *advaitic* thinking as encouraging harmonious social relations and rank love as the greatest Christian virtue. In this sense mission takes place "in the Spirit" – it is a spirituality of love and unity. The re-thinking of mission attitudes to other faiths, which has been developed particularly in reflection on the Indian context, is evident in TTL in its descriptions of "transformative spirituality" which creates just and inclusive communities (paras 29-35, 91, 104, 109).

Second, the framework of pneumatology encourages a holistic approach to missions that is life-affirming. Whereas Samartha had entitled his 1991 book *One Christ – Many Religions*, in 1995, Knitter – also reflecting on Indian experience – considered *One Earth Many Religions* and looked at how multi-faith dialogue could promote global responsibility.[51] But in beginning his reflection of the Spirit from "life,"[52] Samartha had already laid the foundation for this shift and anticipated the approach of "finding out where the Holy Spirit is at work and joining in." Informed by reflection on the creed and encouraged by Orthodox theology, reflection on the Spirit and life in ecumenical circles came to fruition in TTL, which described mission as affirming life wherever it is found (1, 3, 4, 102, 107, etc) and understood it as discerning the mission of the Spirit in order to join in (1, 24, 25, 43, 90, 97, etc). Although Dupuis confined his reflection on the Spirit's work to humanity, rather than the whole cosmos, his theology of convergence equally encouraged building interreligious relationships for the common good.

---

[51] Samartha, *One Christ- Many Religions*; Knitter, *One Earth Many Religions*.

[52] S.J. Samartha, "The Holy Spirit and People of Various Faiths, Cultures and Ideologies."

Third, TTL reflects the Indian reflections of the leading figures of Samartha and Dupuis in its attention to dialogue and its setting of evangelism in the context of dialogue (paras 93-96). Samartha tended to shy away from evangelism because of its association in his mind with exclusivism. The new document accepts the central place of evangelism in Christian faith but, in keeping with Samartha's legacy of dialogue, it seeks to discipline the practice of evangelism to be authentic and humble in the way of Christ (paras 86-92).[53] Like Dupuis, TTL recognises positive value in other religions and divine purpose in the existence of plural societies (paras 9, 90, 96, 97, 110).

Finally, on the question of the freedom of the Spirit versus the need for faithfulness to classical doctrines of the Trinity and the Incarnation, which divide Samartha's and Dupuis' approaches, TTL both celebrates the blowing of the Spirit who gives life to all and at the same time identifies Jesus Christ as the criterion for what Christians recognise as fullness of life and as the embodiment of the Spirit of God. While focusing on the mission of the Spirit, TTL does not depart from the trinitarian framework of *missio Dei*. Any Christian pneumatology must reconnect with christology and therefore with the church that is the body of Christ. However, the connection between the Holy Spirit and Christian mission is not that of the colonial era in which the Spirit was regarded as supplying the power for some uncritical support of colonial ventures. Owing partly to Indian theologians in pluralistic contexts, such as Samartha and Dupuis, in TTL, mission is as wide as the mission of the Spirit to bring life. To join in with that mission is to discern the presence and activity of the Spirit by the criterion of the fullness of life brought by Jesus Christ. In pluralistic contexts, participating in this mission is to follow in the way of Christ by evangelising in a dialogical way and embracing a spirituality that is mutually transformative.

---

[53] This section draws heavily on another document that is indebted to Samartha's approach that was jointly developed by the PCID, WCC and the WEA, *Christian Witness in a Multi-religious World: Recommendations for Conduct* (2011). Available from the respective websites.

9

HOLY SPIRIT AND CHRISTIAN MISSION: A RE-READING OF STANLEY J. SAMARTHA'S THEOLOGY OF THE HOLY SPIRIT IN THE PLURALISTIC CONTEXT OF INDIA

Samuel George*

Religious plurality is a stark reality of our time. Faced with pluralism and complexity of our age, contemporary societies are either exasperating each other by insisting on affirming their identities in religious fundamentalist accents or splitting into fragments with no unifying religious horizons.

---

* **Samuel George**, DTh, is Professor of Christian Theology at Allahabad Bible Seminary (Serampore University), Uttar Pradesh. He holds a Doctorate in Theology from Serampore University. Earlier he served as the Principal of Master's College of Theology (Serampore University), Visakhapatnam. Some of his major works are: *The Historical Particularity of Jesus: A Dialogue with the Hindu View of History* (2014); *Ekklesia: Indian Conversations* (2015); *Christian Theology: Indian Conversations. Vols. 1 & 2* (2016); *Jesus Beyond Borders: Towards a "Glocal" Christology* (2016). Apart from these, he has contributed in many national and international journals. He also serves as the Editor-in-Chief of *New Life Theological Journal*.

To say that religious pluralism,[1] apart from being a fact of life now and one that has come to stay, will also become more extensive and more complex[2] is not an exaggeration. As Christians, we know that one of the great challenges posed by religious pluralism is how to understand the universality of revelation and salvation in Jesus and, at the same time, without half measures, the revelatory or salvific value-including universal value-of other religions. In a context like India where "plural condition" is an existential reality, Christian faith has to "compete" with many other faiths in the religiously plural market place. Such a context demands a redefining of the core of one's faith statements.

Pneumatology-the deliberation on the "person," nature, and work of the Holy Spirit- is one of the cardinal facts of the Christian faith.

In a pluralistic context, it is important to understand the work of the Holy Spirit irrespective of caste, colour, and creed. It becomes more imperative in the Indian context as to how the work of the Holy Spirit transcends the boundaries of the church and engages with people of other faiths and no-faiths. It is in this context that we find the pioneering role of Stanley J. Samartha, who pushed for a wider outlook to relate the Holy Spirit and people of other faiths.

This paper is an attempt to analyze Samartha's pneumatology especially in the context of religious plurality. The focus of the study will be to assess the appropriateness of Samartha's pneumatology to the religiously plural context of India.

---

[1] The following recent literatures on the subject throw light on the importance of religious plurality in today's context. Cf. Veli-Matti-Karkkainen, *An Introduction to the Theology of Religions: Biblical, Historical and Contemporary Perspectives* (Illinois: InterVarsity Press, 2003); John B. Cobb, *Christian Faith and Religious Diversity* (Minneapolis: Fortress Press, 2002); Gavin D'Costa, *Meeting of Religion and Trinity* (Edinburgh: T&T Clark, 2000); Paul F. Knitter (ed), *Myth of Religious Superiority: Multifaith Exploration of Religious Pluralism* (Maryknoll, New York: Orbis Books, 2005); Evelyn Monteiro, *Church and Culture: Communion in Pluralism* (Delhi: ISPCK, 2004); Imtiaz Ahmad, Partha S. Gosh, and Helmut Reifeld (eds), *Pluralism and Equality: Values in Indian Society and Politics* (New Delhi: Sage Publications, 2000); Paul F. Knitter and Chandra Muzaffar (eds), *Subverting Greed: Religious Perspectives on the Global Economy* (Maryknoll, New York: Orbis Books, 2002); Paul F. Knitter, *Introducing Theologies of Religion* (Maryknoll, New York: Orbis Books, 2002); Marjorie Hewitt Suchocki, *Divinity and Diversity: A Christian Affirmation of Religious Pluralism* (Nashville: Abingdon Press, 2003).

[2] Luiz Carlos Susin, "Introduction: Emergence and Urgency of the New Pluralist Paradigm," *Concilium* 1 (2007), 9.

SAMARTHA: THE MAN AND HIS THOUGHT WORLD

Stanley Jedidiah ("Beloved of the Lord" cf. 2 Sam 12:25) Samartha was born on 7 October 1920 in Karkal, a small village in South Kanara District of Karnataka state in India. His parents Lucas Jonathan Samartha (1891-1959), a pastor, and Sahadevi (1901-1982), a teacher, were from the Basel Mission.[3] Early in life, Samartha was enveloped by a deep Christian spirit, highly influenced by the Basel Mission. He acknowledges in his writings the deep impact of the Basel Mission in shaping his Christian character.[4]

In 1941, he began his theological studies at United Theological College (UTC) in Bangalore. Here, he had a "broadening" experience. Students and staff from different denominations and a mixture of western and Indian teachers had a lasting impact on young Samartha. Paul D. Devanandan, the Professor of Philosophy and History of Religions at UTC, created a great impression on Samartha. In 1958, he earned his PhD for the thesis entitled: *The Modern Hindu View of History According to Representative Thinkers*. In 1963, he delivered a series of lectures on certain select Hindu thinkers and their response to Jesus Christ, which later became an important book on Indian christology.[5] Being associated with the Christian Institute for the Study of Religion and Society (CISRS), Bangalore, Samartha got himself involved in many dialogues and seminars on social, economic and religious issues. In 1967, he attended an important consultation on "Christian Dialogue with Men of Other Faiths," held in Kandy, Ceylon. This consultation was a significant step forward in the ecumenical movement with regard to Christian attitude toward other religions.

Samartha's contribution to the cause of dialogue resulted in the creation of the Sub-unit on Dialogue with People of Living Faiths and Ideologies (IDE). He became its founding director in 1971 and worked with it till 1980. The initiative to start in this vein was his own primarily as

---

[3] For a detailed biographical note cf. Eeuwout Klootwijk, *Commitment and Openness: The Intereligious Dialogue and Theology of Religions in the Work of Stanley J. Samartha* (Zoetermeer: Uitgeverij Boekencentrum B.V, 1992), 19-57.

[4] Stanley J. Samartha, "Digging Up Old Wells: Reflections on the Legacy of the Basel Mission in India" in Godwin Shiri (ed), *Wholeness in Christ: The Legacy of the Basel Mission in India* (Mangalore: KATHRI, 1985), 86.

[5] Stanley J. Samartha, *Hindu Response to Unbound Christ* (Madras: CLS, 1974).

he was particularly peeved by the western framework and policing attitude in understanding other living faiths. He was not happy with the fact that theological questions about people of other faiths were asked without any real dialogical experience. He called for a widening of the Christian theological approach to other religions, noting that "an emphasis on "discontinuity" does not help to provide a positive theological framework for Christians and people of other faiths to meet together on a personal plane."[6]

In the World Council of Churches (WCC) as the first secretary of the dialogue unit, he became then an open proponent of dialogue among Christians and people of other living faiths. It was during this time he interacted with the following themes such as the quest for human community in a religious-pluralistic world; peace, justice and religion; the development of a christology in a world of religions, especially, in the Indian context.[7]

A word about his method is fitting here. In his own words, he wrote, "[m]y method was to state the problem in contemporary terms, raise questions, identify issues and suggest possible lines of approach to consider them."[8] During his time of interaction with different Christian groups and people of other faiths, he made an interesting comment that without "this enriching experience, my understanding of Jesus Christ who 'suffered outside the gate' would have been far too narrow and my notion of God far too limited to sustain an extended Christian ministry."[9]

In 1981, he returned to India and joined CISRS as a consultant on ecumenical issues in inter-cultural relations. In 1982, he joined UTC as a visiting professor in the Department of Religion, Culture and Society. He was also involved with South Asia Theological Research Institute (SATHRI), Bangalore. It was in 1991 that his magnum opus on christology

---

[6] Stanley J. Samartha, "The Word of God and the Living Faiths of Men: Plans for Further Study SME 68:12, 1968," Typescript, UTC 1C.19, 1968, Bangalore.

[7] Klootwijk, *Commitment and Openness*, 48.

[8] Stanley J. Samartha, "Letter to Dr. J.B. Cobb Jr., 20 April, 1983," UTC, SJS 7 Correspondence, 1949-1984, Bangalore.

[9] "Director's Report," *Minutes of the Fourth Meeting of the Working Group Hungary, April 1980* (Geneva: WCC, 1980), 35, cited by Klootwijk, *Commitment and Openness*, 49.

One Christ-Many Religions[10] came out signifying his refined and matured stand on christology in a religiously plural context. In 2001, Samartha went to be with the Lord.

HOLY SPIRIT IN THE WRITINGS OF SAMARTHA

For Samartha, the interest in the Spirit arises from his main focus of theology, the Theology of Religions. To a great extent, this special interest in the Spirit has to do with the Indian background, which lends itself to pneumatology. His choice of *advaita* as the philosophical framework for his theology means that he tends to understand the Holy Spirit against the background of the spirit as *atman*.[11]

Knitter characterizes Samartha as moving towards a "pneumatocentric" theology of religions, which to a broader extent he accepts.[12] Samartha believed pneumatology has great potential for theology of religions.[13] His pneumatological positions can be gleaned from two papers with almost identical titles, though written nearly twenty years apart: "The Holy Spirit and People of Various Faiths, Cultures and Ideologies,"[14] and "The Holy Spirit and People of Other Faiths."[15]

Samartha's pneumatology cannot be gleaned without first delving into his theology of dialogue. The following sentences explain his theology:

- His theology of dialogue has its origins in the Indian context.

---

[10] Stanley J. Samartha, *One Christ Many Religions: Towards a Revised Christology*, 2nd Indian edn. (Bangalore: SATHRI, 1994).

[11] Kirsteen Kim, *Mission in the Spirit: The Holy Spirit in Indian Christian Theologies* (Delhi: ISPCK, 2003), 13.

[12] Paul F. Knitter, "Stanley Samartha's 'One Christ-Many Religions': Plaudits and Problems," *Current Dialogue* 21 (1991), 25-30; Paul F. Knitter, "Stanley Samartha's *One Christ-Many Religions*: Plaudits and Problems," *The SATHRI Journal* 1 (1993), 1-9; Stanley J. Samartha, "'In Search of a Revised Christology.' A Response to Paul Knitter," *Current Dialogue* 21 (1991), 30-37.

[13] Stanley J. Samartha, *Between Two Cultures: Ecumenical Ministry in a Pluralist World* (Geneva: WCC Publications, 1996), 144, 153, 185.

[14] Stanley J. Samartha, "The Holy Spirit and People of Various Faiths, Cultures, and Ideologies" in Dow Kirkpatrick (ed), *The Holy Spirit*, Papers of the Oxford Institute on Methodist Theological Studies, 1973 (Nashville, Tennessee: Tidings, 1974), 20-39.

[15] Stanley J. Samartha, "The Holy Spirit and People of Other Faiths," *Ecumenical Review* 42/3-4 (1990), 250-263; Stanley J. Samartha, "The Holy Spirit and People of Other Faiths" in Emilio Castro (ed), *To the Wind of God's Spirit: Reflections on the Canberra Theme* (Geneva: WCC, 1990), 50-63.

- Dialogue takes place "in community." For him, dialogue is between adherents of faiths not religious systems. Therefore, he preferred to call them, "Neighbours of other faiths."[16] For him such dialogue is possible by recognizing "the spiritual" as the "basic, the underlying, all-pervading factor."[17]

- He stressed the experiential nature of dialogue. For him, it was the people not the system that was paramount.

- For him, dialogue is pneumatological. He saw the basis for dialogue as threefold: the incarnation as God's dialogue with humanity; the open nature of the new community in Christ; and the Holy Spirit's leading into all truth described in John 16:13. For him, the Holy Spirit "not only makes it necessary for us to enter into dialogue, but also to continue in it without fear, but with full expectation and openness."[18]

- In his theology, the existential approach of dialogue in a pluralistic society preceded the theoretical formulation of a pluralist theology of religions.

Samartha's dialogue was not a method but "a mood, a spirit, an attitude of love and respect" for "our neighbours of other faiths."[19] For him, it takes place in the "milieu of the Spirit."[20]

SPIRIT OF DIALOGUE

For Samartha, the Spirit is indeed the Spirit of God.[21] It, therefore, helps (according to him) in overcoming the limitations of exclusive claims. It also helps in being more sensitive to the outreach of the Spirit's presence

---

[16] Stanley J. Samartha, *Courage for Dialogue: Ecumenical Issues in Inter-Religious Relationships* (Geneva: WCC Publications, 1981), 1.

[17] Stanley J. Samartha, "The Nature and Purpose of the Consultation" in Stanley J. Samartha (ed), *Towards Wolrd Community: The Colombo Papers* (Geneva: WCC, 1975), 6-11.

[18] Samartha, *Courage for Dialogue: Ecumenical Issues in Inter-Religious Relationships*, 1-14.

[19] Samartha, *One Christ Many Religions: Towards a Revised Christology*, 57.

[20] Samartha, *Courage for Dialogue: Ecumenical Issues in Inter-Religious Relationships*, 73-75.

[21] He presented John 16:13 as his pneumatological basis for dialogue.

and works beyond a christocentric revelation and outside the visible boundaries of the church in the world.[22]

For him, a pneumatological route might provide a more viable theological space and greater spiritual freedom to grasp the outreach of God's revelation in the world. He wrote, "[t]he Spirit could become the hinge to open the door of Christian hospitality to neighbours of other faiths and ideological convictions seeking fullness of life in emerging India 2000."[23]

Surprisingly enough, he regards this route a new frontier, which is more tentative and exploratory.[24] It is surprising because Samartha first wrote on the relation of the Holy Spirit and people of other living faiths in 1973 that:

> [i]t would be premature and less than helpful to attempt any systematic treatment of the topic before us. The data are insufficient, criteria have to be developed responsibly, and the insights gained through actual dialogues have to be carefully evaluated.[25]

Even after eighteen years, he was not able to systematize this relationship. Is it because the nature of the Holy Spirit itself is such that it defies systematization or Samartha kept this relationship fluidly to maintain the theocentricity of his theology of dialogue?

It is interesting to note that on the Holy Spirit, Samartha was largely influenced by the Orthodox theology. Metropolitan George Khodr of Lebanon's address in 1971 to the Central Committee of the WCC meeting in Addis Ababa had a lasting impact on Samartha. Orthodox theology speaks of the Holy Spirit as proceeding from the Father alone whereas the western Protestant theologies talk about the Spirit proceeding both from the Father and the Son. As an Indian theologian, Samartha said that this debate is of very little relevance to Christian theologians working

---

[22] Stanley J. Samartha, "The Holy Spirit and the Revelation of God in Emerging India - 2000 (Keynote Address)" in Paul Puthanangady (ed), *Emerging India and the Word of God* (Bangalore: NBCLC, 1991), 28.

[23] Samartha, "The Holy Spirit and the Revelation of God in Emerging India - 2000 (Keynote Address)," 29.

[24] Samartha, "The Holy Spirit and the Revelation of God in Emerging India - 2000 (Keynote Address)," 29.

[25] Samartha, "The Holy Spirit and People of Various Faiths, Cultures, and Ideologies," 30.

in the religiously plural society of India.²⁶ Recent developments in the study of pneumatology have opened up new and unexpected entries in the exploration of the wider operations of the Spirit not only in the church but also in other religions and secular movements in India.²⁷ He wrote, "[t]he pneumatological route may, therefore, provide us with a threshold to cross the frontier into the outreach of the Spirit's presence and work in the world."²⁸

Following the eastern tradition (Father is the sole source of the Spirit), Samartha wrote,

> there will be greater freedom and far more theological space for the Spirit, proceeding from the Father, to breathe freely through the whole *oikoumene* which includes not only Christians but neighbours of other faiths and ideological convictions as well.²⁹

Before we make any comments about the nature and characteristics or even relevance of his pneumatology in the Indian context, let us briefly look into his theology of the Holy Spirit, however exploratory it is.

The mystery-centeredness of God in Samartha's theology is latently evident. He wrote: "the limitation of words and the inadequacy of conceptual forms are perhaps nowhere more consciously to be acknowledged than in a discussion on the Holy Spirit."³⁰ He pointed out two reasons for this new interest in pneumatology:

- It is increasingly recognized that all human life, not just an artificially isolated segment called the "religious" dimension, comes within the purview of God's activity.

- There is the existential fact that all human beings, not just Christians but people of all living faiths, cultures, and

---

[26] Samartha, "The Holy Spirit and the Revelation of God in Emerging India - 2000 (Keynote Address)," 35.

[27] Samartha, "The Holy Spirit and the Revelation of God in Emerging India - 2000 (Keynote Address)," 35-36.

[28] Samartha, "The Holy Spirit and the Revelation of God in Emerging India - 2000 (Keynote Address)," 36.

[29] Samartha, "The Holy Spirit and the Revelation of God in Emerging India - 2000 (Keynote Address)," 36.

[30] Samartha, "The Holy Spirit and People of Various Faiths, Cultures, and Ideologies," 20.

ideologies, share a common future, either for survival or for annihilation.[31]

For Samartha, this realization makes all of us inter-dependent in our search for the meaning of life and existence. Theologically, the importance of it cannot be ignored any longer. The fact that everyone is open to the activity of God's Spirit seriously challenges a legalistic dogmatism, which limits the work of the Spirit to a narrow segment of time, to an isolated bit of geographic location, and to the history of a particular people.[32]

It is interesting to note that Samartha's usage of pneumatology is to undergird his theo-centric theology. He said,

> [a] more sensitive recognition of the wider work of the holy spirit may also help us to broaden our understanding of God's saving act, thus correcting what our Orthodox friends describe as a 'Christo-monistic tendency' that seems to dominate Protestant theology, and preventing our conceptions of God from becoming too small and static.[33]

Samartha's exploratory pneumatology emerges out of existential circumstances (dialogue with people of living faiths). Therefore, he spoke of existential criteria rather than conceptual criteria to understand the relation between the Holy Spirit and people of other living faiths.[34] In the following lines below, he charts out his pneumatology and its relation with people of other living faiths.

- Inadequacy of scriptural basis for the relationship between the Holy Spirit and people of other faiths. The relation of the Spirit is portrayed in the context of the believing community of that time and should not be regarded as negative judgment on other religious faiths.

- Christianity in itself is not a mono-perspective. There are divergent views on the work of the Holy Spirit in relation to people of other religions. No one particular position can be regarded as the norm to judge others.

---

[31] Samartha, "The Holy Spirit and People of Various Faiths, Cultures, and Ideologies," 20.
[32] Samartha, "The Holy Spirit and People of Various Faiths, Cultures, and Ideologies," 20.
[33] Samartha, "The Holy Spirit and People of Various Faiths, Cultures, and Ideologies," 21.
[34] Samartha, "The Holy Spirit and People of Various Faiths, Cultures, and Ideologies," 30.

- Dialogue is the Spirit's way of awakening and bringing nearer to the fulfilment of what was already implanted in all humanity to participate in the divine life. The Spirit's works cannot be confined to the monotheistic family only. What about the non-monotheistic religions like Hinduism, the primal, and tribal religions of Africa and Asia? What about those who are beyond the peripheries of religions? If Cyrus can be "his anointed...whose right hand I take hold of" (Isa 45:1), why not Gandhi or Fidel Castro or Mao Tse-Tung and others? Does not the Spirit of God touch other people in *their* history to transform a certain moment from being part of mere *chronos* to become a significant *kairos*?

- The Spirit is "boundless freedom" which is its essence and nature. Putting a criteria to discern its activity is to negate the Spirit itself. However, without some discernible "signs" to recognize the work of the Spirit, one could be lost like "a boat without a rudder in a sea of relativism."[35] The scriptures, church tradition, and obedience to the living God provide ample signs to recognize the work of the Spirit today. The Spirit means *life*, not death – and so vitality, creativity, and growth. The Spirit means order, not chaos; and so meaning, significance, and truth become important. The Spirit means community, not separation, and so another mark is sharing, fellowship, bearing one another's burden. One can sense the work of the Spirit wherever they find these marks – life, order, and community. However, the Spirit is not limited to them only.

- Recognition of the work of the Spirit affects our settled theological notions. "Reflection on the work of the Spirit may be subordinated to a readiness to be led by the Spirit together with the partners into the depths of God's mystery."[36] Existential needs take precedence over theological formulations.

---

[35] Samartha, "The Holy Spirit and People of Various Faiths, Cultures, and Ideologies," 33.
[36] Samartha, "The Holy Spirit and People of Various Faiths, Cultures, and Ideologies," 34.

The question of the Holy Spirit must inevitably lead to the doctrine of God himself and of the Trinity in far more inclusive ways than Christian theology has done before. It must take into account the accountability, the incomprehensibility, and the mystery of God and the work of his Spirit among others no less than his revelation in Jesus Christ through the Holy Spirit.[37]

Samartha is right in his assessment that the doctrine of the Spirit and its relationship with other living faiths was never a serious discussion in the history of the Church.

> [I]n the major debates of the councils which touched the Spirit the main concern was to guard the purity of doctrine and preserve the unity of the church. ... The question of the Spirit *and* people of other faiths is therefore, a *new* question that has somewhat aggressively thrust itself on the theological consciousness of the church only in recent years. It has become both a historical demand and a theological imperative for the church.[38]

Lamenting that in the subsequent years since 1973[39] Samartha writes, "one finds very little serious and careful reflection on this matter although it is recognized as an important issue of the churches."[40] He also mentions that even in the WCC circles the relationship between the Spirit and the people of other living faiths has mostly remained a question, which still seeks an answer. It is in the context of the 1991 WCC General Assembly (with the theme: "Come Holy Spirit – Renew the Whole Creation") at Canberra that the third person of Trinity came into the theological and ecclesiological forefront. Samartha points that even though the question of this relationship is noted, they are difficult enough to be avoided. Even when its theological importance for the life and work of the church in a religiously plural world is repeatedly recognized, there is hesitation, even unwillingness, to discuss the theological implications of the question.[41]

---

[37] Samartha, "The Holy Spirit and People of Various Faiths, Cultures, and Ideologies," 20.37.

[38] Samartha, "The Holy Spirit and People of Other Faiths," 250.

[39] He gave a lecture at Oxford Institute of Methodist Studies, Lincoln College, Oxford in July 1973.

[40] Samartha, "The Holy Spirit and People of Other Faiths," 251.

[41] Samartha, "The Holy Spirit and People of Other Faiths," 252.

For Samartha, this reluctance, hesitation, and even hostility are for two obvious reasons: one, the fear of syncretism, and the other is the assumption that any recognition of the presence of God or Christ or the Spirit in the lives of people of other faiths leads to the danger of relativism.[42] He further points out that apart from these two there are even deeper and more complex reasons that make it so difficult to discuss the relation of the Spirit to people of other faiths. Samartha cautions that these are complex and delicate matters touching on the Christian faith. However, he felt that, on the one hand, one has to be very careful in dealing with them because they are connected with the spiritual life, emotions, and feelings of Christians but, on the other hand, one should at least open up and draw attention to these (however, tentative it can be).

The uncertain, vague, and the hazy character of the *person* of the Spirit within the Trinity forces a timid retreat when it comes to the discussion of the relationship between the Spirit and other faiths. Another is the question of the *source* of the Spirit, whether the Spirit proceeds from the Father *alone* or from the Father *and the Son*. The third is the connection between the outpouring of the Spirit on the day of the Pentecost and the work of the Spirit in the ministry of Jesus, and in creation *before* the Pentecost. Yet another reason is the relation between *baptism* and the gift of the Spirit.[43]

Interestingly, Samartha finds the crucial factor for this neglect is the predominance of christology in western ecclesiology. The Spirit is often relegated to an extra, an addendum. The Spirit is largely marginalized in our theologies.[44]

Samartha accepts Hans Huebner's conclusion that the New Testament gives ample evidence that the Spirit of God is understood as a person. He argues that the prayer to the Spirit is the prayer to the Spirit of God. He further writes, "[i]f Christians are themselves doctrinally

---

[42] Samartha, "The Holy Spirit and People of Other Faiths," 252.
[43] Samartha, "The Holy Spirit and People of Other Faiths," 253.
[44] In the Nicene Creed, the reference to the Spirit is minimal. Even though the Nicaea-Constantinople Creed of 381 said far more about the Spirit than the Nicene Creed, it refrains from calling the Spirit *homoousios* with the Father and the Son.

Holy Spirit and Christian Mission: A Re-Reading of Stanley J. Samartha's Theology

hesitant about the person of the Holy Spirit, how can they affirm or deny the presence of the Spirit in the lives of people of other faiths?"[45]

Another interesting argument that Samartha makes in relating the Spirit to people of other faiths is through the discussion on the *gender* of the Spirit. For him, since the Father and the Son are anthropomorphic symbols, to consider the Spirit as feminine, as mother, does not seem outrageous. Referring to the Sheffield conference on the "The Community of Women and Men in the Church" (1981), he speaks of "the maternal office of the Holy Spirit," "the giver of Life." The Spirit (as the feminine principle of God) is a source of new life through baptism, giving birth to new children of God. Even in other religious traditions, feminine aspect of God is emphasized – *Shakti*. However, he rejected Chenchiah's use of *Shakti* to interpret the work of the Holy Spirit in creation in biological and evolutionary terms because he felt that the New Testament does not adequately support it.[46] He writes,

> [i]t looks as if the Trinity of the Father, Son and Mother is far more balanced in relation to human life than the male-dominated formula. The implication of this to the Spirit's relation to people of other faiths may be that the Spirit as Mother would be far kinder, more generous and affectionate towards all her children.[47]

It is interesting to note Samartha, an Indian Protestant theologian, not "accepting" the *filioque*[48] – probably, the cause of "the greatest schism in Christendom." He explains,

> [t]he implication of this for the topic of the Spirit's relation to people of other faiths should be made clear. The question is whether the Father is the *sole* source of the Spirit as the Orthodox insist, or *jointly* with the Son as the Vatican and the West in general affirm. If it is the latter, then the flow of the Spirit is restricted to the Christomonistic channel, and limited to the church and only through the agency of the church

---

[45] Samartha, "The Holy Spirit and People of Other Faiths," 254.

[46] Samartha, Hindu Response to Unbound Christ, 131.

[47] Samartha, "The Holy Spirit and People of Other Faiths," 254.

[48] It literally means "and [from] the Son." It is a Latin term added to the Nicene-Constantinopolitan Creed, which is not in the original version. It has been the subject of great controversy between eastern and western Christianity. Filioque describes the double procession of the Holy Spirit and is translated into the English clause "and the Son" in that creed. It reads: "We believe in the Holy Spirit, the Lord, the giver of life, who proceeds from the Father (and the Son). With the Father and the Son he is worshiped and glorified."

to the rest of humanity. If it is the former, then there will be far more theological space for the Spirit proceeding from the Father to breathe freely through the whole *oikoumene* that includes neighbours of other faiths as well.[49]

What might be the reason for such a position by Samartha? It is our contention that to maintain the "primacy of theocentricity," he positioned himself in this fashion. It is in this light he maintains that the church is constituted both christologically and pneumatologically. He also points out how the Vatican and the WCC in its later studies have corrected themselves and recognized that the Holy Spirit was at work in the world *before* Christ and "was glorified," thus, making it possible to broaden the field of operation of the Spirit. In the Old Testament, we find the Spirit has spoken through *the prophets of Israel*. If so, that includes the Jews. He writes that "[b]y acknowledging that the Spirit was at work and spoke through the prophets of Israel *before* Christ, the door is perhaps a little more open for the prophets of other faiths to be smuggled into God's *oikoumene*."[50]

Another area where Samartha sees the potential of relating the Spirit and people of other faiths is the connection between baptism and the gift of the Holy Spirit. Samartha notes that in the early church there were instances of pouring out of the Spirit without baptism or before it (cf. Acts 4:17; 10; 19:1-7). He writes that "[t]his means that the possibility of the Spirit being present and active among those who are not baptized, and in communities outside the visible boundaries of the institutional

---

[49] Samartha, "The Holy Spirit and People of Other Faiths," 255.
[50] Samartha, "The Holy Spirit and People of Other Faiths," 256.

church, should be left open rather than closed."⁵¹ In theological circles this notion is called anonymous Christians/Christianity.⁵²

Another very important area where Samartha sees this relationship meaningfully cohabiting is the recent phenomenon of willingness to recognize the presence of the Spirit in secular movements and societies. He asks,

> [i]f Christian theologians are willing to discern the presence of the Spirit in societies where the existence of God itself is denied, why is it so difficult for some of them to admit the presence of the Holy Spirit in predominantly religious societies where the existence of God has been affirmed for many long centuries, in some cases ever earlier than Christianity?⁵³

He rightly questions that if the presence of God can be found in the context of "No God" then why can it not be traced in the context of "Numerous Gods"? Why this refusal?

TOWARDS A PNEUMATOLOGY IN THE CONTEXT OF RELIGIOUS PLURALITY

Samartha refuses to chart out a doctrine that discusses the Spirit's relation to people of other faiths. It does not mean that doctrines are not important, but he points out that the Spirit defies control and systematization; therefore, they may have to be subordinated to the discernment of the

---

⁵¹ Samartha, "The Holy Spirit and People of Other Faiths," 256.

⁵² Anonymous Christian is a notion introduced by the Jesuit theologian Karl Rahner (1904–1984) that declares that people who have never heard the Christian gospel might be saved through Christ. Non-Christians could have "in [their] basic orientation and fundamental decision," Rahner wrote, "accepted the salvific grace of God, through Christ, although [they] may never have heard of the Christian revelation." This notion is also called as churchless Christianity. Herbert Hoefer in his book, *Churchless Christianity*, has compiled hard data from people living in rural Tamil Nadu (S. India) and in urban Chennai (Madras) who are devoted followers of Christ who have not joined a Christian church and, indeed, remain within the Hindu community. Cf. Herbert Hoefer, *Churchless Christianity* (Pasadena, CA: William Carey Library, 2001) 96. Hoefer cites at least 156,000 "non-baptized believers in Christ" (30,000 high caste, ie, Brahmin; 70,000 middle castes, ie, Kshyatriya and Vaishya; 56,000 Scheduled Castes, ie, Shudra and Dalit). See Appendix II - V, 277-352. For more, cf. Timothy C. Tennent, "The Challenge of Churchless Christianity: An Evangelical Assessment," *International Bulletin of Missionary Research* 29/ 4 (2005), 171-177; Samuel George, *Jesus Beyond Borders: Towards a "Glocal" Christology* (New Delhi: CWI, 2016), 133-158.

⁵³ Samartha, "The Holy Spirit and People of Other Faiths," 257.

actual working of the Spirit in the lives of people.[54] The fruit of the Spirit should be found in the lives of people in a religiously plural context. "Life must get precedence over doctrine."[55] For him, it is existence over doctrine. He opines that a doctrine of the Spirit in the context of religious plurality may have to emerge out of theological reflection on the experience of people in history.[56] Samartha provides few pointers toward this pneumatology in the context of religious plurality.

It is to the Bible that Samartha turns to find the signs of the work of the Spirit and its relation with people of other faiths. He observes that "[t]here are several characteristics of the Spirit attested in the Bible, which may become pointers to this matter."[57] These are:

- The mark of *freedom*, spontaneity, unpredictability.
- The mark of *boundlessness* of the Spirit.
- The power to bring *new relationships* and, as a consequence,
- To create *new communities* of people cutting across all barriers of religion, culture, ideology, race and language.

> As fire, the Spirit destroys all that stands in the way of the emergence of new life – outmoded dogmas, meaningless rituals, obsolete customs, oppressive institutions, barriers that separate people of one community from another. It is the Spirit who provides inspiration, energy and power to humble folk to rise up in righteous anger against tyranny, oppression and injustice in society. As the Giver of life it is the Spirit who moves them to demand fullness of life, freedom, self-respect and human dignity.[58]

Arguing through a number of living examples of "acts of friendship, courage, and self-sacrifice" by people of other faiths in the midst of religious riots and violence, Samartha raises a fundamental question. "When similar acts are so obviously performed by neighbours of other faiths as well, are there serious theological reasons to *deny* the presence of the Spirit among them?"[59]

---

[54] Samartha, "The Holy Spirit and People of Other Faiths," 257.
[55] Samartha, "The Holy Spirit and People of Other Faiths," 258.
[56] Samartha, "The Holy Spirit and People of Other Faiths," 258.
[57] Samartha, "The Holy Spirit and People of Other Faiths," 258.
[58] Samartha, "The Holy Spirit and People of Other Faiths," 258.
[59] Samartha, "The Holy Spirit and People of Other Faiths," 259.

Samartha states that for Christians, the ethical fruits are rooted in their faith in God through Christ and in the power of the Spirit. For Christians, to be in Christ is indeed to be in God. But in a religiously plural context, to be in Christ is not the *only* way to be in God.[60] The discernment of the Spirit among people of other faiths is a contentious issue for Christians. Samartha writes, "Christians are called upon to *discern*, not to *control* the Spirit."[61] For him, the quality of discernment is itself a gift of the Spirit that is perhaps most needed to recognize and bring out the positive dimensions to the topic – The Holy Spirit and people of other faiths.[62] He maintains that "[t]o discern the movement of the Spirit not only in the church but also in the communities of people outside the visible boundaries of the church is perhaps the most challenging demand of our time."[63] Hence, he asks, "[w]herever the fruits of the Spirit are to be found – 'love, joy, peace, patience, kindness, goodness, faithfulness, gentleness, self-control' (Gal. 5:22) – whether in the lives of Christians or neighbours of other faiths, is not the Spirit of God present?"[64]

He not only turns our attention to the above mentioned visible signs of the Spirit but also to less visible signs too. These are not so easily recognizable but perhaps they are more profound marks of the Spirit. One such mark is inwardness, interiority, the power to root people's lives in the depth of God's being. Interestingly, this quality of inwardness is found in all religions. It is perhaps in the Hindu and Buddhist traditions that this inwardness of life is most emphasized.[65]

VIABILITY OF SAMARTHA'S PNEUMATOLOGY FOR MISSIONS IN INDIA

Kim writes that in the course of nearly forty years of Samartha's theology, there seems to be a shift from the "unbound Christ" to the "unbound Spirit."[66] He felt that focusing on the Spirit opens new avenues in the theology of religions. Such a positioning provides a way out of the

---

[60] Samartha, "The Holy Spirit and People of Other Faiths," 259.
[61] Samartha, "The Holy Spirit and People of Other Faiths," 260.
[62] Samartha, "The Holy Spirit and People of Other Faiths," 260.
[63] Samartha, "The Holy Spirit and People of Other Faiths," 260.
[64] Samartha, "The Holy Spirit and People of Other Faiths," 260-261.
[65] Samartha, "The Holy Spirit and People of Other Faiths," 261.
[66] Kim, *Mission in the Spirit: The Holy Spirit in Indian Christian Theologies*, 71.

salvation-historical thinking in Christianity, and other dogmas, and recognizes truth and goodness in the lives of neighbours of other faiths. However, even though he vouched for the Spirit, and heavily criticized the western Protestant theology for basing its ecclesiology on christology, he ended up relating people of other faiths with christology – *One Christ, Many Religions*.

It is interesting to note that Samartha wishes to keep the discussions on the Spirit in the context of the Trinity. He believes that by keeping it this way he is able to "anchorage in history," which Hinduism tends to lose and the religious dimension, which Christian activism tends to neglect.[67] This is a very positive position. Missional theology should be anchored in the triune God.

There are two aspects in Samartha's pneumatology namely: the Spirit's role in the secular arena, and the mark of the Spirit as inwardness, interiority, which we feel has relevance for our missional pneumatology in the Indian pluralistic context.

He writes that "[t]he outreach of the Spirit of God cannot be confined only to religions. One can discern the initiatives of the Spirit as divine energy even in situations where people do not recognize them as such."[68] Secular movements are related to social and economic justice where religion does not have a major role. However, Christians can recognize "seeds" or "signs" of the Spirit among them if it helps them to provide a theological grounding to co-operate with others for human wellbeing.[69]

This engagement of the Spirit stimulates Christians to be engaged in the universal search for economic, social justice and all ethical ideals. In the outreach of the Spirit the work of the Christians for the above mentioned works is linked with similar work done by neighbors who sometimes are not from any religious affinities.

---

[67] Kim, *Mission in the Spirit: The Holy Spirit in Indian Christian Theologies*, 73.
[68] Samartha, "The Holy Spirit and the Revelation of God in Emerging India - 2000 (Keynote Address)," 39.
[69] Samartha, "The Holy Spirit and the Revelation of God in Emerging India - 2000 (Keynote Address)," 39.

Another area in the secular world where Samartha sees the influence of the Spirit is in the field of ecology. For him, the Spirit of God links nature, humanity, and God in the community of creation. The Spirit as *shakti* or divine energy and as divine breath keeps creation alive and holds together the community of creation.[70]

Samartha writes that "one of the less visible, not so easily recognizable, but perhaps more profound, marks of the Spirit is inwardness, interiority, the power to root people's lives in the depths of God's being."[71] For him, the Spirit as the indwelling God enables people to abide in God. For Christians, this rootedness takes place through Christ in the power of the Spirit. Ethics is rooted in theology and theology is rooted in inner life. It should be noted that this mark of inwardness is not exclusive to Christianity. In the missionary activities in India, the inward role of the Spirit is extremely paramount.

India has been in the forefront of missions for centuries now. Christian missionary activities are intensively undertaken in our country. In the context of an upsurge of a right-wing nationalistic and Hindutva ideology today, serious debate and dialogue on missions has to be undertaken. This is not to be done because of the creation of a fear psychosis but because this ought to be the way forward for missions in India.

India, which is economically poor, is strangely rich in cultural and religious diversity. Nowhere else in the world is the influence of religions so pervasive, so pluriform, so powerful that it affects the existential life of every Indian in a very profound manner.[72] For an Indian theologian/missiologist, the Indian situation is indeed a daunting one. One is involved in missions to a very large, intensely varied, and densely populated subcontinent, which holds over 15 per cent of the world's population. The awesome size of her population is uniquely matched by its bewildering diversity. With less than 3 per cent of its population Christian, India is one of the least Christian nations of the world. Diversity is the hallmark

---

[70] Samartha, "The Holy Spirit and the Revelation of God in Emerging India - 2000 (Keynote Address)," 39-40.

[71] Samartha, "The Holy Spirit and People of Other Faiths," 261.

[72] Samuel George, *The Historical Particularity of Jesus: A Dialogue with the Hindu View of History* (Kolkata, India: Punthi Pustak, 2014), 305.

of this great nation in almost every aspect: culture, religiosity, language, and people. It has been the cradle of the great religions of Hinduism, Buddhism, Jainism, Sikhism, and many other religious sects.[73]

For centuries, various religious communities have peacefully coexisted in this land. However, any unifying efforts in the name of cultural-religious identities, regional aspirations, or any such hegemonizing activities have led to communal disharmony and destruction of communities. Mathew writes that:

> [t]hese efforts and resultant disturbances have challenged the peaceful co-existence and attempted to bring forth different communal and ideological interest groups, in which some have become highly malicious and extremist in intention style and operation. Christian mission operations are also not an exemption from such an attitude. Amidst such a challenging situation it is our genuine human responsibility to bring peoples of all religions, ideologies, political parties, regions, with varied interests to build up a New India, where Christian Gospel and witness also has to play an important role.[74]

The present context of India is such an explosive one where divisive politics has become the hallmark of the present government and communal flare-ups are so common that we do not even bother to notice it. In such a situation, the idea of plurality, conversion and missions demands our utmost attention. If not, we as a community are heading towards more difficulties. What we need is a sincere introspection and an "in-reach," which is possible with an "intra-Christian dialogue" of different churches within themselves and between one another.[75]

I am often reminded of the Peter-Cornelius event in the book of Acts chapter 15 where the Spirit of God was granted to "others" irrespective of their cultural, religious, geographical status. Such availability of the Spirit of God to "others" is what Samartha has vouched for in his pneumatology.

---

[73] George, *The Historical Particularity of Jesus*, 301.

[74] Prasad Mathew, "The Context Decides the Agenda and Pace for the Mission of the Church: A Case Study of the First Christian in the Western Hemisphere (Acts. 16:6-15)" in Koshy P. Varughese (ed), *Challenges and Prospects of Mission in the Emerging Context: Essays in Memory of the Rev. Mathew Thomas* (Faridabad, India: Dharma Jyoti Vidya Peeth, 2010), 109.

[75] Mathew, "The Context Decides the Agenda and Pace for the Mission of the Church," 109-110.

This is extremely relevant in the discussion of the missions of the Church in India where religious and cultural pluralism is a living fact. The explicit understanding that "God shows no partiality and whoever fears God and does what is right is acceptable to God," should lead the Indian church to get converted in our approach to people of other religions and cultures and acknowledge the richness in them, and mutually enrich, encourage and get corrected and guided. Remember, it is the heavenly beings that direct the earthly actions throughout the Peter-Cornelius story, illustrating the abiding truth, that "God made it his business" to accept Gentiles as his people (cf. Acts 15:14). It did not happen on human initiative.[76] Samartha rightly points out that "[t]he question today is how to state the Christian commitment to God through Christ in the power of the Spirit in such a way that commitment does not lead to fanaticism and tolerance does not mean shallow friendliness."[77]

Samartha can be called one of the pioneers of relating Christian faith to people of other living faiths. In the Indian context, his constructive role in this relation-building has been enormous. However, it is in the field of pneumatology and Christian missions that we see his contribution in a much more pioneering manner. We have noted above that his theocentric position helped him to see the Holy Spirit as pervading every religion, culture, secular field, and ecology. The boundless Spirit permeates and works among all. This Spirit of truth leads all to the Ultimate—God.

Samartha sounds a clarion call to the church in India for the work of the Holy Spirit in the inner life of individuals and institutions. In this approach, the inter-connectedness of inward conversion and outward missions is to be rightly understood and emphasized in unequivocal terms. The church in India has lost its focus on missions because it has neglected the aspect of inner conversion. She can reflect (*missions*) only that which she possesses. A shallow church offers a shallow gospel to the people. Such a gospel is a gospel of *status quo*. Missions of the church reflect her inner life and standards. A shallow-blunt life can only reflect

---

[76] Richard J. Dillon, "Acts of the Apostles" in Raymond Edward Brown, Joseph A. Fitzmyer, and Roland E. Murphy (eds), *The Jerome Biblical Commentary* (Bangalore: Theological Publication in India, 1982), 745.

[77] Samartha, "The Holy Spirit and the Revelation of God in Emerging India - 2000 (Keynote Address)," 34.

such a mission mandate. The church in India needs to get back to the act of introspection and action for an inner cleansing. There has to be a realization that God is the author of both conversion and missions. The Spirit of God pervades every aspect of humanity and nature. The church needs to understand that an inner conversion leads to missions outside. What is reflected outside is an inner converted life. Missions is Church's "converted" life. Conversion and missions go hand in hand. There cannot be an over emphasis on any one at the expense of the other. A radical missions demands a radical conversion on the part of the faith community. A radically transformed community (the Spirit-led community) would lead to radically transforming missions, which in turn would create a radically converted society and nation. That ought to be the focus of missions in India.

10

THE HOLY SPIRIT AND THE CHURCH AS THE ORDINARY MEANS OF SALVATION

Steven Griffin[*]

The American historian of religion Darryl Hart has observed that while sixteenth century Protestants like John Calvin and Martin Luther assumed that the church was "an objective medium of grace outside of which there was no ordinary possibility of salvation," later Protestants like Jonathan Edwards and Charles Hodge came to think of it as an essentially "subjective, invisible quality shared by the truly converted."[1] The impact of this shift on the modern evangelical movement should not be underestimated. Many followers of Jesus today assume that a personal relationship with Christ might begin and be maintained with little or no reference to the church. Faith statements of not a few denominations define the church primarily, if not exclusively, in invisible terms. And the ordinary language we use to speak of the means to be saved suggests

---

[*] **Steven Griffin**, PhD, is Professor of Christian Doctrine and World Christianity at Ryle Seminary in Ottawa, Canada, and visiting lecturer in Theology at the West Africa Theological Seminary in Lagos, Nigeria. He earned his doctoral award in Historical Theology, McGill University. Raised in Mexico, and with training in Russian studies, his interest in theology and world cultures is reflected in works published in *Doon Theological Journal, Journal of Asian Mission,* and *The Ecumenist.*

[1] D.G. Hart, "The Church in Evangelical Theologies, Past and Future" in M. Husbands and D. Treier (eds), *The Community of the Word: Toward an* Evangelical Ecclesiology (Downers Grove, IL: InterVarsity Press, 2005), 25.

an exaggerated concern to avoid confusion between the church and salvation. One example will suffice. On a Sunday morning some years ago in a large international, evangelical church in South East Asia, I took note of these words from one of the elders: "Salvation does not come through the Church, but through a relationship with Jesus." Just the following Sunday, as my family and I were being welcomed into that congregation, another elder read a statement that conveyed something rather different.

> The Church is of God, and will be preserved to the end of time, for the conduct of worship, the due administration of His Word and Sacraments, the maintenance of Christian fellowship and discipline, the edification of believers, and the conversion of the world. People of every age and circumstance stand in need of the means of grace which it alone supplies.[2]

While the point made on the first Sunday was surely meant to remind us that the church is not the source of salvation, sadly it reinforced the all-too-common notion that knowing, trusting and following Jesus is an essentially unmediated, church-free affair. In the end, whether it was true or not that God reaches out to sinners and keeps them as his own precisely through the church as an external means—as proclaimed on the second Sunday—was left unclear.

Protestants are not alone in undermining the idea that sinners should not expect to be saved apart from the Church—that is, apart from that visible community that is gathered by, and sent into the world through, the proclamation of God's Word and celebration of the gospel sacraments.[3] Embracing the notion that non-Christian religions are taken up and fulfilled in the revelation of God in Christ, Karl Rahner spoke on behalf of those who are prepared to consider these, to varying degrees, valid ways of salvation. That is, on the assumption that non-Christian religions contain "supernatural elements arising out of the grace which is given to men as a gratuitous gift on account of Christ," Christians

---

[2] See *The United Methodist Hymnal: Book of United Methodist Worship* (Nashville, TN: The United Methodist Publishing House, 1993), 45.

[3] According to John Calvin, "[w]herever we see the Word of God purely preached and heard, and the sacraments administered according to Christ's institution, there, it is not to be doubted, a church of God exists." J.T. McNeill (ed), *Institutes of the Christian Religion*, vol. 20 of The Library of Christian Classics, F.L. Battles (trans.) (Philadelphia: Westminster Press, 1960), 1023.

could approach members of those groups as "anonymous" Christians who in and through their respective traditions participate in the same salvation.[4] With more pluralistic assumptions about the religions, ie, without assuming that the religions find their fulfilment in Christ but still speaking in christocentric terms, R. Panikkar spoke for those who would see the religions as complementary, drawn by Christ towards a single end which has not yet been revealed. Thus Panikkar claimed that we cannot say "how Christianity will look when the present Christian waters and the Hindu river merge into a bigger stream, where the peoples of the future will quench their thirst – for truth, for goodness, for salvation."[5] Whether we follow Rahner or Panikkar in this matter, however, we tend to think of the Holy Spirit not primarily as one who is sovereign in relation to the nations, with the liberty to confront or fulfil this or that element within culture "from above" or "from without," through means of his choosing, but rather as the One who works directly and immediately "from below" or "from within," ie, in the heartbeat of religion itself. Hence the tendency to overlook the ways in which the religions have a way of distorting "the light that gives light to everyone" (John 1:9) and, as Joseph Ratzinger pointed out in *Dominus Iesus*, to disregard the "superstitions and errors" in them that "constitute an obstacle to salvation" (21).[6]

Under the circumstances, a more Chalcedonian way forward is called for if we are to understand the relationship between the church and salvation rightly. That is, we must strive neither to confuse realities that have their own integrity nor to separate realities that are meant to be held together. Thus, on the one hand, the church and salvation are not to be confused, for to say that the church is God's ordinary instrument of

---

[4] K. Rahner, "Christianity and the Non-Christian Religions" in *Theological Investigations*, vol. 5 (London: Darton, Longman and Todd, 1966), 121, 131-133.

[5] R. Panikkar, "The Unknown Christ of Hinduism" in *Christianity and Other Religions* (Glasgow: Collins, 1980), 144.

[6] J. Ratzinger, *Dominus Iesus* [On the Unicity and Salvific Universality of Jesus Christ and the Church]. http://www.vatican.va/roman_curia/congregations/cfaith/documents/rc_con_cfaith_doc_20000806_dominus-iesus_en.html (accessed 15 December 2016). Numbers in parentheses refer to the particular section in the document. Mark Heim's proposal raises a similar problem regarding standards for discernment of truth and error in the religions. He argues that what God has in mind is not one particular religious end for all (ie, "Salvation"), but multiple ones ("salvations"), all of which are rooted in the same salvific purpose of God. See Mark Heim,*The Depth of the Riches: A Trinitarian Theology of Religious Ends* (Grand Rapids, MI: William B. Eerdmans, 2000), 77.

salvation is not to imply that God is bound by the regular outward means, for he may save through external means of his choosing those outside the church who call on him for mercy. As J.I. Packer explains, although the Bible "sets forth Jesus Christ as the only Saviour from sin," we are not permitted to set limits "to the dealings of the merciful God with individuals, even within non-Christian religions."[7] On the other hand, to drive a wedge between the two realities is to imply that "life in Christ" or "life in the Spirit" might be regarded as something quite separate or distinct from "life in the Church." It is one thing to acknowledge that, "God had some friends in the world outside the commonwealth of Israel," as Heinrich Bullinger put it when he wished to account for those who might, through necessity or human weakness, obtain salvation apart from the regular sacramental life of the church.[8] It is quite another, however, to encourage the idea that the salvation that according to Peter in Acts 4 is found only in Jesus might be sought apart from the visible, apostolic fellowship of prayer, worship, teaching and remembering that we meet in Acts 1-2, and that is the creation of the "Lord and life-giver" (Nicene Creed) that Jesus himself promised.[9]

If the church, through its ministry of the Word and sacraments, is to serve as the Holy Spirit's ordinary means to give new life to sinners and to keep them in Christ's fellowship, then at the most basic level the church is called to be a visible sign of Christ's kingdom. Just what sort of sign, however, remains a central question, because some proposals fall short of attributing to the church a proper instrumental role in salvation. Restrictivists propose a church as an ark of salvation model that effectively collapses salvation into the church. So the Council of Florence (1442), e.g., argued that "those not living within the Catholic church, not only

---

[7] J.I. Packer, *The Thirty-Nine Articles: Their Place and Use Today* (Oxford: Latimer House, 1984), 73.

[8] H. Bullinger, *The Second Helvetic Confession*, Chapter 17. https://www.ccel.org/creeds/helvetic.htm (accessed 15 December 2016).

[9] Proponents of a "pneumatological" approach to the religions will no doubt object to my "ecclesiocentric" assumptions. However, to the extent that the former approach rests on a view of the economy of the Spirit as something quite distinct from that of the Son (based in part on a rejection of the filioque), its trinitarian (and Chalcedonian) framework will require further study. In practical terms, the proposal to discern the work of the Holy Spirit within non-Christian religions without reference to Christ and his church remains problematic. See e.g., Chapter four of K.E. Johnson, *A 'Trinitarian' Theology of Religions? An Augustinian Assessment of Several Recent Proposals* (Ph.D. Thesis, Duke University, USA, 2007).

pagans but also Jews and heretics and schismatics, cannot participate in eternal life, but will depart 'into everlasting fire which was prepared for the devil and his angels,' unless before the end of life the same have been added to the flock."[10] Proponents of the pluralist thesis reduce the church to an illustration of the salvation that is at work in all cultures under different names, and in so doing collapse the church into salvation—in which case the latter is understood generically as transformation from self-centeredness to God-centeredness.[11] Proponents of the fulfilment or inclusivist thesis suggest that the church is to be seen as a vanguard of a salvation that is latent in human cultures and therefore not fundamentally served by the church, but only named by it. As Rahner put it, the church is that "historically tangible vanguard and the historically and socially constituted explicit expression of what the Christian hopes is present as a hidden reality even outside the visible church."[12] A proper instrumental role of the church in relation to salvation comes into view, however, when we come to the Roman Catholic model of the church as sacrament of salvation, as expounded by Popes Paul VI, John Paul II and Benedict XVI. In what follows, I offer an overview and appreciation of that model from a Protestant perspective with a view to considering the relevance of the matter for Christian unity and mission.

THE CHURCH AND THE FULLNESS OF SALVATION

In Lumen Gentium (1964), or the "Dogmatic Constitution on the Church" that expounds the church's role in relation to the nations,[13] Pope Paul VI sets forth at the outset a sacramental model, according to which the church serves as the light of Christ in the world in the power of the Holy Spirit. Being in Christ who is the "Light of nations," the church bears brightly on its countenance the light of Christ, and as such is held to be a "sign and instrument" of salvation, understood as union with God and with the whole human race (1). Through the Holy Spirit's outpouring

---

[10] Cited by H. Netland, *Dissonant Voices: Religious Pluralism and the Question of Truth* (Vancouver, B.C.: Regent College Publishing, 1991), 13.

[11] See John Hick, "A Pluralist View" in D. Okholm and T. Phillips (eds), *Four Views on Salvation in a Pluralistic World* (Grand Rapids, MI: Zondervan, 1995), 43.

[12] Rahner, "Christianity," 131-133.

[13] Vatican Council II, Lumen Gentium [Dogmatic Constitution on the Church]. https://www.ewtn.com/library/councils/v2church.htm (accessed 15 December 2016). Numbers in parentheses that follow refer to the particular section in the document.

(2), and being indwelt, empowered, equipped, directed, and aided by the same Spirit (3), the Church as a "structured" society is neither confused with nor separated from the mystical body of Christ (8); rather, what is invisible is built up by what is visible, under the Holy Spirit's direction (8). In this way, the Church is to be held as the ordinary means of salvation, for whoever comes to know that God has made it indispensable for man's salvation may not seek to be saved apart from it: "Whosoever, therefore, knowing that the Catholic Church was made necessary by Christ, would refuse to enter or to remain in it, could not be saved" (14).

While appropriating in this way the classical teaching that outside the church there is no salvation, Lumen Gentium did not overlook the fulfilment theme.[14] In fact, some have found that the "spirit" of Vatican II encourages the idea that non-Christian religions might function as "legitimate paths of salvation for their members."[15] Some support for this is suggested in Section 16, which acknowledges that elements of truth and goodness which may be found in non-Christian religions are to be reckoned as forms of *praeparatio evangelica*. However, in the same section it is affirmed, to echo Paul in Romans 1, that "often men, deceived by the Evil One, have become vain in their reasonings and have exchanged the truth of God for a lie, serving the creature rather than the Creator" (16). It is for this reason that H. Van Straelen argues that in Lumen Gentium the positive elements within non-Christian religions are considered to be forms of preparation for the gospel at best, since "natural religion cannot be more than a groping for the truth," and that in Acts 17, pagans in general are seen to be on the wrong path.[16] On this point van Straelen differs rather sharply from Karl Rahner, who suggested that in the modern

---

[14] Since they believed that the world was already permeated by the gospel message, defenders of the axiom *extra ecclesiam nulla salus* had in mind those who had fallen away from the gospel having heard it, and not the status of non-Christians or their religion as such. See Gavin D'Costa, "'Extra ecclesiam nulla salus' revisited" in *Religious Pluralism and Unbelief: Studies Critical and Comparative* (London: Routledge, 1990), 130.

[15] J. Dupuis, *Toward a Christian Theology of Religious Pluralism* (Maryknoll, NY: Orbis Books, 1999), 170.

[16] H.J.J.M. Van Straelen, *The Church and the Non-Christian Religions at the Threshold of the 21st Century: A Historical and Theological Study*, R. Nowell (trans.) (London: Avon, 1998), 270, 275. Van Straelen adds that the seeds of Logos theology (e.g., in Justin Martyr) support the idea that "some philosophers had reached insights which contain a partial truth. But the idea of canonizing pagan religions was totally alien to them" (276).

era we need no longer share Paul's pessimism regarding the salvation of non-Christians."[17]

Whatever the case may be, it is clear that in their writings on the subject Popes John Paul II and Benedict XVI would not seek like Rahner to get beyond Paul's supposed first-century cultural limitations when it came to the fact of other religions. On the contrary, by upholding the Second Vatican Council's reluctance to speak of non-Christian religions as ways of salvation, and in seeking to expound the nature of the church as described in Lumen Gentium as the "sacrament" of salvation, they demonstrated that their aim was to clarify the way in which the church remains central in God's plan to save sinners, even in cases where individuals have no apparent contact with the Church.

To establish the church's instrumental role in salvation, in *Redemptoris Missio* (1990) John Paul II notes, in the first place, the threat which the pluralist thesis represents for that conviction.[18] He challenges the idea that salvation might be reduced to a benefit which remains "within the confines of the kingdom of man" (ie, within strictly human efforts for liberation), for by restricting the work of the Church to the promotion of peace, justice and dialogue which is aimed merely at mutual enrichment, the so-called theocentric approach to the religions effectively collapses the church into the kingdom, thereby reducing the church to a mere sign of salvation (17). In the second place, against a fulfilment thesis found in the vanguard model of the church in relation to salvation, he insists that dialogue with members of other religions is to be "conducted and implemented with the conviction that *the Church is the ordinary means of salvation*" (55, Emphasis original). Thus, the church is sent to the ends of the earth by the Holy Spirit, who is the "principal agent of the whole Church's mission" (21), with the confidence that "*she alone* possesses the fullness of the means of salvation" (55, Emphasis original) and that those who are finally saved apart from it will enjoy a "mysterious" relationship

---

[17] K. Rahner, *Mission and Grace: Essays in Pastoral Theology*, vol. 3, C. Hastings (trans.) (London: Sheed and Ward, 1966), 6, cited by Van Straelen, 271. Van Stralen notes that the Council did not accept Rahner's position (277).

[18] John Paul II, *Redemptoris Missio* [On the permanent validity of the Church's missionary mandate]. http://w2vatican.va/content/john-paul-ii/en/encyclicals/documents/hf_jp-ii_enc_07121990_redemptotis-missio.html (accessed 15 December 2016). Numbers in parentheses that follow refer to the particular section in the document.

with the church that is mediated by the same Spirit and based on Jesus' sacrificial death on the cross, but in ways known to God alone (10).[19]

In *Dominus Iesus* (2000), Pope Benedict XVI (as Cardinal Ratzinger) develops John Paul II's concerns with his affirmation that "God has willed that the Church founded by him be the instrument for the salvation of all humanity" (22). He begins with a sharp critique of the relativistic assumptions which guide the pluralist approach to the religions. Those who understand the fundamental truth regarding the definitive character of the revelation of Jesus Christ to be superseded, he notes, are motivated by the erroneous presupposition that what might be true for some might not be for others, or that the incarnation represents "a mere appearing of God in history" (4). Here we recall John Paul II's insistence that "Christ is none other than Jesus of Nazareth" (*Redemptoris Missio*, 6). Benedict XVI's challenge to the inclusivist proposal is made with reference to the nature of the sacraments. Thus, while God may use "some prayers and rituals" of other religions to prepare individuals to receive the gospel, these are not to be understood as coming from God in the same sense that the sacraments convey, *ex opere operato*, the benefit to which they point. The distinction between the two kinds of external things is based on the fact that while the latter serve as efficacious means to apply the benefit of Christ's sacrifice to the believer by faith, the former are inevitably mixed with other rituals that stand in the way of salvation to the extent that "they depend on superstitions or other errors" (*Dominus Iesus*, 21).

To the theme of fulfilment understood in a qualified way, Benedict XVI adds the theme of fullness of salvation that is made available in and through the Church. In this way, the classical extra *ecclesiam nulla salus* remains true, for the fullness of salvation is held to be available only in sacramental fellowship with the Roman Catholic church. Benedict XVI recalls from Lumen Gentium that the church is the "universal sacrament of salvation," mystically inseparable from Christ (20), and called to announce "the necessity of conversion to Jesus Christ and of adherence to the Church through Baptism and the other sacraments in order to participate *fully* in communion with God, the Father, Son and Holy Spirit" (22, Emphasis

---

[19] As Van Straelen argues, "[t]he fact that the followers of other religions can receive God's grace and be saved by Christ apart from the ordinary means which he has established does not thereby cancel the call to faith and baptism which God wills for all people" (280).

added). Moreover, while it is acknowledged that adherents of other religions "can receive divine grace, it is also certain that *objectively speaking* they are in a gravely deficient situation in comparison with those who, in the Church, have the fullness of the means of salvation" (22, Emphasis original).

In Benedict XVI's teaching, it is specifically to the church that is in fellowship with Peter and those overseers considered to be his successors that one is to look for the fullness of salvation. It is clear, however, that fullness is to be understood only in relation to Christ. That is, it is only as the church finds itself in Christ that it enjoys the fullness of the means of salvation. This is based on the truths, as Paul says in Colossians 2:9 that the fullness of divinity dwells in Christ (*Dominus Iesus*, 5), that the fullness and centre of salvation is found in Christ (13), and that the church possesses "the fullness of Christ's salvific mystery," being one with him (16). Here Benedict introduces a welcome Chalcedonian affirmation: "[J]ust as the head and members of a living body, though not identical, are inseparable, so too Christ and the Church can neither be confused nor separated, and constitute a single 'whole Christ'" (16).

To the christological basis of the Church's identity Benedict XVI adds the qualification that the church remains a pilgrim people. In *Truth and Tolerance*, he encourages a view of the religions—including Christianity—as dynamic, not static, entities. Thus, he suggests that we do well to approach religions not so much as realities which exist in "one single form," but as a complex of traditions which may or may not be related to the gospel.[20] Thus, he explains that in our day Islam can be encountered in forms which reflect "a certain proximity to the mystery of Christ" as well as destructive ones.[21] Since the direction of a religion is more important than its shape in a given moment, Benedict XVI includes Christianity among the religions which are not to be canonized as they already exist, as if to excuse the faithful "from any deeper searching."[22] In the light of this, he can assert that "salvation does not lie in religions as such, but it is connected to them, inasmuch as, and to the extent that, they

---

[20] J. Ratzinger, *Truth and Tolerance: Christian Belief and World Religions*, H. Taylor (trans.) (San Francisco: Ignatius Press, 2003), 53.

[21] Ratzinger, *Truth and Tolerance*, 53-54.

[22] Ratzinger, *Truth and Tolerance*, 54.

lead man toward the one good, toward the search for God, for truth, and for love."[23]

THE CHURCH AND THE ASSURANCE OF SALVATION

It is from Benedict XVI's claim that salvation does not lie in religions as such that a Protestant appreciation of papal contributions to the topic might take its point of departure, for there is much to welcome and affirm in that body of teachings. The first is the model of the church in relation to salvation that comes into view. As a sacrament of salvation, the proposal which we have surveyed presents to us an image of the church as that city set on a hill (Matt 5:14-16). The people whom Jesus describes as "light of the world" are called through their good works to let their light shine for all to see. And lest the glory be attributed to that city—lest the nations assume that the light that saves is to be found in the city's own resources—Jesus declares: "[L]et your light shine before others, that they may see your good deeds and glorify your Father in heaven." At the same time, the image of an established city speaks to the truth that salvation is here and now; that insofar as it finds its identity in Christ, the church becomes the Holy Spirit's means to draw sinners to the light of Christ's fellowship.

In the second place, the teaching that the church is God's ordinary means to save sinners echoes an important theme found in the Reformed tradition. Bullinger wrote that just "as there was no salvation outside Noah's ark when the world perished in the flood, so we believe that there is no certain salvation outside Christ, who offers himself to be enjoyed by the elect in the Church."[24] Similarly, the Westminster Confession of Faith would speak of the visible church as "the house and family of God, out of which there is no ordinary possibility of salvation."[25] Implicit here is the refusal, in the words of Lesslie Newbigin, both "to limit the saving

---

[23] Ratzinger, *Truth and Tolerance*, 205. A similar dynamic is at work in Gavin D'Costa's quest for the "ecclesial significance of the presence of other religions." Given that according to Redemptoris Missio 29 the Spirit's universal work is "not to be separated from his particular activity within the body of Christ, which is the Church," D'Costa suggests that the Spirit's work in the world is ecclesiological in the sense that it is through non-Christian religions that the Holy Spirit wishes to challenge, develop and deepen the church's devotion to God. See G. D'Costa, *The Meeting of Religions* (Maryknoll, NY: Orbis, 2000), 12, 108, 117.

[24] Bullinger, *Second Helvetic Confession*, Chapter 17.

[25] *The Westminster Confession of Faith*, Chapter 25, Section 2. http://www.reformed.org/documents/wcf_with_proofs/ (accessed 15 December 2016).

grace of God to the members of the Christian Church" and to reduce the matter of salvation to a question "about our destiny as individual souls after death."[26] As important as such personal assurance is, Benedict XVI is surely right to insist that salvation is not to be reduced to a question about who finally gets into heaven. Rather, Christians are justified in asking "what heaven is and how it comes upon earth," since "future salvation must make its mark in a way of life that makes a person 'human' here and thus capable of relating to God."[27]

In the third place, Benedict XVI introduces into the discussion regarding the church's sacramental nature a welcome distinction between prevenient grace and special (or efficacious) grace. Without assuming that salvation takes place strictly within the sphere of religion,[28] he is nevertheless confident that God may use elements within non-Christian religions ("some prayers and rituals," as noted above) as forms of preparation for the gospel. However, the promise of efficacious grace is not attached to these external things, which are in any case ambiguous on their own.[29] In this way, Benedict XVI can draw the distinction between those who, on the one hand, enjoy the fullness of the means of salvation in the church and those, on the other, who may be saved apart from it but who are in "a gravely deficient situation," since it is only to the sacraments that God attaches the promise of saving grace.[30]

This last point is particularly welcome, for it introduces the theme of confidence based on God's promise that is central to Protestant reflection on the relationship between the church and salvation. That tradition has tended to recognize the devastating nature of sin in the lives of individuals, and on that basis has acknowledged the sinner's need to

---

[26] L. Newbigin, *The Gospel in a Pluralist Society* (Grand Rapids, MI: William B. Eerdmans, 1989), 182, 179.

[27] Ratzinger, *Truth and Tolerance*, 205.

[28] Ratzinger, *Truth and Tolerance*, 53.

[29] To these external things we could add elements which lie outside the sphere of formal religion, such as the hospitality shown to Joshua's spies, whom Rahab welcomed "by faith" (Heb 11:31).

[30] Chalcedonian logic applies here too: just as we should not confuse common (or prevenient) grace with saving grace, neither should we distinguish them radically. As Richard Mouw says: For all "any of us can know – much of what we now think of as common grace may in the end time be revealed to be saving grace" See Richard J. Mouw, *He Shines in All That's Fair: Culture and Common Grace* (Grand Rapids, MI: William B. Eerdmans, 2001), 100.

embrace God's promise personally, and therefore to enjoy the assurance of God's pardon. In the light of this emphasis, the Protestant has been drawn not primarily to the church as a city on a hill that mediates the fullness of salvation, but rather as a herald that announces the promise of a salvation that, while anticipated in the here and now, belongs properly to the city which is yet to come (Heb 13:14).[31] As John Webster put it, "the active life of the church is best understood, not as a visible realization or representation of the divine presence but as one long act of testimony – as an attestation of the work of God in Christ, now irrepressibly present and effective in the Spirit's power."[32]

As a model which approaches the church as the Holy Spirit's means to assure sinners of their salvation, the Protestant model complements the sacramental one in three main ways. The first has to do with the church's nature as a sign and of the salvation that it signifies. While the herald model has, here and there, tended to reduce the church to a sign that "simply points" to the city that is yet to come, and therefore to undermine the sacramental model,[33] properly speaking, it announces benefits from God which are present as well as future. In this way, it is to be approached, in Newbigin's words, as a "sign, instrument, and foretaste of God's redeeming grace."[34] Thus, salvation is precisely all about how heaven "comes upon earth" (Benedict XVI), for it is, following Newbigin once again, "the completion of God's whole work in creation and redemption, the summing up of all things with Christ as head (Eph. 1:10), the reconciling of all things in heaven and earth through the blood of the cross (Col. 1:20), the subjecting of all hostile powers under the feet of Christ (1 Cor. 15:24-28)."[35]

---

[31] In developing ecclesial models this way, I am indebted to A. Dulles, *Models of the Church* (Dublin: Gill & MacMillan, 1987).

[32] J. Webster, "The Visible Attests the Invisible" in M. Husbands and D. Treier (eds), *The Community of the Word: Toward an Evangelical Ecclesiology* (Downers Grove, IL: InterVarsity Press, 2005), 96.

[33] "Testimony is astonished indication. Arrested by the wholly disorienting grace of God in Christ and the Spirit, the church simply points. It is not identical or continuous with that to which it bears witness, for otherwise its testimony would be self-testimony and therefore false. Nor is its testimony an action which effects that which it indicates; the witness of the church is an ostensive, not an effective, sign; it indicates the inherent achieved effectiveness which the object of testimony has in itself" (Webster, "The Visible Attests the Invisible," 106).

[34] Newbigin, *The Gospel*, 233.

[35] Newbigin, *The Gospel*, 178-179.

A related concern about the Protestant model is that with its emphasis on the personal encounter with God in Christ it tends to render the church an occasional, less than historically continuous, reality: "practically a series of totally disconnected events" brought about through the ministry of the word and sacraments (Newbigin).[36] However, to the extent that Christianity is concerned not simply with events in history, but also with the meaning of those events, then historical continuity would properly be sought in the church's confessing tradition as a means to safeguard the integrity of that interpretation.

The second way in which the Protestant model complements the Roman Catholic model has to do with the importance of assurance in the life of the believer. Here again the church's nature as a sign is relevant, for apart from being "the light of the world", the church is also called to be "the salt of the earth" (Matt 5:13-16). If the "scattered" identity is established through the Holy Spirit's sending of the church as witnesses to the ends of the earth (Acts 1:8), the image of salt highlights the temporal dimension of that work (to the end of time as we know it). This is because salt introduces the virtue of anticipation, for it serves to preserve. Paul says, "[l]et your speech always be gracious, seasoned with salt, so that you may know how to answer everyone" (Col 4:6), indicating that godly conversation requires the kind of restraint that is proper to listening and waiting. And this virtue is linked, in turn, to holding on to God's promise: "[B]ecause I know whom I have believed, and am convinced that he is able to guard what I have entrusted to him until that day" (2 Tim 1:12; see also Job 19:25, Rom 5:2). It is in the light of faith understood as "a most firm trust and a clear and steadfast assent of the mind" with regard to God's promise that Bullinger speaks of the church as the only certain means of salvation.[37]

Called to be both salt and light in the world—to taste as well as to see "that the Lord is good" (Ps 34:8)—the Protestant model's conception of the relationship between word and image suggests a third way in which it complements the sacramental model. The Psalmist's declaration that "the unfolding of your [God's] words gives light" (Ps 119:130, Parenthesis

---

[36] L. Newbigin, *The Household of God* (New York: Friendship Press, 1954), 48.
[37] Bullinger, *Second Helvetic Confession*, Chapters 16 and 17.

added) reminds us that illumination depends on God's Word (rather than the other way around), and reflects the logical priority of sound over sight which we find throughout Scripture. With the Word incarnate now removed from our sight, and, as long as the pilgrim "is in this mortal body", as Augustine put it, "he is far from the Lord; so he walks by faith, not by sight" (2 Cor 5:7).[38] On this basis, the herald model of the church serves as a safeguard against the notion that God's chosen instrument (the bread and wine of the Lord's Supper, or the church itself) might be understood simply to contain within itself that to which it points, thereby inviting the faithful to confuse the instrument with the source. To this necessary reduction of the sacrament from "container-sign" to instrumental sign we might add the reduction of the rite of ordination, on which the sacramental model rests in part. While it is one thing to affirm baptism and the Lord's Supper as sacraments, since by faith, and on the authority of Christ's promise, they mediate what they signify, it is another to attribute sacramental status to the ordained ministry and other lesser signs which, as the Thirty- Nine Articles of the Church of England put it, "have not any visible sign or ceremony ordained of God."[39] As such, a Protestant may very well appreciate and welcome the concern for historic continuity to which the papacy bears witness without having to assume that it is primarily the See of Peter that the church is to consider as its focus and instrument of unity. In the Protestant model, it would be primarily to faithful overseers in council, such as those we meet in Acts 15 that the church would look to as the Holy Spirit's outward means to keep his people in fellowship.

In conclusion, having suggested some of the implications of our survey for Christian unity, what might the lessons learned here mean in practical terms for the Church's message in the world? To review, we have understood salvation as everything that God has done, is doing, and will do to bring all things under Christ's lordship. We have understood the church as the society throughout the world that professes faith in Christ as Lord and that remains in the apostles' teaching, fellowship, breaking of bread and prayers. Finally, we have affirmed that the church is God's

---

[38] Augustine of Hippo, *The City of God against the Pagans* (XIX.14), R.W. Dyson (ed. and trans.) (Cambridge: Cambridge University Press, 1998), XIX.14.

[39] The Thirty-Nine Articles, article 25. https://www.churchofengland,org/prayer-worship/worship/book-of-common-prayer/articles-of-religion.aspx (accessed 15 December 2016).

ordinary instrument of salvation. I think that three practical implications follow.

First, with the focus in salvation being on the whole objective, historical movement of God, once we have sensed that God has called us into fellowship through the ministry of his people, we are not to expect or to look for salvation apart from that fellowship. In positive terms, we are to announce with confidence that the reconciliation of all things under Christ's authority is to be worked out in history precisely through the fellowship that he has provided in the church; by the same token, we are to preach that individuals may find assurance that they belong to Christ precisely in that fellowship. Individuals who, as far as we can tell, are intellectually incapable of embracing the truth that they belong to God are not thereby left out, and neither are those individuals who, as far as we can tell, have never been given the opportunity to embrace the hope of the gospel, simply the lost. If they were, then God would be bound by human instruments (both external and inward) in reaching them.

Second, the truth that God may reach some through extraordinary means does not mean that for some individuals salvation is relatively easy (since, e.g., they were born into a Christian family), but hard for others because they have more cultural barriers to negotiate along the way. "Make every effort to enter through the narrow door" (Luke 13:24) applies to all. Moreover, the fact that God may reach individuals in an extraordinary way—since Jesus promises that there will be surprises (same passage)—does not mean that God is reaching them apart from Christ. To be reached is to be reached by God in Christ, because all salvation is in Jesus Christ, through him, and for him; and if anyone is saved without ever hearing of Jesus it will be because God's love, mercy and forgiveness was made known through a means that we'll only know about on the other side.

Third, and finally, the evangelistic proclamation of the church will not be motivated by a sense of panic (which is the logical implication of restrictivism), but by an experience of the love of the Father that compels believers to invite others to know the same forgiveness and freedom that they have experienced. Such forgiveness is never less than urgent, because we are miserable sinners as long as we do not receive divine pardon, and because the promised freedom will have a wider impact that cannot be measured on this side of Jesus' return in glory.

11

THIRD ARTICLE THEOLOGY AND APOLOGETICS

*Aruthuckal Varughese John**

Apologetics has often reflected the very culture it has sought to reach—an abrasive, rationalistic, human project. A shift towards prioritizing the Spirit can radically reshape apologetics to being a humble, God-dependent, exercise. This essay explores the shape of apologetics if we started with the Spirit by highlighting the oft-unacknowledged epistemic role of the Spirit as the agent who leads humans into truth.

A CASE FOR A THIRD ARTICLE THEOLOGY

The Holy Spirit, the third article in the Niceo-Constantinopolitan creed, following the Father and the Son, has only recently come into theological focus. The "third article" is *the Spirit* in the Nicene Creed. Arguing for a Third Article theology, Habets writes, "Western Christianity has inherent

---

* **Aruthuckal Varughese John** PhD is the RZIM Chair of Apologetics and Professor of Theology at SAIACS, India. He is currently a Post-doctoral Research Fellow with Langham, UK. His interests include Kierkegaard Studies, Pneumatology, Apologetics and Public Theology. He is the author of *Truth and Subjectivity, Faith and History: Kierkegaard's Insights for Christian Faith* (Orlando: Pickwick, 2012). He is also the co-editor of *Christians in the Public Square* (Bangalore: SAIACS Press, 2013) and *Exclusion and Inclusion in Changing India* (Bangalore: SAIACS Press, 2015). This paper was originally presented at the IAMS Conference in Seoul, South Korea.

two great theological traditions—as a heuristic device they may be termed respectively a theology of the First Article and a theology of the Second Article of the creed. A First Article theology is typified by medieval scholasticism, a Second Article theology by Reformation theology. These two trajectories have dominated the theological landscape."[1] However, the contemporary times can manifestly be seen as belonging to the third article, the Holy Spirit.

Whether it is an intentional acknowledgement of the Spirit's ontological presence or of his decisive epistemic function, a Third Article theology brings the life and ministry of the church and theological inquiry within the scope and purview of the Pentecost. A Third Article theology rests on animplied inadequacy of the first two without discounting their significance. Amos Yong believes that the move from the Second Article theology to a Third Article theology is commendable, "since the theological enterprise has been dominated traditionally by the symbol of the Word (or the Logos), resulting in part with a textually constructed theology (*theo-logia*) whereby emphasis is placed on the internal coherence of the Christian scheme of understanding rather than on the full correlation of the biblical text with the realities which the text reflects or points to."[2]

Given that theological controversies and heresies from the time of the early church have been related to the deity of Christ, apologetic preoccupations, expectedly, have remained christologically focused. The deity of the Spirit faced fewer problems and came to be settled along with the formalization of the trinitarian doctrine in the council of Nicaea. Yet it may be noticed that the discussion surrounding each person of the Trinity has a bearing on the other members of the Trinity. For instance,

---

[1] Myk Habets, *The Anointed Son: A Trinitarian Spirit Christology* (Eugene: Pickwick Publications, 2010), 231.

[2] Amos Yong, *Spirit-Word-Community: Theological Hermeneutics in Trinitarian Perspective* (England: Ashgate Publishing Limited, 2002), 8. Yet, it is often true that when we undertake such corrective shifts in our theological thinking, we are prone to over-corrections plunging us onto an error on the opposite end of the spectrum. Some cases of pneumatological priority have tended to move away from the exclusive and definitive nature of Christ's work toward a more nebulous inclusivism in locating the Spirit's activity in all of world history, including world religions.

some discussions on Spirit christology have not left the doctrine of Trinity unaffected.[3]

While present in the early theological engagements, the Spirit disappeared from modern discussions, especially from the discussions of the western church. The eastern churches still maintained a relative importance of the Spirit in their theological engagements. Speaking about the general Christian response to the Holy Spirit, James Forbes writes,

> many Christians are Holy Spirit-shy. For some, conversations about empowerment of the Spirit in one's ministry are occasions of anxiety and intimidation. Some preachers hesitate to speak of the Spirit in relationship to what they do. Others talk about the Spirit in traditional language of faith, but without personal meaning. Hence, many of the biblical provisions for Holy Spirit empowerment often are left unrealized like unclaimed packages or unopened letters.[4]

However, through the past several decades, there is a noticeable recovery from this loss. As Alister McGrath records, "the Holy Spirit has long been the Cinderella of the Trinity. The other two sisters may have gone to the theological ball; the Holy Spirit got left behind every time. But not now."[5] Since McGrath wrote these words, much has been written on the subject.[6] My effort is to conceive apologetics within a pneumatological framework by envisioning Spirit as a starting point for Christian ministry in general and for evangelism undergirded with apologetics in particular.

---

[3] The term, "Spirit christology" has not had a fixed, singular meaning. Habets identifies two models that have informed discussions surrounding Spirit christology. The *replacement model*, which replaces logos christology with Spirit christology, sees the Spirit as "the divine element in the incarnation" (Habets, *The Anointed Son,* 195.) and denies intrinsic divinity to the second person. Thus, the replacement model collapses Trinity into some form of binitarianims. Whereas, the *complementary model* seeks to use Spirit christology to complement Logos christology and thus remains faithful to orthodox commitment to trinitarian beliefs. For further discussions on the Spirit christology and Trinity, see Ralph Del Colle, *Christ and the Spirit: Spirit-Christology in Trinitarian Perspective* (New York: Oxford University Press, 1994); Habets, *The Anointed Son,* 188–227; Roger Haight, "The Case for Spirit Christology," *Theological Studies* 53 (1992), 257–287.

[4] James Forbes, *The Holy Spirit & Preaching* (Nashville: Abingdon Press, 1989), 21–22.

[5] Alister McGrath, *Christian Theology: An Introduction*, 5th edn. (Oxford: Wiley Blackwell, 2011), 227.

[6] For a detailed survey of various attempts of a Third Article theology, see Habets, *The Anointed Son*, 228–257.

MODERN SECULARITY AND THE DEMISE OF THE SPIRIT

The demise of the Spirit from the human realm can only be properly understood in correlation to the spirit of the age. A unique feature of modernity is the increased secularization of societies and a corresponding disappearance of (a sense of) transcendence. This is not only true of western societies, but is increasingly true of every society that has adopted secularism. The *Secular Age,* Charles Taylor argues, is characterized by an "exclusive humanism," which dispenses with the very idea of transcendence and thus with it, dispenses with the idea of God, the miraculous, and a divinely instituted moral order. "For the first time in history" Taylor argues, "a purely self-sufficient humanism came to be a widely available option. I mean by this a humanism accepting no final goals beyond human flourishing, nor any allegiance to anything else beyond this flourishing. Of no previous society was this true."[7]

What John Lennon sang in 1971: "Imagine there's no heaven. It's easy if you try. No hell below us, above us only sky"— has today become the norm and thus needs neither imagining nor trying. Rather, to imagine there is a heaven would require trying. On the reception of religious belief, or the lack thereof, within *a secular age,* James K.A. Smith elaborates saying,

> [t]he standard picture, we might say, sees religion as a sort of addendum to being human: *all* humans eat, sleep, breathe, have sex, wear clothes, are citizens of some nation, and engage in play. Then, in addition to that, *some* (perhaps even *many*) homo sapiens are 'religious': they are 'believers' who participate in religious rituals and practices, identify with religious communities, and hold religious beliefs. These beliefs and practices are generally taken to be tied to certain established traditions and institutions (Buddhism, Christianity, Islam, etc). Those who study 'believers' are often those without this extra-human supplement: they are 'just' human, that is, 'secular.' 'Believers,' to them, are kind of exotic; they have conspicuous growths, like two heads. From the perspective of the secular scientist, who lacks such growth (who has been healed of such lesions, as it were), this religious addendum is a curious supplement to being human—a kind of deformation.[8]

---

[7] Charles Taylor, *A Secular Age* (Massachusetts: Harvard University Press, 2007), 18.
[8] James K.A. Smith, "Secular Liturgies and the Prospects for a 'Post-Secular' Sociology of Religion" in Philip Gorski, et al. (eds), *The Post-Secular in Question: Religion in Contemporary Society* (New York: New York University Press, 2012), 166.

The secularist, therefore, zealously commits himself to the task of *exorcising* religious belief from the public spaces and discourses. Bowing before his modernist altar and committed to the enlightenment dogma of "pure reason," the secular *exorcist* commissions himself as the apostle to *disenchant* (to use Taylor's term) the world.

The spirit of *a secular age* cannot but greatly influence the Christian faith and theology. Exorcism of religious belief from a culture entails immeasurable losses, foremost of which is the demise of the self-effacing Spirit. The secularist dis-enchanting of the world of transcendence entails an expulsion of the Spirit where Christians turn into practical deists, subscribing to a belief that retains nothing more than some metaphysical notion of the ultimate reality, rather than a robust spiritual communion with God. The practical day-to-day lives are lived within the logic of immanence and within the naturalistic calculus.

In such a scenario, one's reading of the scriptures is trapped into accessing meanings that are the lowest common denominator picked up by the natural eye rather than an illumination by the Spirit. By way of over correction to the problem of *eisegesis*, where indiscriminate and often self-serving meanings were quickly attached to texts, we would now rather err on the side of caution and draw minimally out of the text. So, we have a problem where biblical interpretation almost looks as if it is an attempt to make sense to a naturalist rather than seeing them as life-giving words to the believer.

In short, the loss of the transcendence from a culture is maximally a loss of the Spirit. After all, unlike the Holy Spirit, the other two members of the Trinity have a visible trail—the Father, his created order (natural theology) and the Son his historical presence (theology of redemption). Whereas, the self-effacing Holy Spirit is neither seen nor known by the world (John 14:17) or by the church that succumbs to the spirit of the age. In short, the cultural influence of naturalism has left the church Spirit-impoverished.

Consequently, the Spirit has been absent from theological discussions until recently. The modern framework, which sought rational legitimation for knowledge purely within the logic of immanence, would not accommodate the "uncertainties" associated with the

Spirit. Apologetics as the twin sister of theology also understandably preoccupied herself with christological concerns, influenced by the modern rationalistic framework both in its content and method.

The rationalistic bias of modernity rejected what were earlier acceptable sources of knowledge as illegitimate, thus shifting the framework of apologetics towards propositional truths. Penner gives a telling critique of the modern apologetics and its implicit epistemological commitment, with which he finds something intrinsically problematic. However, I would locate modern apologetics within the framework of contextual theology, which ascribes to it relevance within a defined time frame and theological method. But Penner is right on target in analyzing that:

> [i]n the modern philosophical paradigm, then, reason forms what I will call the 'objective-universal-neutral complex' (OUNCE) . . . . So the move to propositions as the main bearers of Christian truths and revelation is important . . . because propositions are exactly the kinds of entities that must exist if one is to communicate and defend truths according to the demands of OUNCE.[9]

Within the modernist framework, apologetics reduces Christian faith to "a set of propositional asseverations that can be epistemically justified" rather than as "a set of practices—a way of life, a confession, etc."[10] Penner argues that such apologetics fail to see that modern "apologetic paradigm is *itself* a product of modernity."[11] In a sense, modern apologetics takes natural theology to its logical conclusion in that the metaphysical scaffoldings of the logico-semantic discourse become as fundamental as the doctrine itself. In a similar commentary, Hauerwas writes that "[t]he problem is not that kind of metaphysical testing but is, rather, when metaphysics becomes an attempt to secure the truth of Christian convictions in a manner that makes the content of those

---

[9] Myron Penner, *The End of Apologetics* (Grand Rapids, MI: Baker Academic, 2013), 32. Penner's target is the modernist commitments in the works of William Lane Craig, J.P. Moreland, and others. However, a modernist commitment seems to become explicit only from hindsight. That there are no good answers to bad questions is only evident when, in time, they are so recognized. It is still not evident on Penner's view as to what sort of realistic responses might have been given to modern critique of Christianity without such hindsight.

[10] Penner, *The End of Apologetics*, 42.

[11] Penner, *The End of Apologetics*, 43.

convictions secondary. Such a project, I fear, has been legitimated for some time in the name of natural theology."[12]

In short, the modern apologetic paradigm has to endorse the authority of the modern philosophical framework and the method of justification it frames to make apologetics valid. This has led to twisting the earlier theological reasoning to fit the modern agenda. Penner rightly points to the case of Thomas Aquinas's "Five Ways" which is often invoked as "natural theology without paying much attention to the theological (and what is the same to Thomas, philosophical) assumptions that underlie them—or making even a passing reference to the premodern context that informs Aquinas's thought."[13] Whereas, far from providing his arguments as standing on its own right, Aquinas believed, as Timothy Smith argues, that:

> [t]he reasoning upon the faith will typically but not exclusively involve the manifestation of that faith where reason cannot attain of its own accord. Revelation, however, provides the more certain and complete knowledge. The argument from authority never gives up its place to rational argument, though rational argument may be employed where the authority of revelation is retained ... The argument from authority, that is, from the authority of revelation, always reigns as the more certain and complete.[14]

Hauerwas argues that "the *Summa* must be read as a theological, not a philosophical, text."[15] This dismantles the burden of proof in the philosophical sense of justification and locates the *Five Ways* within a theological scheme. Aquinas's own position is telling in this regard:

> The truth about God such as reason could discover would only be known by a few, and that after a long time, and with the admixture of many errors. Whereas, man's whole salvation, which is in God, depends upon knowledge of the truth. Therefore, in order that the salvation of men might be brought about more fitly and more surely, it was necessary that they should be taught divine truths by divine revelation. It was therefore

---

[12] Stanley Hauerwas, *With the Grain of the Universe* (Grand Rapids, MI: Brazos Press, 2001), 37.

[13] Penner, *The End of Apologetics*, 43.

[14] Cited by Hauerwas, *With the Grain*, 30. Cf. Timothy L. Smith, "Thomas Aquinas's *De Deo*: Setting the Record Straight on His Theological Method," *Sapientia* 53/203 (1998), 135–136.

[15] See Hauerwas, *With the Grain*, 36.

necessary that, besides philosophical science built up by reason there should be a sacred science learned through revelation.[16]

Apologetics that seek to justify beliefs within a modernistic framework themselves end up serving those assumptions rather than the gospel. While the gospel needs to be made intelligible to people, the adoption of the rationalistic calculus tends to become syncretistic in defining meaning fundamentally within immanence. Thus, a believer is left with the choice to either justify her beliefs within the logic of immanence or forfeit them.

Adaptation of apologetics to fit the modern framework may then be understood as a contextual attempt within a certain historical and philosophical milieu that became syncretistic. Viewing modern apologetics as a form of contextualization thus helps us appreciate where it is helpful and critique where it is not.

STARTING WITH THE SPIRIT

Today, given where we are within the theological landscape, the question, "what happens if we intentionally begin our apologetics with the Spirit?" is unavoidable. Starting with the Spirit,[17] especially when it pertains to evangelism, missions or apologetics, seems fundamental within the Lukan account, which records the final words of Jesus to his disciples that commands them not to leave Jerusalem until they received the Holy Spirit. Although the command to go and make disciples carried great urgency, it was to be undertaken only after the reception of the Holy Spirit. Clearly, there was a functional purpose in Jesus' instruction. The disciples were to receive the Holy Spirit as had Jesus himself before beginning his ministry. This recognizable priority ascribed to the Spirit in mission legitimates a similar priority of the Spirit within theological methodology.

The Spirit priority also seems to follow the structure of function within the economic trinity. That is, while the trinitarian order follows the Father sending the Son to complete the work of redemption followed by

---

[16] Cited by Hauerwas, *With the Grain*, 30. Cf. Aquinas, *Summa Theologica*, 1.1.
[17] Habets records several theological initiatives that focused on the question: "What happens when we intentionally start the task of systematic theology with pneumatology?" See Habets, *The Anointed Son*, 230–231.

the sending of the Spirit to sanctify the church, human encounter seems to always require an inverse trinitarian order. It is the Spirit who testifies to the Lordship of Christ, for "no one can say, 'Jesus is Lord,' except by the Holy Spirit" (1Cor 12:3), and it is in Jesus in whom "all the fullness of the Deity lives in bodily form" (Col 2:9), that we see the face of the Father (John 14:9). Spirit is thus the epistemic agency as well as the starting point in turning the gospel into an intelligible account for the individual for any subsequent transformation. Given the self-effacing nature of the Spirit who points humans toward Christ, who in turn points us towards the Father, a Spirit priority inherently provides a *trinitarian mould* for theological thinking and practice.

However, wherever the enlightenment framework has governed the apologetic discourse, it had either been conceived within a rational and logico-semantic conceptual scheme to the exclusion of Spirit as the vehicle of truth, or it had naturalized the Spirit's activity within the rationalistic discourse. This not only requires us to restore to the Spirit the position due within the Godhead, but also recognize how the Spirit claims his position in terms of content and method in apologetics as a discipline. A Third Article theology brings this pivotal shift by properly distributing the economic activity of the second and third persons of the Trinity, facilitating a better understanding of God and his mission.

Spirit's Epistemic Mediation between God and Humans

A pneumatological explorationis not really about making the Holy Spirit an *object* of human inquiry; rather, it is, shall we say, a "circular" way of understanding the function of the Spirit revealed to us in the scriptures, which in turn is revealed by the Spirit. Spirit–revealed knowledge follows an internal method of justification, where, what the Spirit reveals is justified by the scriptures and what the scriptures reveal is justified by the Spirit. This *intra-ecclesial* calculus is inaccessible to the world, given that "[t]he world cannot accept him, because it neither sees him nor knows him. But you know him, for he lives with you and will be in you" (John 14:17). The world's inaccessibility of revelation entails that it also has no method of verifying a revelation and is thus bound to reject it.

However, if knowledge is justified true belief, a Spirit-revealed belief may still function as religious knowledge although the justification for such a belief is shared only within the body of Christ. That is, despite it being an *intra-ecclesial* exercise, given that there is a method of verification, Spirit revealed beliefs are to be legitimately considered *religious knowledge*.

As Habets writes, "[i]n the theological prolegomena the epistemological role of the Holy Spirit is the unique contribution a Third Article Theology may make. A key function of the Spirit is to mediate knowledge of God to human creatures through the incarnate Word. In so doing Christ and the Spirit mutually mediate one another."[18] This we find in John's record of Jesus' promise to intercede before the Father to send "another advocate…be with you forever" (John 14:16) and also that "when he, the Spirit of truth comes, he will guide you into all the truth" (John 16:13). This promise alone warrants a robust Spirit dimension to any Christian epistemology.

The beliefs we hold within our cognition and our relationship with God the Father through Jesus are both made possible only because of the mediation of the Holy Spirit. Although they are not separate functions, both the ontological and epistemological mediation remain distinct functions of the Spirit. Ontological mediation leads toward a life that dwells within Christ and the epistemological mediation leads one toward the possession of the true doctrine. Together, both being and thought, as the essence of Christian faith, obtain their validity through the witness of the Holy Spirit.

What does it mean to ascribe such mediation between humans and God to the Spirit? We may begin by considering the promise that the *Spirit will guide you into all the truth*. Guiding us into *all the truth* would encompass all realities pertaining to God, the world, and humanity. Clearly therefore, the Spirit is at work in delivering proper knowledge concerning nature, humans and God. However, given the claim in John 14:6, we could infer that the immediate meaning to the referent "all truth" is Jesus himself, who *is* the truth. Christ is the truth because in him "all the fullness of the Deity lives in bodily form" (Col 2:9). Since all truths with a small 't', including those concerning "things [that] were created: things

---

[18] Habets, *The Anointed Son*, 239–240.

in heaven and on earth, visible and invisible, whether thrones or powers or rulers or authorities—all things have been created through him and for him" (Col 1:16, Parenthesis added) are subsumed in Christ, the causal principle, they only have their significance derived from the Truth with *capital 'T'*. Therefore, while Christ, as the intercessor is the mediator to the Spirit, the Spirit who guides us into all truth is the mediator to Christ.

Yet, because the bodily dwelling of the deity entails a historical appearance, truth claims pertaining to the historical presence attain no small significance making it a necessary part of the true doctrine. To be guided into *all the truth* thus would include on the one hand, being led into Christ by abiding in Christ (John 15:4)—a spiritual communion, and on the other, being guided to the right knowledge of the nature and the realities pertaining to the being of God—the true doctrine.

SPIRIT AND THE POSSIBILITY OF DIRECT KNOWLEDGE

Given that we are bequeathed with a modern-rationalist epistemology and pedagogy, we may reasonably conclude that much remains to be understood as regards the epistemic role of the Spirit in mission and apologetics. In this scheme, religious beliefs are visualized as *objects out there* for our brains to cognitively process, for all knowledge, including religious knowledge, are processed and obtained as a consequence of cognitive and rational engagement. This would, generally speaking, preclude the Spirit's activity in human epistemic pursuits. And even where the Spirit's role is acknowledged, it is often as one who ennobles human rationality and thus is still conceived within a rationalistic framework.[19]

The role of reason in assessing truth claims leading to possible religious belief/knowledge is immediately acceptable to the children of modernity. But what remains outside the purview of the rationalist epistemology is the acceptability of immediate or direct knowledge as warranted beliefs.[20] This lack of reception of direct knowledge entails that

---

[19] The picture may not look very different in the contemporary times where emotional intelligence is seen as an equally important faculty for processing knowledge. Whether it is human rationality or human emotions, both remain within the logic of immanence if untouched by the Holy Spirit.

[20] This is generally the case except in the articulations of *basic beliefs* within reformed epistemology by Alvin Plantinga, Nicholas Wolterstorff, and others.

such passages as Romans 1:20 are interpreted *via* natural theology, which inadvertently ascribes a modern rationalist frame to the gospel. However, as Kelly James Clark argues, "[t]he crucial question is how knowledge of God is communicated through these phenomena. Does this text indicate that knowledge of God is communicated *directly* or *via an argument*?"[21] Of course, not every case of direct knowledge is mediated by the Spirit nor does the Spirit preclude the use of rationality to mediate knowledge. Yet, an epistemology that prioritizes the Spirit recovers the possibility of direct knowledge as viable.

Similarly, divine revelation becomes impossible precisely because the secular anthropology dispenses with the idea that humans possess a spirit or that they are spiritual beings. In short, it redefines all of life purely within the framework of immanence. "Human spirit" is morphed to take a restricted meaning as some kind of *collective human fortitude* that can be deployed in the face of struggle and human suffering. Thus, we may talk of a resilient human spirit in the face of a natural disaster; yet, absent from this view is a notion of humans as spiritual beings with a distinct spirit.

A Third Article theology reclaims the human spirit as a vehicle of knowing, which is unimaginable within a secular, naturalistic framework. As James D.G. Dunn writes,

> [t]he spirit of a person is that aspect through which God most immediately encounters him (Rom 8:16; Gal 6:18; Phil 4:23; 2 Tim 4:22; Phlm 25; Heb 4:12; Jas 4:5), that dimension of the whole person wherein and whereby he is most immediately open and responsive to God (Matt 5:3; Luke 1:47; Rom 1:9; 1Pet 3:4), that area of human awareness most sensitive to matters of the spiritual realm (Mark 2:8; 8:12; John 11:33; 13:21; Acts 17:16; 2 Cor 2:13; 7:13).[22]

Epistemic mediation of the Holy Spirit may be understood only by recovering a biblical anthropology that includes a robust idea of the human spirit.

---

[21] James Kelly Clark, *Return to Reason* (Grand Rapids, MI: William B. Eerdmans, 1990), 49.

[22] James D.G. Dunn, *The Christ and the Spirit* (Grand Rapids, MI: William B. Eerdmans, 1998), 3-4.

Conversely, a re-assessment of our knowledge formation could indicate that the status ascribed to human rationality as the vehicle for truth is overrated. Martin Heidegger explicates how we construct our knowledge of the world in general, which I believe is also helpful to understand how we construe religious knowledge. "In contrast (to Husserl)," James K.A. Smith argues, "Heidegger emphasized (1) that our relation to the world is always already a *construal*, a take on the world; and, more importantly for us here, (2) that such construal happened at a precognitive level." While the former entails that to be in the world is to interpret the world, the latter "emphasizes that such construal and interpretation happen on an order or register that is not cognitive or intellectual—a register that is not even, in a way, '*conscious*'. Thus Heidegger can suggest that the world is construed on the order of 'mood.'"[23]

This moodedness, which Heidegger calls "attunement" is a precognitive understanding of the world, where, "Dasein cannot know anything of the sort because the possibilities of disclosure which belong to cognition reach far too short a way compared with the primordial disclosure belonging to moods."[24] Accordingly, "mood discloses the world for us in a primordial way; it effects a construal of the world *before* our cognitive, intellectual 'knowledge' of the world comes into play. And we do an injustice to this 'understanding' that is effected by mood/attunement if we require it to answer to our more familiar criteria for 'knowledge.'"[25] As Smith elaborates, "it's not just that mood is a kind of immature, prior disclosure that needs to be articulated and then superseded by cognitive disclosure; rather, such mooded disclosure is both primordial and irreducible. The heart, we might say, has reasons of which reason knows nothing."[26] Smith further illustrates how Heidegger's intuition about being attuned in a pre-cognitive sense is affirmed by contemporary studies in cognitive science.[27] It may thus be concluded that there is much to be explored about the exact nature of knowledge formation in the

---

[23] Smith, "Secular Liturgies and the Prospects," 169.
[24] Martin Heidegger, *Being and Time*, John Macquarrie and Edward Robinson (trans.) (Oxford: Basil Blackwell, 1978), §29, 173, cited by Smith, "Secular Liturgies and the Prospects," 170.
[25] Smith, "Secular Liturgies and the Prospects," 170.
[26] Smith, "Secular Liturgies and the Prospects," 170.
[27] Smith, "Secular Liturgies and the Prospects," 169–172.

human mind. Yet, it seems to me, that Heidegger provides a helpful grid to envisage knowledge formation that is direct and pre-cognitive.

Spirit as the Provider of Truth and the Condition for Truth

Moving specifically to Christian religious knowledge, a Kierkegaardian pneumatology would identify the Spirit not only as the provider of *truth* but also as the provider of the *condition* to receive truth when we encounter it.[28] The reasoning is that truth still remains inaccessible to anyone who does not have the right condition to receive it. Consequently, the Spirit is conceived as the agent who brings the human cognitive faculty to a position where the truth of the gospel becomes intelligible by aligning human affections, cognition, and volition in a manner that is able to receive truth.

Notwithstanding this, a Heideggerian conception of knowing as "the order of mood" could conceive of the Spirit as the direct mediator without necessarily involving a rationalistic process of making the gospel intelligible. Rather, the truth of the gospel is suddenly impressed upon the individual and consequently the gospel becomes intelligible and rational. As Bruce Marshall says, the Spirit does not "persuade by adding something to the totality of belief, by giving us reasons or evidence we do not already have, but by eliciting our assent to a way of structuring the whole."[29]

For one to be led into all the truth, the Spirit's function in human lives seems uniquely structured to act in particularized ways in each individual. In this sense, the Spirit, who knows our deepest thoughts, intentions and affections, functions as a personalized trainer or a resident counselor by participating alongside each individual in the process of conversion and transformation. Unlike God the Father who functions as the creator of the whole universe and "achieves an end which is universal" and God the Son who redeems through Word becoming flesh and "works

---

[28] For further discussion on this, see my *Truth and Subjectivity, Faith and History: Kierkegaard's Insights for Christian Faith.*

[29] Bruce D. Marshall, *Trinity and Truth* (Cambridge: Cambridge University Press, 2004), 204.

a work which is for the benefit of the entire mass of humankind and for the cosmic order," McIntyre writes, "[i]n the Holy Spirit, however, God relates himself to the intricacies of this person's sin and salvation, and his or her responsibilities to God and neighbor, as they occur within the created natural order and in human history."[30]

The personalized nature of the Spirit's work affirms each individual, one's physical and psychological condition and one's learning style. The Spirit's pedagogical method is tailored to each individual. As McIntyre writes,

> His [Spirit's] care, his oversight, his will, his demands particularize themselves in the most precise fashion, and make themselves relevant to the multiplicities and idiosyncrasies of his or her being, so that they, as persons, become aware that it is particularly their redemption which is God's ultimate aim, and not that of the whole human race or all humankind everywhere and in all times.[31]

Thus, the Spirit's revelation to humans is by way of searching and examining the human soul—human affections and human desires (Ps 139:23-24; 1 Cor 2:10-11). Pivotal to this assumption is the biblical pedagogical framework that seeks to transform rather than merely inform the individual. Here, the assurance to "guide you into all the truth" (John 16:13) is combined with the promise of true freedom as "where the Spirit of the Lord is, there is freedom" (2 Cor 3:17). Thus, there is a strong sense of *character/spiritual formation* associated with the provision of truth.

The Spirit, through this sort of examination, enables an audit of the human soul as to where we stand before God. This results in recognition of the human need for forgiveness and salvation. But, beyond the function of revealing to us who we really are, the Spirit performs another pivotal function of being the comforter. Without his comfort, we would be crushed beneath our sense of inadequacy and sinfulness. In short, it is the same character that we see in Christ, who is full of *grace and truth* that we also see in the Spirit of truth, the comforter. The twin qualities of grace and truth, held together, show us both our wretchedness and our position as God's children by walking the journey with us toward perfection.

---

[30] John McIntyre, *The Shape of Pneumatology: Studies in the Doctrine of the Holy Spirit* (Edinburgh: T&T Clark, 1997), 173.

[31] McIntyre, *The Shape of Pneumatology*, 174, (Parenthesis added).

Spirit Revelation: Recollection and Repetition

In addition to teaching, John (14:25) records that the Holy Spirit delivers the truth *via recollection/memory/remembrance*. What does recollection mediated by the Spirit entail? Biblical recollection is facilitated by at least two modes: the **first** type of recollection is associated with intentional *repetition* of practices and disciplines. Any act of repetition in itself cannot be construed as Spirit mediated. Yet, spiritual disciplines developed under the guidance of the Holy Spirit are a necessary part of being guided *into all the truth*. This is the reason that repetition of disciplines is viewed as the epitome of religious commitment.

Thus, the repetitive practice of the Lord's Table, in addition, to defining a believer's identity in Christ is also a means of recollecting Christ's death for the present in such a manner that the present is altered because of this recollection. Constantin Constantius (a pseudonym deployed by Kierkegaard) in *Repetition*, argues, "[r]epetition and recollection are the same movement, except in opposite directions, for what is recollected has been, is repeated backward, whereas genuine repetition is recollected forward."[32] Thus, both recollection and repetition are at once practiced in the historical memorizing, where the cross is *repeated* in the eucharistic *recollection* as the cross is *recollected* in the eucharistic *repetition*. Both recollection and repetition is for the sake of the present—to live as Christ did, and for the future—to anticipate his return. Both recollection and repetition are combined in the eucharistic celebration in the present as it looks to the past as well as to the future.

A **second** type of recollection is a Spirit-inspired event where the Spirit "will teach you all things and will remind you of everything I have said to you" (John 14:26). This is affirmed by John as he recalls Zechariah 9:9 as referring to Jesus' triumphal entry. He writes that, "[a]t first his disciples did not understand all this. Only after Jesus was glorified did they *recollect*[33] that these things had been written about him and that these things had been done to him" (John 12:16). While the fact that the meaning was unveiled only after the glorification of Jesus, it may be

---

[32] Søren Kierkegaard, *Fear and Trembling and Repetition*, Howard and Edna Hong (eds and trans.) (Princeton: Princeton University Press, 1983), 131.

[33] The term "recollect," in italics, is the author's rendering in place of the original word "realize."

understood in conjunction with John 14:26, which locates the agency of meaning-recovery to the Holy Spirit who brings to their memory both the content and meaning of his teaching.

Similarly, Jesus uses parables that deliberately veiled meaning from those who were not to receive the Spirit (Matt 13:34; Mark 4:34). John repeats this truth again (10:6) when he says, "Jesus used this figure (the parable of the good shepherd) of speech, but the Pharisees did not understand what he was telling them."As the perplexed disciples wondered why Jesus spoke to them in parables, Jesus answers, "[b]ecause the knowledge of the secrets of the kingdom of heaven has been given to you, but not to them…. This is why I speak to them in parables: 'Though seeing, they do not see; though hearing, they do not hear or understand" (Matt 13:10–13).[34]

The second kind of recollection is clearly used to denote that divine truths, even those pertaining to what we've heard or read, continue to be veiled from our cognition unless the Spirit brings to remembrance and unravels the meaning of Jesus' teaching. Human opaqueness to the "secrets of the kingdom of heaven" is not something that is introduced at the moment of narrating the parable, but is a pre-condition where, "people's heart has become calloused; they hardly hear with their ears, and they have closed their eyes. Otherwise they might see with their eyes, hear with their ears, understand with their hearts and turn, and I would heal them" (Matt 13:15). In short, the secrets of the kingdom of heaven are knowable only by the mediation of the Spirit.

TOWARD A CONSTRUCTIVE SPIRIT-SHAPED APOLOGETICS

If apologetics has often been found trapped in the very method of the ideology that it seeks to respond to, prioritizing the Spirit can function as an antidote. If in a secular age the loss of transcendence were maximally the loss of the Spirit, then an intentional priority of the Spirit would also maximally help recover what is lost as a result of secularity. This reversal starts by an intentional reinstating of that which is lost. Consequently, a theological and practical integration of the Holy Spirit in the day-to-day affairs of the mundane and secular life would recover the spiritual,

---

[34] Also see Mark 4:10-13; Luke 9:44-45.

transcendental, and an everyday integration of the divine within the mundane. By reclaiming the Spirit's role within the mundane life, Christians would now "re-enchant" the world from within the purview of the Pentecost that changes everything in the world.

Apologetics that is Spirit-shaped follows from the very nature of the Spirit-filled Christ. Christ, as is revealed in the scriptures, is always within the mediating presence of the Holy Spirit. Jesus' birth is instanced by the trinitarian presence, with the Father sending the Son and a birth caused by the overshadowing presence of the Spirit upon Mary. At his baptism, we notice the trinitarian presence again—the testimony of the Father and resting of the Spirit upon Jesus, from which time the Spirit's presence manifestly remained (John 1:32–33) as the empowerment for his prophetic ministry.[35] Consequently, a Spirit-shaped apologetics is fundamentally trinitarian.

Ontologically, trinitarian mutual co-existence is understood in terms of perichoresis—a relationship of mutual indwelling[36] where each member of the Trinity is always indwelling the other two. Understood as the bond of love—the go-between God, the Holy Spirit, shapes both the apologist and apologetics where truth and love are held in balance. For the apologist, this provides a blueprint for a ministry that emanates from love, rather than morph into a debate machine, created for the destruction of the opponent.

Functionally, the co-activity of the members of the Trinity provides an important blueprint for the practice of apologetics. Each member is present in the work of the other members of the Trinity. This presence is not merely a presence of solidarity but one of functional unity. John McIntyre, in his *Shape of Pneumatology*, provides a useful way to understand the function of each member of the Trinity as co-activity with

---

[35] Thiselton writes, "The saying of R. Aha (Leviticus Rabbah 15:2) is often cited: 'The Holy Spirit, who rests on the prophets, rests on them only by measure.' He adds that the immeasurable gift of the Spirit to Jesus 'corresponds to the perfection of the revelation through him'." Anthony C. Thiselton, *The Holy Spirit — in Biblical Teaching, Through the Centuries, and Today* (Grand Rapids, MI: William B. Eerdmans, 2013), 138.

[36] John 17:21, "That all of them may be one, Father, just as you are in me and I am in you. May they also be in us so that the world may believe that you have sent me."

other members of the Trinity, yet as terminatively completed by one of the members. He writes,

> Thus the creation of the world is the work of the whole Trinity, with the fiat of the Father, the creation being 'by the Word' and the Spirit as a brooding presence, but it terminates or has its completion through the Father. In the case of the incarnation, it is a work common to the whole of the Trinity, having its source in the will of the Father, with the Holy Spirit appearing at the conception, and through the life, death and resurrection of Jesus Christ, but in its goal and ultimate issue it is the work of the Son. The presence of God in believers, in the Church, in history and in the world is the work of the entire Trinity, but in its implementation it is fulfilled by the Spirit.[37]

Consequently, one does not need to labor to see how Christian apologists ought to function not as independent, lone-rangers, but as a team characterized by togetherness and functional oneness.

This further lends itself to the affirmation of a relational dimension to apologetics. Rather than singularly target an idea or a question, a Spirit-guided relational approach would prioritize the person behind the question along with his/her commitments to written or unwritten liturgies. Within this calculus, human life is captured within the ebb and flow of familial, social and political realities, which are intermixed with creedal and liturgical faith life. After all, as Forbes argues, "[t]he anointing of Jesus cannot be separated from his nurture in his family and in his faith community."[38]

A Spirit-shaped apologetics flows out of the communion of the Spirit emphasized in Ephesians 2:22 and 2 Corinthians 13:14, which is fundamentally relational. This *communion of the Holy Spirit*, oft-used in Christian benediction, could mean a "communion with the Holy Spirit" or fellowship of unity that exists among Christians or "that the communion which exists among the Christians *is* the Holy Spirit."[39] A Spirit-shaped apologetics thus functions relationally *as* an activity of the Spirit and under the *direction* and as an *extension* of the communion of the Spirit.

---

[37] McIntyre, *The Shape of Pneumatology*, 82.
[38] Forbes, *The Holy Spirit & Preaching*, 31.
[39] McIntyre, *The Shape of Pneumatology*, 183-184.

A Spirit-shaped apologetics also affirms a soteriology in which it is the same Spirit, which caused the birth of Jesus that causes the re-birth of an individual.[40] The Pauline expressions of the new-life in Christ or being clothed with Christ are primarily ascribed to the Spirit's indwelling presence and life in the Spirit. It is in this "new life" that a believer shares the likeness of Christ. The apologetic task is fundamentally redrawn in the light of the language of *life and death*, where the goal is to draw people from death to life rather than merely rearrange the cognitive pieces of data in their brain. The apologetic task thus stems from a position of total dependency on the work of the Holy Spirit. Acknowledging the epistemic role of the Spirit in human conversion and transformation has the potential to reshape our evangelistic and apologetic efforts in terms of total Spirit-dependence.

A Logo-centric apologetics that preserves a propositional shape to "truth" tends to retain logos as logos and fails to fully acknowledge the incarnation both that of the Christ and of the Spirit. As Habets writes, "Scripture contains truth statements but not the Truth, which is exclusively the being and act of God himself. Theological concepts, including Scripture, point beyond the statements themselves to the Truth and do so through levels of cognition: the level of experience, the theological level, and the meta-scientific level."[41]

Finally, a Spirit-shaped apologetics actualizes both the objective and subjective ways of human knowing. While the Christian faith demands affirmation of the objective fact of incarnation and the truth of the scriptures, it also at the same time, demands a subjective and personal assent to a personal God. The (objective) reality of Christian beliefs becomes personal (subjective) beliefs when the Holy Spirit leads an individual into truth. "In the moment of faith," as Mark C. Taylor using Kierkegaardian calculus points, "the sinner (the temporal self) is saved (becomes eternal). Faith is, thus, the inverse image of the Incarnation. In the incarnation the Eternal becomes temporal but remains eternal; in the moment of faith, the sinner realizes the possibility of eternal blessed-

---

[40] Forbes, *The Holy Spirit & Preaching*, 30.
[41] Habets, *The Anointed Son*, 239.

ness (immortality), but remains temporal."[42] A Spirit-shaped apologetics uniquely caters to both the objective and subjective aspects of Christian faith.

In conclusion, we may state that a Third Article apologetics is robustly trinitarian. In bringing the focus upon the Holy Spirit, it essentially recaptures the whole of Trinity rather than remain merely christologically focused. A Third Article apologetics also affirms a more biblically rooted epistemology by attributing to the Holy Spirit his rightful epistemic role as the Spirit of truth who mediates humankind to God and God to humankind. It also dismantles every human criterion of validation—be it human rationality or human volition—leaving the sole authority of justifying belief primarily as a function of the Spirit. While it does not make philosophical justification entirely redundant, it nevertheless makes it subservient to the function of the Holy Spirit.

---

[42] Mark C. Taylor, *Kierkegaard's Pseudonymous Authorship: A Study of Time and the Self* (Princeton: Princeton University Press, 1975), 10.

12

HOLY SPIRIT AND CHRISTIAN MISSION IN A PLURALISTIC CONTEXT

Paul Swarup*

Christian mission in India has always been done in a pluralistic context of many faiths, cultures, languages and religious practices. The question that we are looking at is how the Holy Spirit enables Christian mission to be done in this kind of a context. Once we have understood the context, then we need to explore a relevant missions practice from an evangelical charismatic foundation. The work of the Holy Spirit is most critical in any mission context. Mission always needs to be trinitarian: *missio Dei*, *missio Christi*, and *missio Spiritūs Sancti*. Once we understand the triune God at work in missions, then we will be able to establish a relevant missions practice for our context. This paper looks at three main sections: The first section looks at the current context for doing missions; the second section looks at two specific challenges particularly with regard to our theology

---

* **Paul Swarup**, PhD, is the Presbyter in Charge of the Cathedral Church of the Redemption, New Delhi. He is a member of the fifteen member international team of translators for the NIV called the Committee on Bible Translation (CBT). He is also one of the Old Testament editors of the recently released *South Asia Bible Commentary* and had written the commentary on Jeremiah, Lamentations, Proverbs and co-authored Exodus in that volume. He holds a PhD in OT Theology/Dead Sea Scrolls from the University of Cambridge, UK.

and missions; and the final section looks at the role of the Holy Spirit for doing missions in a pluralistic context.

THE PLURALISTIC CONTEXT OF MISSION IN INDIA

India is a multi-cultural, multi-religious, multi-ethnic nation. This variety creates a beautiful tapestry of bright colours and combinations. The *adivasi* people such as the Munda, the Ho, the Santal, the Khuruk, and others have, since pre-historic times, practiced *Sarna*, their indigenous religion. Later several religions, particularly Hinduism, Jainism and Sikhism, originated here. Others like vedic religion and classical Buddhism gradually became extinct and whatever remained of them was assimilated into Hinduism.

Christianity has been in India from the first century AD onwards with the coming of St. Thomas in AD 52. In this sense, it is the oldest minority religion in India. Islam has also been in India from the seventh century AD onwards. The firmness of their presence is evident from the sacred places of their traditions to which adherents of all faiths and no faiths are welcome.

According to official statistics, a vast majority of the billion plus Indians are Hindus (80 per cent) followed by Muslims (14 per cent), Christians (2.3 per cent), and Sikhs (1.95 per cent).[1] However these statistics are contested by the *Sarna* followers in the *adivasi* belt who want to remain distinct from Hindus. Moreover, India has, following Indonesia, the second largest Muslim population in the world. People are faced with such a mix of religions and the worldviews associated with them that it is almost impossible to hold such a society together. People also very often abuse religion to polarise and gain votes.

The different faith groups face the challenges of how to approach the other, whether for dialogue or mission, in confrontation or indifference, or with coercion, allurement, or threat. Religious pluralism is also a challenge for contemporary society. How can people of different faiths co-exist in harmony? How can the festivals and holy days of each faith tradition be held and kept? Another challenge is inter-religious marriage

---

[1] censusindia.gov.in/Census_And_You/religion.aspx (accessed 13 October 2016).

which is viewed with suspicion through terms like, "Love *Jihad*" and "*Bahu Bachao*."

THE CURRENT SITUATION

One of the most important areas to address in the current context is the caste system. Indian culture with all its diversity is marked by the cultural practice of caste. In this context, one of the agendas for Christian mission has been set significantly by two people, namely Jyoti Rao Phule and B.R. Ambedkar. The exploitation of *dalit* women, men, and children is evident every day in our newspapers. Some missionaries addressed both the immediate challenges like *Sati* and the practice of untouchability in the caste system.

While Jyoti Rao Phule and B.R. Ambedkar set the agenda for long term reform with regard to the caste system, many notable names can be brought to mind for having addressed immediate issues. For instance, Pandita Ramabai addressed the situation of subordination both of women by men and of India by the British, and Bishop V. Samuel Azariah addressed the problem of the subordinated Indian Church. Raj Kumari Amrit Kaur addressed the context of independence, and Fr. C.F. Andrews raised his voice against indentured Indian labourers. Verghese Kurian dedicated his entire professional life to empower Indian farmers through co-operatives. He helped to lay the foundation of democratic enterprises at the grass roots and showed the way to ensure economic justice with people's participation. He believed that by placing technology and professional management in the hands of the farmers, the standard of living of millions of our poor people can be improved.[2] Likewise, Mother Teresa addressed the needs of the poor who were dying on the streets of Kolkata with no one to care for them.

We must remember that it was in the context of addressing the immediate challenges of backwardness, illiteracy, famines, lack of health care, and poverty that the missionaries started some of the world-renowned institutions for higher education like St. Stephen's College in Delhi, St. Xavier's College and Wilson College in Mumbai, and Loyola

---

[2] http://www.amuldairy.com/index.php/about-us/2013-04-10-04-22-16/dr-kurien (accessed 26 September 2016).

College and Madras Christian College in Chennai and Christian medical colleges in Vellore and Ludhiana to address issues of health care. The Allahabad Agriculture College was established to address the problem of mass starvation due to bad cultivation practices. All these examples show that missionaries in the past tended to address immediate issues but failed to engage with the more long term and deep rooted issues of caste and social injustice.

The Caste System

The caste system has been the bane of Indian society. For instance, the fierce persecution in Kandhamal is rooted in the sanskritisation of *adivasi* tribes who began to treat the tribals who converted to Christianity as menials. The resistance of the tribal Christians who exerted their human dignity led to envy in the dominant tribe. Missions addressed the problems of the victims, but nobody dealt with the root cause which was the caste system. Ambedkar strongly emphasised the point that sanskritisation (a term later coined by M.N. Srinivas, a renowned sociologist[3]) established society on the system of caste. He described caste as an unjust social system which is marked by graded inequality, fixity of occupation, and fixation by birth.[4]

The Hindu religion organises society into four tiers—*Brahman, Kshatrya, Vaishya,* and *Shudra*—in a descending order of purity. The Brahman priests are the purest and most superior, whereas the *Shudras* are the service class for all the other castes. The Brahman language Sanskrit was considered to be the purest and superior to all other dialects like Prakrit and Pali. Speaking about the Hindu social order, Ambedkar says,

> Does the Hindu social order recognise equality? The answer must be in the negative. That men are born equal is a doctrine which is repugnant to the Hindu social order. In the spiritual sense it treats the doctrine as false. According to the Hindu social order though it is true that men are the children of Prajapati the Creator of the Universe, they are not equal on that account. For, they were created from the different parts

---

[3] https://en.wikipedia.org/wiki/Sanskritisation (accessed 26 September 2016).
[4] Hari Narake (ed), *B.R. Dr. Babasaheb Ambedkar Writings and Speeches,* vol. 3, 2nd edn., reprint (New Delhi: Ministry of Social Justice & Empowerment, Government of India, 2014), 111-113. https://www.mea.gov.in/Images/attach/amb/Volume_03.pdf (accessed 9 October 2016).

of the body of Prajapati. The Brahmins were created from the mouth, the Kshatriyas from the arms, the Vaishyas from his thighs and Shudras from his feet. The limbs from which they were created being of unequal value the men thus created are as unequal.[5]

The system was re-enforced by Manu who wrote *Manu Smriti*, one of the religious law codes of the majority community in India. The problem with the law code is that it reinforces social inequality by regulating marriage and penal loss on the basis of caste system. Take for example the punishment of offences as laid down by Manu for defamation: VIII.267. "A soldier, defaming a priest, shall be fined a hundred *panas*; merchant thus offending, a hundred and fifty, or two hundred; but for such an offence a mechanic or servile man shall be whipped."[6]

Every alternate system or religion which challenges the caste system with its purity system divide is usually persecuted. Their deities and religious symbols tend to be dishonoured, and what they cherished as sacred is frequently desecrated. Such acts are symbolic of discrediting and subjugating particularly the egalitarian religions. It is in this light we need to understand that burning of churches like St. Sebastian's church in Delhi or the desecration of another church in Ghaziabad. So the first major issue for missions practice in India's pluralistic context is the issue of caste.

Challenge to Secularism

Another key issue that needs to be understood as part of the context of mission is the challenge to secularism. The Oxford dictionary defines secularism as "the principle of separation of the state from religious institutions." The challenge we need to address as a nation is the issue of maintaining the secular fabric of India in spite of all the efforts by fundamentalist hardliners to make India into a homogeneous unit of Hindus. The word "secular" is being questioned and challenged. In the parliamentary debate on 26 November 2015, the Home Minister, Rajnath Singh said that because of the rampant misuse of the word secularism, there have been instances of tension in the society. He also said that

---

[5] Narake, *B.R. Dr. Babasaheb Ambedkar Writings and Speeches*, 106.
[6] Narake, *B.R. Dr. Babasaheb Ambedkar Writings and Speeches*, 108.

B.R. Ambedkar never thought of putting the term "secularism" in the constitution as it was inbuilt in the system. The words were incorporated through an amendment in 1976.[7] Responding to this, Sitaram Yechury of Communist Party of India-Marxist (CPI[M]) told reporters, "Rajnath Singh has made it clear that secularism and socialism, which were added (to the Preamble) as an amendment, should be removed. And then they (Bharatiya Janata Party [BJP]) have to prepare ground to establish Rashtriya Swayamsevak Sangh (RSS) Hindu Rashtra (nation) in place of the constitutional system. This is their main aim."[8]

ANTI-CONVERSION LAWS

Another key issue Christian missions have to address is that of conversion. In India today, "conversion" has been a hot point of friction between the many religious communities. Bharatiya Janta Party is now ruling in the centre, and many BJP ruled states like Gujarat, Orissa, Madhya Pradesh, Chhattisgarh, and Himachal Pradesh, have passed laws against forcible conversions and have even gone to the extent of defining force as that which "includes show of force or a threat of injury of any kind, including threat of divine displeasure or social ex-communication."[9] The state governments even want to have a monopoly over God! They try to gag God, and even he does not have a choice over what he can be displeased about!

The irony of this bill is that it is coined as the Freedom of Religion Bill but it fails to address the caste divisions within the Brahmanical system that ostracises the poorest of the poor and socially excommunicates them. The *Sangh Parivar*[10] has been carrying out the *Ghar Wapsi* (*Returning home*) programme in parts of India. They represent the Hindu nationalist movement. It includes the RSS and several dozen affiliated organisations,

---

[7] See Parliamentary Debates Text for Rajnath Singh's view, 50-54, http://164.100.47.132/debatestext/16/VI/2611.pdf (accessed 29 October 2016).

[8] http://indiatoday.intoday.in/story/bjp-wants-to-establish-hindu-rashtra-oppn/1/532421.html (accessed 3 November 2016).

[9] South Asia Human Rights Documentation Centre, "Anti-Conversion Laws: Challenges to Secularism and Fundamental Rights," *Economic and Political Weekly*, 43/2 (12-18 January, 2008), 64.

[10] The "Sangh Parivar" refers to the family of Hindu nationalist organizations which have been started by members of the Rashtriya Swayamsevak Sangh (RSS) or drew inspiration from its ideology.

whose members' expressed opinions have been diverse over a range of topics. *Ghar Wapsi* has been their way of forcing people to reconvert back to Hinduism under threat or force. Last year, the Rajya Sabha was seized with the matter of forced conversions and the *Ghar Wapsi* programme. The Catholic Bishops Conference of India (CBCI) in its press release said,

> [t]he Ghar Wapsi programmes, the saffronisation of education and culture, and the demands for a Hindu Rashtra are again posing challenges to the secular ethos of our beloved country. Conversions of a religious nature are an exercise of one's free will and one's constitutional/ fundamental rights and freedom of conscience and of religion. Ghar Wapsi is a political process, carried out by the powerful exponents of religious nationalism – much against the principle of Secularism. It does not even have the legitimacy of freedom of political expression.[11]

However the *Ghar Wapsi* programme is one of the ploys used to make sure that the oppressed have no alternatives or choices left for them. In an article about *Ghar Wapsi*, Kancha Ilaiah states,

> [t]he real intention of the RSS is to terrorize the Dalits, OBCs who have been converting into several evangelical Christian denominations who do not have any centralized structure. After B.R. Ambedkar opened the lock of conversion at Nagpur in 1956 to Buddhism, the right to convert to a religion that they find useful or beneficial has become a respectable, spiritual and democratic right. Though Ambedkar expected Dalits to convert to Buddhism, most of them, across the country preferred Christianity. Hardly any tribal or OBC converted to Buddhism. This worries the RSS most.
>
> The most significant issue is that the historical untouchables and oppressed OBCs found a spiritual home in Christianity. The only thing they lost after conversion was the right to reservation.[12]

The effort to bring a pan-India anti-conversion bill has to be opposed at every forum and particularly in Parliament as it would impinge on our fundamental rights. However, the government may be able to force such a bill through sheer majority, in which case we may

---

[11] CBCI Press release, 21 January, 2015, "Government urged to uphold the secular nature of India," http://cbci.in/FullNews.aspx?ID=1495 (accessed 5 October, 2016).

[12] Kancha Ilaiah, "No Ghar So No Wapsi," http://www.deccanchronicle.com/150105/commentary-op-ed/article/no-ghar-so-no-ghar-wapsi (accessed 27 October, 2016).

have to challenge them in the court in order to retain the secular fabric of our country.

Constitutional Provision for the Freedom of Religion

What does the constitution of India say about the Freedom of Religion? Article 15 says: "*The State shall not discriminate against any citizen on grounds only of religion, race, caste, sex, place of birth or any of them.*"[13] Article 25 of the constitution of India defining the right to Freedom of Religion states in clause 1: "*subject to public order morality and health and to other provision of this part,* **all persons are equally entitled to freedom of conscience** *and the* **right freely to profess, practice and propagate religion.**"[14]

Freedom of religion is enshrined in our constitution, and it is the fundamental duty of governments and individual citizens to protect it. Every individual in a democratic country like ours should have the right to choose our faith and practice it free of persecution and discrimination. In the current situation, we see a denial of the rights of conscience and choice of religions to people of scheduled caste background, especially *dalits*. They lose their reservations and benefits of scheduled castes or *dalits* the moment they become Christians. Changing their religion does not alter the socio-economics of the people who do so. But they lose their privileges the moment they become Christians. They are disadvantaged because of their faith.

So, as we look at the background in which Indian missions happens we note that the first and foremost context is that of the caste system. How does Indian missions work through this maze without itself being subsumed by it as in the past? The second area of concern in the present context is the challenge to secularism. The idea of separating the state from religious institutions seems to be anathema for the present regime and they would rather have the religious institutions running the state and forming a Hindu *Rashtra*. A third issue, we noted is the growing number of anti-conversion laws euphemistically called as "Freedom of Religion Bills." These are being implemented in numerous states with an effort to curb any conversion even if it is genuine transformation of the

---

[13] *Constitution of India*, Article 15, 7.
[14] *Constitution of India*, Article 25 (1), 13, (Bold added).

heart. The right to choose a religion of one's choice seems to be slowly disappearing. The constitutional provision is that all have the right to freedom of conscience and to profess, practice and propagate religion in India. Even though this is enshrined in the constitution, it is slowly being eroded.

In the following part we will address two specific challenges in doing missions in such a context. Our theology and our mission are both challenged and therefore we will be looking at the challenges on these two fronts.

CHALLENGES TO MISSION

In our context today, we are challenged in two specific areas. The first is in our theology when we talk about the uniqueness of Christ and his claims. How can Jesus be the only way to God? Do not all roads lead to the same God? Most Hindus would be quite comfortable to see Jesus as one of the gods and as one of the ways. The second challenge is to our missional activities. Any work done to uplift the poor is seen suspiciously as though the sole intent of such activity is conversion or soul winning. This challenge particularly came to light in the killing of Graham Staines, a medical doctor, and his young sons who were burned alive. Staines was involved in a healing ministry for leprosy patients and was also a practicing Christian.

CHALLENGE TO THEOLOGY: THE EXCLUSIVE CLAIMS OF CHRIST

Christians in India have been challenged about their dogmatic and exclusive claims about Jesus Christ. Most Indians from other faiths would be more than happy to accept Jesus as one of the gods but not as the only God, or as the only way to receive salvation. Once while I was conducting a Bible study for students from other faiths, they told me that they were quite happy to receive Christ as their Saviour, but their immediate question was, "Does that mean I have to leave my faith and all that I have grown up with all these years? Will the Spirit of God reside in me or leave me if I do keep my faith as well?" The only answer that I could give them was that the Holy Spirit is the Spirit of truth and that God's Spirit would lead them into all truth as long as they earnestly sought the truth.

In a pluralistic society like India, this is the lynchpin: *How does one not compromise on the exclusive claims of Jesus Christ, but at the same time be involved with others in a common programme for establishing justice, peace, and the transformation of lives?* The accusation of the world is that whatever programmes we are involved in, all are covert operations to convert people from one religion to another. Also, the efforts of the hardliners are to portray Christianity as a western religion and that Christians are subject to Rome and work as anti-nationals. Moreover, the RSS, the parent body of the BJP, the ruling party in India, has been calling for "Indianising" the church in India. Because of their ideologies and activities, many would consider them to be right-wing parties with strong fascist tendencies. However, in the current situation, the so-called fringe elements have come to centre stage. Sudharshan, the former leader of the RSS, in a speech called the church in India to pursue a path of Indianising herself and becoming one with the mainstream of Indian culture. C.V. Matthew rightly points out that the assumption here is that there is one culture that is called Indian culture, and all the religious minorities should adopt this Indian culture after severing their relationship with any other body outside India. The call has been given to become a Swadeshi church (church of one's own land or native church). On the surface there seems to be nothing wrong with this call. But as one analyses what their understanding of mainstream and Indian are, then we know what their agenda is.[15] Gandhiji himself was concerned about such ideology and communicated his anxiety to the RSS members that, "if the Hindus felt that in India there was no place for anyone except the Hindus, and if non-Hindus, especially Muslims, wished to live here, they had to live as the slaves of the Hindus, they would kill Hinduism."[16]

The call of the RSS to join the mainstream is a call to sever all connections with the world-wide church and have native gods like Ram and Krishna as their heroes while celebrating festivals like Diwali and Holi as their festivals. C.V. Matthew again rightly points out that Ram and Krishna are deities of the majority community, and they are not to be mixed up with national personalities like Ashoka, Akbar, Mahatma

---

[15] C.V. Matthew, "Christian Identity: To Be or Not to Be" in Richard Howell (ed), *Free to Choose* (New Delhi: EFI, 2002), 56.
[16] R. Guha, *India After Gandhi: The History of the World's Largest Democracy* (London: Picador, 2007), 18.

Gandhi, or Mother Teresa; Diwali and Holi likewise are their religious festivals, unlike Independence Day and Republic Day. Therefore, a call towards Indianisation and joining the mainstream is a call to worship what the Hindus worship and celebrate Hindu festivals while having no connection with the global church. What is astonishing is that national festivals are not even mentioned.[17]

Therefore, in setting the agenda for Christians, the Hindu extremists contradict the basic constitutional right of every Indian citizen who is entitled to freedom of conscience and deny them the opportunity of changing from one religion to another. The more serious casualty in this whole matter is the *truth*. We have already noted that the anti-conversion Acts in several states aim to even domesticate God by saying that any threat of divine displeasure would be seen as a show of force! Moreover, social excommunication is what takes place under the garb of the caste system. Preaching the gospel to the underprivileged and the social outcastes is primarily to invite them to be part of God's kingdom where there is no social excommunication, to invite them to celebrate life as guests of the king of kings and to lead lives of dignity and self-worth.

The answer to the exclusive claims of Christians comes from Christ himself. He himself made the claim, "I am the way and the truth and the life. No one comes to the Father except through me" (John 14:6). God who sent his Son Jesus to reconcile people to himself has made Jesus the way to enter into his kingdom. The terms and conditions are set by God himself to enter his kingdom rather than by Christians. This is very similar to visa stipulations that each country sets up for entry into their land. Each nation sets her own conditions for entry. Likewise, God the Father has said that entry into his kingdom is by faith alone, through Christ alone and by grace alone. It is a free gift which God gives us, but we need to receive it by faith. The need to hear the gospel about Jesus and his offer of life is a fundamental human right. Each person is entitled to hear this good news. What they do with it is their decision, but we are commanded to share this good news. So while we are engaged in common issues of justice and peace, we cannot forget the exclusive claims of Christ. However, these claims should not be forced on others in

---

[17] Matthew, "Christian Identity," 56.

a patronising manner but shared with great humility as being recipients of grace ourselves.

CHALLENGE TO MISSION: SOCIAL ACTION

We now move on to the second specific challenge – which is to our missions. The advice to Christians has been not to engage in a mission of preaching Jesus Christ and to convert the nationals into foreigners, for Christian mission is considered an anti-national and subversive act. Christian charity and social services are considered to be unethical and motivated programmes, "inspired, funded and controlled by nefarious foreign powers that work towards the disintegration of our glorious country."[18]

All social action by the Christian community is viewed with suspicion as though the only agenda of our schools and hospitals is to convert people to Christianity. Why are we involved so much in uplifting the poor and the downtrodden, the oppressed and the outcastes? Why are we doing what we are doing? Many in the church see all our outreach programmes to the poor and the downtrodden as wonderful opportunities for preaching the gospel to them and to see them come to faith in Christ. Some feel that these are wonderful opportunities for conversion. However, they do not see the whole picture of engaging with the poor, supporting them, and giving them an education as part of the mandate God calls us to do in and through Jesus Christ. When Jesus was in Palestine, he broke down social barriers forming around himself a community drawn from the marginalised people of the Palestinian society. Jesus freely mingled with those who were sinners and those who were considered unclean. Jesus came to call the sinners, not the righteous. The sinners are the beneficiaries of God's liberating rule. The outcastes Jesus befriended experienced God's extravagant love and acceptance. Many of these were virtually untouchables of that time and not very different from the lowest castes in the Hindu social system. Jesus' claim saying that he had come for the sake of sinners itself is unique. Similarly, we too are called to show God's love to the poorest of the poor and to the outcastes.

As far as people of other faiths are concerned, they are more than willing to join hands with Christians in working towards justice and

---

[18] Matthew, "Christian Identity," 57.

peace and for the transformation of the lives of the underprivileged. They are very happy with the lead that many of our Christian organisations, both Roman Catholic and Protestant, have given in the fields of medicine and education. The numerous schools and hospitals set up by Christian institutions are always in big demand. In fact, most people of other faiths would prefer to have their children go to a convent or a Christian school due to their higher standards of education. Many of India's top bureaucrats and ministers have been educated in Christian schools and colleges. Loving our neighbours as ourselves, which is mandated by Christ, is seen always as a channel to convert rather than as reaching out to them because God in Christ has first loved us. Unfortunately, many Christians see these activities only as channels to convert rather than through the broader perspective—as following the mandate of Christ to love our neighbours as ourselves because God in Christ first loved us, and encouraging our neighbours of other religions to work to transform our entire society by doing the same. So we need to see our mission as holistic which addresses not only the spiritual area but the physical, mental and social areas as well. Missions that is not holistic can lead to accusations of conversion.

THE WORK OF THE HOLY SPIRIT IN CHRISTIAN MISSION IN A PLURALISTIC CONTEXT

In the first section of this paper, we looked at the context for Christian mission in India today. It is a context where the caste system is predominant and breaking through it would be quite a challenge. It is also a time when the secular fabric of India is being challenged and religious ideologies tend to drive the state. Numerous states have brought in anti-conversion laws curbing the freedom to propagate one's religion. Even though the constitution in Article 25 guarantees the freedom of religion to profess, practice and propagate, the laws seem to be contrary to them. In this kind of a hostile environment, how can Christian missions work? In the second section, we noted two specific challenges for doing Christian missions in a pluralistic context, namely, the challenge to our theology (ie, the exclusive claims of Christ) and a challenge to our mission (the accusation that all our good deeds are covert acts of conversion).

In this kind of a context, how does the Holy Spirit help us in partnering with the mission of God? The Holy Spirit is the one who continues the mission of God after the resurrection and ascension of Jesus. We are to look at the four key issues that were raised in the previous two sections about the context and challenges for missions in a pluralistic setting. Firstly, we need to see how the Holy Spirit helps us as we address the issues of caste and subjugation. Secondly, how do we engage in Christian missions in a hostile environment where there are anti-conversion laws and persecution and where the constitutional provisions are being ignored? Thirdly, we need to address the challenges to our theology, particularly to the uniqueness of Christ and he being the only way to salvation. Finally, we have to see how the Holy Spirit helps us in the challenge to our mission – particularly to works of service.

Caste System – The Holy Spirit Affirms Each Individual as Members of One Body

We have observed that the caste system is one of the key challenges in our context for Christian missions. Since people were believed to have been made from the different body parts of *Prajapati*, they all had different values and were not equal. The comparison of the body with human societies was a rhetorical commonplace in the ancient world. The analogy was usually used to urge members of subordinate classes to stay in their places in the social order and not to upset the equilibrium by rebelling against the higher classes. This thinking was not only used in the ancient world but is used today in the Indian caste system to keep the *dalits* or the lower classes out of the social system. But Paul reverses the rhetoric of the analogy. Instead of appealing for subordination, he appeals for affirmation of each other's gifts as co-equals complementing each other in the body of Christ.

Paul says, "[j]ust as a body, though one, has many parts, but all its many parts form one body, so it is with Christ. For we were all baptised by one Spirit so as to form one body – whether Jews or Gentiles, slave or free – and we were all given the one Spirit to drink" (1 Cor 12:12-13).

Paul's argument against the subjugate system of the body analogy is that we are all members of the one body because we were all baptized into that same body and were made to drink of the same Holy Spirit. The Holy Spirit, therefore, makes us equal members of this body, though our gifts may be diverse. In a context where the caste system plays such a significant role, we are to see that the Holy Spirit reverses the idea of subjugation and instead affirms each person's gifts. Therefore, there is no Jew or Greek, slave or free, Brahmin or Dalit. In Christ no social or racial distinction can act as a barrier for anyone, whether they are from the North or South, East or West. We have all been made in the image of Christ – the whole human race and all the more within the body of Christ. There is no room for prejudice within the body of Christ. So, the Christian community is called and empowered by the Holy Spirit to challenge the caste system which is prevalent both within the Christian community and outside.

The Holy Spirit's Work in a Hostile Environment

1. *Helps to evangelise*

A second area that we observed is that Christian mission in India today will have to be done in a hostile environment. The idea of India as a secular state is slowly being eroded, and a nation state based on religious ideologies is being attempted to be brought in as centre stage. In a context where the constitution of India provides the freedom to profess freely and propagate one's own religion, there are anti-conversion laws that are being brought in. How does one evangelise and share the good news in such a hostile context? Jesus' disciples were asked to wait for the empowering of the Holy Spirit (Acts 1:8) after which they would be witnesses to the ends of the earth. The Holy Spirit was given to all believers. Luke records for us how this was fulfilled in the lives of Peter, Stephen, Barnabas and Saul along with numerous other believers. We can see the work of the Holy Spirit in evangelism as is characterised by boldness (4:13, 31) and wisdom (6:10). Their message was not always accepted, but the evangelists experienced joy (13:52). The contents of their message and its presentation are described as a cause of wonder (4:13; 13:12), unstoppable (6:10), associated with supernatural phenomena (6:15; 7:55-56; 13:9-11), and having no national boundaries.[19] We see these same characteristics

---

[19] K. Warrington, *The Message of the Holy Spirit*, BST (Nottingham: InterVarsity Press, 2009), 122.

when we minister in a pluralistic context. The Holy Spirit works signs and wonders as people are healed or miraculously delivered from the bondages of Satan. Many a time people from other faiths have come to know Jesus because of the signs and wonders they have experienced in their lives. Without the active presence of the Holy Spirit, our evangelism would be in vain. The message may not always be accepted but the good news is preached with boldness and confidence.

2. Helps us stand firm in the midst of persecution

Persecution of those who preach the gospel is a reality in many parts of India. Kandhamal, Odisha is an example of how terrible persecution can be. But Jesus prepares us as his disciples to be ready for it. Jesus told his disciples that a time was coming when those who would kill them would think that by doing so they were offering worship to God, the same kind of service offered in sacrifice and prayer. The persecutors would do so because they do not know the Father or Jesus. Christians would be persecuted in their own places of worship, Jesus also warned. The Jews who stoned Stephen thought that what they were doing fulfilled the law (Acts 7:58-60). Josephus records the death of James, the brother of Jesus, and his companions who were also accused by their fellow Jews of being breakers of the law and were stoned to death (Josephus, *Antiquities* XX ix:1).[20] Similarly, persecution will come to the followers of Christ within churches and without.

There have been disturbing reports of pastors being beaten up in many parts of India, and we are seeing a slow but steady increase in violence against the followers of Christ. We as the body of Christ need to remind ourselves that we are not alone in this. God's Holy Spirit remains with us constantly, and we as members of Christ's body need to remind ourselves that if one part of the body suffers, then the whole body suffers. We need to respond as a body and help wherever we can.

The Holy Spirit who comes to reside within us is the Spirit of truth and love. He will always lead us in the paths of truth and to the ultimate truth – Jesus Christ. Jesus reminds his disciples that following the path

---

[20] William Whiston, (trans.), *The Works of Flavius Josephus* (Grand Rapids, MI: Associated Publishers and Authors Inc., n.d.).

he trod is going to be very difficult. The calling to be a follower of Jesus seems scary! But we need to take heart because we are not alone in this. God the Holy Spirit, the Spirit of truth and the Spirit of love, empowers us and enables us to stand firm in moments like this.

THE HOLY SPIRIT'S WORK IN THE MIDST OF A CHALLENGE TO OUR THEOLOGY – THE UNIQUENESS OF CHRIST

1. *Affirms "Jesus is Lord"*

A third area of challenge is to our theology, particularly to the unique claims of Christ. How can we say that Jesus is the only God? How can we actually say "He is Lord"? The confession of the early church was "Jesus is Lord," and they too did that in a pluralistic context. Paul writing to the Corinthians says, "[n]ow about the gifts of the Spirit, brothers and sisters, I do not want you to be uninformed. You know that when you were pagans, somehow or other you were influenced and led astray to mute idols. Therefore I want you to know that no one who is speaking by the Spirit of God says, 'Jesus be cursed,' and no one can say, 'Jesus is Lord,' except by the Holy Spirit" (1 Cor 12:1–3).

In these three verses, Paul lays the foundation for the gifts of the Spirit. Paul addresses the brothers and sisters in the church at Corinth saying that he does not want them to be ignorant about spiritual gifts. He reminds them that when they were Gentiles, as many translations have it, they were enticed and led astray to worship idols that could not speak. Paul sets the stage for all that follows by talking to the Corinthians about their former experience as idolaters and their current experience as followers of Christ. He wants to make clear what the genuine work of the Spirit of God is. In the past, they were not rooted and were blown about by every spiritual power they came across. But now they have been rooted and grounded in Christ. The situation in Corinth is very similar to the pluralistic context in which we live. As well as the Christian faith, the city contained many faiths and many different idols. These need not be physical statutes but are anything that takes the place of God. In another place, Paul points out that greed is a form of idolatry (Col 3:5).

Paul goes on to say that no one speaking by the Spirit of God ever says, "'Jesus be cursed,' and no one can say, 'Jesus is Lord,' except by the

Holy Spirit" (1 Cor 12:3). The confession "Jesus is Lord" was the radical confession of the early Christians. The use of this phrase meant absolute allegiance to Jesus as one's deity. It set the believers apart from the Jews for whom it would have been blasphemy and from pagans who had many deities. For Paul, the ultimate criterion of the Spirit's activity was not the power and the gifts available but the exaltation of Jesus as Lord through those gifts.[21] Anything which moves away from that exaltation, though they may be legitimate expressions of the Spirit, begins to move away from Christ to a pagan fascination with spiritual gifts and spiritual activity as ends in themselves. The purpose of the gifts is to proclaim that Jesus is Lord – not just a verbal witness – but also a witness through service and lifestyle by which Jesus is truly shown as Lord. Paul, therefore, sets the stage for the Corinthian church as well as for our churches before he goes on to talk about the gifts of the Spirit.

In a context, where the uniqueness of Jesus is considered unacceptable, the Holy Spirit enables us to confess "Jesus is Lord." As we saw earlier, this means absolute allegiance to Jesus as one's deity which sets believers apart from others. This allegiance is unacceptable in our context where people believe that all roads lead to the one God and that there are different paths to reach this one true God. The real question, however, is not about the paths that are available to reach this one true God but who this one true God is. This God cannot be seen or experienced without the presence of the Holy Spirit. He is the one who affirms for us that Jesus is indeed God in human flesh. So in contexts where we are called to give up unique claims for Jesus Christ as the only Lord and God, the Holy Spirit endorses that he is indeed the only Lord and Saviour.

2. *Lead us into all truth (John 16:8-15)*

As Jesus came down to the earth to reconcile sinful humanity and a righteous God, so also the Holy Spirit functions as a mediator between the unbelieving world and its creator. The Spirit powerfully convicts unbelievers of their sin primarily of unbelief on God's only Son Jesus. Without the intervention of the Spirit no genuine conversion can take

---

[21] Gordon Fee, *The First Epistle to the Corinthians*, NICNT (Grand Rapids, MI: William B. Eerdmans, 1996), 582.

place. People will not be able to respond to the gospel because their eyes are covered with veils, and only the Holy Spirit can remove them.

In the Old Testament, the early prophets were kings and judges of God's people. They wrote God's law, revealed God's will, ruled God's people, and arbitrated in disputes. The Spirit continues that work. He discerns God's mind. Paul, writing to the people at Rome, says, "[a]nd he who searches our hearts knows the mind of the Spirit, because the Spirit intercedes for God's people in accordance with the will of God" (Rom 8:27). Similarly, the writer of Hebrews says, "[f]or the word of God is alive and active. Sharper than any double-edged sword, it penetrates even to dividing soul and spirit, joints and marrow; it judges the thoughts and attitudes of the heart" (Heb 4:12). The Holy Spirit of God is indeed the Spirit of truth who judges the world and knows our innermost thoughts. We cannot fool the Holy Spirit.

- *He judges with regard to sin–because people do not believe in Christ:* The sin the Holy Spirit will judge is that of unbelief. It is not God who makes believing hard; we do. We are the ones who are obstinate. We cover our eyes and ears, turn our backs, and stiffen our necks, while all the time God is whispering our name and calling us back to himself. He wants to teach us his truth and reveal his way for us if we will like young Samuel simply say, "[s]peak, for your servant is listening" (1 Sam 3:10).[22] We see this openness in the example of the Ethiopian eunuch who was reading Isaiah 53. Even though he was reading the sacred text, he did not understand who the prophet was talking about. He needed help, and the Holy Spirit gave that help through Philip (Acts 8:31). The greatest sin that the Holy Spirit will convict us of is the sin of unbelief against God's only Son Jesus.

- *In regard to righteousness – because Jesus was going to the Father:* Our righteousness can come only through the person and work of Christ on the cross and not through our own works. So when Christ judges, he will judge us according to whether

---
[22] Chris Hancock, Sermon Notes.

we have appropriated the righteousness he has made available to us. In our context, righteousness is seen in terms of *karma* or the amount of good deeds we have done that will take us to a better position in the next cycles of life until we merge with the *brahman*. The Holy Spirit makes it amply clear that our righteousness is only imputed to us through Christ's righteousness. Salvation is given to us when we appropriate the righteousness of Jesus given to us freely rather than that earned by our good works.

- *In regard to judgement – because the ruler of the world stands condemned:* In other words, those who follow the ruler of this world and persist in sin will be judged and punished. The Bible makes it clear that there are spiritual realities opposed to the will of God who lead people away from God. Satan has already been defeated on the cross, and his final wiping out will happen when Christ returns. Those who choose to reject Christ and follow the ruler of this world will in the end be judged and condemned.

In pluralistic mission contexts where truth seems to be the casualty and there is rampant corruption all around, the Holy Spirit presents the truth to us: both the truth of Jesus as God in human flesh and truth and integrity in our daily lives as his followers. The Spirit helps us to stand up for the truth.

The Holy Spirit's Work in the Midst of a Challenge to Our Mission – Works of Service

The Holy Spirit is the one who empowers us to be engaged in works of service. Our works of caring for the poor, opening hospitals, educating the weak and the backward, or caring for people affected with leprosy or HIV/AIDS can only be done through the indwelling power of the Holy Spirit. It is the Spirit who gives us the grace to carry out these ministries as he floods us with the love of God and Jesus which moves us into compassion and helps us to engage with those in need. Social work done by its own steam will die a natural death. Sustaining such projects without the rejuvenating power of the Holy Spirit will either make them collapse or turn them into money-making institutions in which the idea of service is totally lost.

In conclusion, as we look at the context of our country, we are confronted with the caste system within every strata of society and faith. We cannot change this outlook towards people without a deep-rooted work of the Holy Spirit. He is the one who can make us see that all of us are made in God's image, and all of us are equal before him. The Holy Spirit affirms our diverse gifts and shows that God is deeply interested in each one of us. A second challenge is that of a hostile environment for Christian mission. Secularism is slowly being eroded away, and the right to follow the religion of one's choice is slowly being taken away under the freedom of religion bills. As we have seen, the constitution of India protects the fundamental human right to follow the faith of one's choice. The anti-conversion laws are all aimed at curbing any missionary activity. However, we must remember that real conversion is the transformation of the heart which only the Holy Spirit can do.

The challenges to our theology and mission also need to be seen in and through the work of the Holy Spirit. People may question the uniqueness of Christ and his claim to be the only Lord and Saviour. This attitude, too, is something we cannot change with our own strength. Only the Holy Spirit can remove the veil from eyes and hearts and make people see Jesus as the only God. The confession "Jesus is Lord" is made possible only by the Holy Spirit. The challenge that our social services are only means and ways of converting others also needs to be addressed through the presence of the indwelling Holy Spirit. It is he who pours out the compassion of God in our lives and enables us to serve others. The Holy Spirit also gives us the boldness to evangelise and to go and make disciples, baptising them in the name of the Father, Son and Holy Spirit. Finally, we will be persecuted for our faith which Jesus already warned us about. When we are persecuted, the Holy Spirit is the one who will stand with us and give us the words to speak and the courage to be bold and stand up for the truth. We can only be actively engaged in the mission of God in a pluralistic context with and by the power of the Holy Spirit.

13

CHRIST-DEVOTEE MOVEMENT: A PENTECOST AT BANARAS

Cyril Kuttiyanikkal*

The wind that blows in the firmament of heavens does not stop with our boundary walls. The birds that fly in the sky do not have the awareness of our physical borderlines and confines. Fire has no concern for our territorial ambits. All these are above our boundaries, walls and limits that we keep for ourselves. Scripture speaks about the arrival of the Holy Spirit with the above mentioned images of "wind," "tongues of fire" (Acts 2:1-3), and "dove" (Mark 1:10). Wind is able to cross every threshold set by human beings. Like wind, God's Spirit is not restricted by human will or desire. We cannot manipulate the direction of the wind or stop its force, any more than we can control a hurricane or squall. We cannot grab, contain, control, or confine it. At the time of creation, the Spirit of God was hovering over the waters (Gen 1:2). At the time of baptism of Jesus, the Holy Spirit descended on him like a dove (Luke 3:22). During Pentecost, God's presence in the form of the Holy Spirit was accompanied by the sound of wind and tongues of fire (Acts 2:1-3).[1] The outpouring of the Spirit at Pentecost enabled the disciples to be fearless witnesses to

---

* **Cyril Kuttiyanikkal**, PhD, is a young Catholic scholar based in Rishikesh, Uttarakhand, where he functions as the animator of theology students. He earned his doctoral award from the Netherlands in Practical Theology. He teaches at Samanvaya Theology College, Bhopal and Jagdalpur, and St. Joseph's College, Khammam.

[1] Wind and fire are tremendously powerful natural forces, which Luke uses to indicate the power which God was giving to the apostles. See John Hargreaves, *A Guide to Acts* (Delhi: ISPCK, 1993), 16.

the Jews first and then to the Gentiles. Just like the Spirit was poured on Jewish Christians, the Gentiles too received the same outpouring of the Spirit (Acts 10:47). Paul and Barnabas were impelled by the Holy Spirit to go to the Gentiles (Acts 13:46-48). One could say that the Spirit pressed the early Church to break down the barriers between Jews and Samaritans, and Gentiles and Jews.[2]

In the context of several religions and cultures in India, many Christians agonise over the lack of growth in Christian population. They wonder how to go about with their missionary mandate in the anti-Christian environment. One might ask: Where has that blowing, swirling, burning, life-giving power of the Spirit gone? Was not the Spirit active in the days of the first Christian community of Acts? If yes, will not the Spirit guide us into new frontiers of mission? Will not the Spirit enable us to break the barriers between Christians and non-Christians just like it was in those days when the barrier between Christians and Gentiles were broken? In this article, I would like to explore the role of the Holy Spirit in the Christ-devotee movement and the Spirit's possible intervention in the church's mission *ad gentes* in the larger Indian context. First of all, I shall briefly familiarise you with the Christ-devotee movement by describing the religious practices of the Christ-devotees. It will be followed by a short presentation of the religious experiences of the devotees. After these descriptive segments, I shall discuss the role of the Spirit in the lives of the devotees and the movement at large. Subsequently, I will discuss the lessons we can learn from this movement in terms of Christian mission in any pluralistic context.

CHRIST-DEVOTEES - AN EMERGING FORM OF CHRISTIAN DISCIPLES

In the North Indian multi-religious and multi-cultural context, on every Sunday of the week and on the second Saturday of every month thousands of people, who are not baptised as Christians come to worship Jesus in Matridham, a Roman Catholic *āśram* in Banaras/Varanasi, Uttar Pradesh, North India. These people who are now called Christ-

---

[2] For more details, see Manjackal James, "Towards a Charismatic Spirituality: Holy Spirit and Evangelization," *Indian Journal of Spirituality* 12/2 (1999), 314-328.

devotees (*Khrist Bhaktas*) are mainly Hindus belonging to several *varṇa/caste*[3] groups, who gather in the āśram in order to listen to the Word of God preached to them, to be cured of all their diseases, to sing praises to the living God in Jesus, and to experience the loving touch of a loving God. They come from the neighbouring villages, cities and districts, and even from neighbouring States. The total number of devotees has grown enormously to be called *Khrist Bhakta* or "Christ-devotee Movement." [4]

In this movement, an interesting interaction is taking place between Christianity and Hinduism. It is fascinating as it enables people from Hindu culture to remain faithful believers in Christ without discarding their loyalty to Hindu culture. However, this new assemblage brings with it fresh challenges to both Christianity and Hinduism. The Christ-devotees are reluctant to receive baptism despite maintaining a deep desire to receive the eucharist. The church is willing to admit them to the Eucharist only after their reception of baptism. This kind of hybrid way of life opens up new frontiers in the Christian *ad gentes* mission albeit the unresolved theological issues lying herein. In this short article, I am not able to take up all these issues. Hence, I limit myself to the role of the Holy Spirit in this movement. However, for clarity, it is important to gather the work of the Spirit in this movement by having an overview of this movement.

In the North Indian context, becoming a Christ-devotee or publicly professing faith in Christ or even going to a Christian *āśram* invites disapproval from family as well as society at large. In this movement also, mostly, in the initial period many devotees were beaten up, scolded or prohibited by their family members from going to the *āśram* or becoming devotees of Jesus. However, since the devotees do not officially

---

[3] The term caste is the equivalent to the Sanskrit term *jāti* used in the Indian sub continent to refer to "race," "breed," or "lineage." *Jātis* are the sub-divisions of the four basic *varṇas*. The numbers of *varṇas* are four (*Brahmaṇs, Kṣatriyās Vaiśas* and *Śūdrās*), or five when those outside (*pañcama*) are included as a category. The number of castes which are in fact known as *jāti*, including sub-castes, is numerous and cannot be counted, as their number grows even today. Both *varṇa* and *jāti* are hierarchical orderings. The ranking among the four *varṇas* are fixed, while *jāti* has a lot of fluidity.

[4] A detailed research work on Christ-devotee movement has been published. For more details and discussion on theological issues about the movement see C.J. Kuttiyanikkal, *Khrist Bhakta Movement: A Model for an Indian Church? Inculturation in the Area of Community Building* (Münster: Lit Verlag, 2014).

change from one religion to another, ie, from Hinduism to Christianity, the opposition has subsided. Presently around four to five thousand devotees attend the weekly Sunday *satsaṅg* (prayer-meeting) and around six thousand devotees attend the second Saturday *satsaṅg* at Matridham, Banaras. On Sundays, many devotees go to the other small āśrams and parishes run by the diocese of Varanasi. There are a number of devotees who attend the prayer meetings at several small and big Protestant and Pentecostal churches or assemblies. The second Saturday *satsaṅgs* at *Matridham Āśram* is special for the Christ-devotees and so they come to the *āśram* on that day. The total number of devotees of the movement is around 60,000 (in 2006 it was 30,000 and had well out numbered the local Roman Catholic population [19,169] of the area). It is growing day by day. Every year, at the time of the annual charismatic convention, more people join the movement as devotees. It is noted that the devotees belong to all the caste/*varṇa* groups of both rural and semi-urban areas.

THE RELIGIOUS PRACTICES OF THE CHRIST-DEVOTEES

Faith, although it is an internal matter, cannot be hidden completely. The faith practices of the Christ-devotees will present us with the extent of their commitment to Christ. And when a community starts to live their faith, the expressions become tangible. Christ-devotees courageously display their commitment to Christ in their prayer meetings and other occasions.

1. The second Saturday and Sunday satsangs

The most important and visible place where one can observe the faith practices of the devotees is the *Matridham Āśram*. They come in large numbers on every Sunday, around four to five thousand of them, and on second Saturdays of the month around six thousand devotees come for the prayer-meetings. At the *āśram* they display a variety of faith expressions culturally relevant for them but the content of which are mostly Christian. Touching the ground and prostrating before the Eucharist, performing *ārătī* in the church, sprinkling on themselves the water from the pond, prostrating or garlanding the statue of Mary, offering sweets, fruit, incense, etc, at the holy places in the compound are only some of them.

In the *satsaṅg bhavan* they listen to the preaching of the Word, join the singing of *bhajans* and prayers, listen to the witnesses, raise their voice in praise and worship, participate in the adoration of the blessed sacrament, and join in the healing prayer. While preaching, the preacher makes them repeat the Word of God after him. They sing and praise loudly and shout "halleluia." Most of the devotees have learned by heart the *bhajans*, prayers, quotes from the Bible and hymns by repeating them in the *āśram*.

The devotees remain in the *satsaṅg bhavan* and attend the entire programme from 11:00 to 16:00 on Sundays and from 10:00 to 16:00 on second Saturdays. All the *satsaṅgs* begin with the invocation of the Holy Spirit. Hymns which plead for the showering of the Holy Spirit are sung. While singing those hymns, the community joins with loud voices, by clapping of hands, and beating of symbols. It is a sight to see how the devotees long to behold the blessed sacrament when brought to the *satsaṅg bhavan* for public adoration. Some even try to touch the sacrament, or at least the priest who carries of the sacrament or his cloak.[5] Others express their devotion by prostrating, bowing their head to the ground and so on. Most people bring with them water and oil to be blessed and taken home. The Holy Spirit is invoked before benediction. The majority of the miracles and cures take place at the time of benediction of the blessed sacrament.

Some Christ-devotees from the neighbourhood attend the Roman Catholic liturgy, participate actively in the singing of *bhajans*, and listen to the Word of God. On the last Sunday of every month, around one hundred fifty devotees attend the monthly *satsaṅg* and as part of the retreat, they join the Roman Catholic liturgy. They listen to the preaching eagerly, sing and recite the prayers in loud voices and show more devotion during the liturgy than the baptised Christians. According to Anil Dev IMS, the father of this movement, this has improved the quality of the faith of the Roman Catholics. Those who visit the *āśram* for retreat, and other purposes are impressed by the faith of the devotees. According to many

---

[5] The present writer had the experience of carrying the sacrament. People from both sides tried to touch the sacrament by pulling it towards them and many touched the clock, hands or feet. Some people placed their hands on the way so that while walking he may step on their hands or at least the feet might touch their hands.

priests, this participation of the *Khrist Bhaktas* in the liturgy rekindles the faith of the Christians.

2. *The family prayer*

The devotees have adopted the practice of family prayer now. Before becoming devotees, they did not have any ritual similar to a family prayer. Many of them had a family deity placed in one room where they offered *pūjā* to the deity. The *pūjā* consisted of lighting the lamp (*diya*), incensing deity and saying personal prayers or chanting the mantra and *ārătī*. This was performed by one member of the family, either the father or mother. Other members of the family did not take part in it. Once they became Christ-devotees, they took the family deity to the *āśram* to be buried under the cross of Christ and now keep the picture of Jesus and other Christian symbols at home. They also wear Christian symbols such as the cross, rosary, etc. If the members of the whole family are devotees, then they have a special place for prayer. After becoming the devotees of Christ, all the family members gather for the family prayer, which is done mostly in the evening. It includes lighting of the lamp, intercessory prayer, rosary, sometimes reading from the Bible, *bhajans*, praise and worship. The prayer is concluded with *ārătī*. The more devoted spend one or two hours in prayer. The women mostly lead the prayer and perform *ārătī*. Some devotees, normally, the women pray in the morning also. The morning prayer is a short one where they limit it to lighting of the lamp, small personal prayers, and an *ārătī*. They also display in a prominent place the pictures of Jesus, Mary, Bible,[6] cross, prayer book, and devotional hymns book published by the *āśram*.[7] Before becoming devotees, it was not normal for them to have their religious symbols displayed in the prominent places, but it was limited to one room or placed normally away from the prominent place, where the family deity was installed.

3. *The village prayer meetings*

The Christ-devotees gather in the villages under the guidance of an *aguā* for the common prayer meeting once a week. Conducted normally in the

---

[6] Some people keep the Bible covered in saffron coloured cloth (as in the Hindu custom).

[7] There are also people like Urmila Patel and Prakash, who have rooms meant only for prayer where the room is filled with holy pictures and atmosphere.

house of *aguā* at 12:00 noon, the prayer meetings are mostly attended by women. The gathering is generally small in numbers, sometimes with just ten to fifteen women, and other times, in certain villages, from thirty to fifty people. Additionally, those who wish to become devotees also join and ask for prayers. Some devotees, who are not able to go to the *āśram* due to either objection from families or some other reasons, like sickness, also attend the village meetings. Sometimes the head catechist from the *āśram* joins the prayer.

The prayer meetings begin with the lighting of the lamp and singing of *bhajans*. One person leads *bhajans* while the group repeats after the leader. Sometimes the devotees sing *bhajans* composed by some of the devotees themselves in their local dialect (*bhojpurī*). Such *bhajans* are rather longer and narrate the events and incidents from the gospel. Mostly, while singing the *bhajans*, the devotees join by ringing bells, playing tambourine (*kartāl*)[8] or clapping their hands. Intercessory prayers, praise, and worship follow it. During the prayer meetings the devotees intercede for various needs of the people in the village, especially for the sick. Towards the end of the prayer meeting, the healing prayer is held if sick people are present. The devotees extend their hands towards the sick during the healing prayer. The prayer session lasts for three hours. If a priest is present, he preaches the Word of God and mostly leads the healing prayer. It is concluded with *ārătī* and distribution of *prasād*. The *ārătī* is given to the picture of Jesus and then taken to all present for reception.

4. *Other devotions and faith practices*

There are many other daily as well as occasional faith practices of the devotees. The occasional faith practices include the monthly retreats, fasting, and penance which are optional. Invariably, they are also devoted to Mary, the mother of Jesus. They also regularly participate in the annual programmes like Christmas, Easter, annual charismatic convention, and *Gurupūrṇimā*. The holy week is the time for their spiritual renewal with as many as ten thousand people attending the three-day programmes with much devotion. Without giving much description about these practices

---

[8] *Kartāl* (literally means the rhythm of the hand) is made of wooden blocks with holes for fingers and circular copper plates.

let us now probe their religious experiences of the new-found faith in Christ.

New Religious Experience

After having surveyed the faith-practices of the devotees, it is important that we take stock of their religious experiences as well. The intention of many people when they come to the *āśram* or the movement for the first time is to fulfil their curiosity, since many people speak about it. Some people come to get freedom from evil spirits, while others come to get cured of physical ailments. But once they come, they are captured by the atmosphere, prayers, preaching, and miracles. There are cases of those who had come only for the sake of curiosity but became a devotee at the very first occasion and then an *aguā* not long later. Let us explore how and what is the experience of their new found faith in Christ.

1. Experience of miraculous cures

Several people, especially the rural folks, suffer from various kinds of problems and illnesses. They have either less means to go for the medical treatment in time or the treatments have not yielded any result. At times, the problems of life are such that they do not see any solutions. Mostly people turn to witchcraft or sorcerers who are called *ojhās*. *Ojhās* collect money and materials, like chicken, liquor, and go on with their witchcraft, while the suffering remains. There are also instances when medical treatment for longer periods has not given any progress. Hence, people are desperate for cures from their ailments. When they hear about the miraculous cures happening in the *āśram*, they flock to it. People who are suffering are eager to get cured and as they take part in the prayers and healing services often they get cured miraculously. It is true that many may come to *āśram* just for the sake of physical cure. But once they experience the cure through divine intervention, they become committed Christ-devotees.

2. Freedom from evil spirits

Another important aspect of their experience is the freedom they receive from the spell of evil spirits. There is widespread belief in the existence of evil spirits and the spirits of the dead roaming in the villages. They believe that the spirits of the dead people have to be appeased. People find evil spirits as the source for almost all calamities and sicknesses. In order to get rid of the spell of these spirits or to appease them the people usually go to *ojhās*. When they realise that the *ojhās* could not keep the evil spirits away forever or another evil spirit has come to disturb them, or their enemy has set an evil spirit against them, they come to the *āśram* to get rid of their sufferings and the attacks of evil spirits. The story of Jesus who cures the people from satanic forces is very appealing to these people. When they see the miracles and hear the witness of the people who have received miraculous freedom from the spell of evil spirits, their faith increases and eventually many of them receive freedom from the spell of evil spirits.

3. *Experience of a loving God*

Another experience of the devotees is the experience of God as a friend or a benefactor and not as someone to be feared. When people become Christ-devotees, they take the house deity or the icon of the house-deity and bring it to the *āśram*. They leave the deity in the *āśram* to be buried under the foot of the cross so that it can do no damage to the family. Many times the family members are afraid of taking the deity themselves and ask the staff of the *āśram* to take it away. The deity was seen as someone to be feared. The focus of their spirituality was on propitiating the deities. They often believed in the wrath of God and were careful not to displease the deity. They are now taught that Jesus is the saviour whom they need not fear but love. They are also taught that God is love and that God does not need to be propitiated. Thus, they learn to love God and experience God as loving.

4. *Expressive prayer: charismatic and communitarian*

For the Christ-devotees, expressive prayer and community prayer are something new. In Hinduism prayers are mostly offered silently by individuals. Even when there is a gathering in the temple, each person approaches the deity individually. In the *āśram*, the *Khrist Bhaktas* are taught to pray loudly as one family and to pray for one another. Unlike the Hindu temple where the *pūjā* is offered for each individual, there is only one liturgy, one adoration, and one healing prayer for all the devotees.

The charismatic form of prayers said aloud and in community are new experiences for them. It seems that the charismatic method of prayer and preaching of the Word of God leads them into a different level of spiritual freedom and inner healing. They seem to experience the power of the Spirit during the *satsaṅgs*. The people who are afflicted by poverty, social oppression and having lots of physical and psychological problems find solace in these prayer meetings. The physical and psychological healing that is happening during prayers adds to their devotion and faith. They are also freed from various superstitions and bondages, which lead to peace in their personal and family lives.

5. *Experience of heavenly visions*

Although not extensive, a few devotees receive visions of Jesus, Mary, etc. Some of them have frequent visions, while some have only occasionally. One medical student Meena who receives frequent visions states that Mary feeds her quite often and then she feels no more hunger for the rest of the day even if she does not take any physical food. Other devotees approach the visionaries with requests for prayer as the devotees think that the prayers of the visionaries have more effect.

ROLE OF THE SPIRIT IN THE CHRIST-DEVOTEE MOVEMENT

The showering of the Holy Spirit on the disciples of Jesus happened at the time of Pentecost. Those present in the upper room to receive the Spirit were all Jews who had accepted Jesus as their Lord and Master. Moreover, those who accepted the baptism at the preaching of the apostles at Pentecost and became part of the community of disciples were also Jews themselves. However, they could not imagine what the Spirit had in store for the Gentiles. Hence, they were "astonished that the gift of the Holy Spirit had been poured out even on Gentiles" (Acts 10:45). Now, we shall see how the Spirit is active among those who do not belong to any of the ecclesial communities by way of baptism and membership. It seems that the Spirit is pouring out on all who believe in Jesus no matter which region or religion one belongs to.

PRAYER-MEETINGS AS OCCASIONS FOR ENCOUNTERING THE SPIRIT

The Christianity of the Christ-devotee movement sees everything in the life of devotees as the gift of the Holy Spirit. The showering of the Spirit does not depend on the recipient's ability, but is a free gift of God. The *satsaṅgs* provide a context for encountering the Spirit. All the *satsaṅgs* in the *āśram* and the prayer meetings in the villages begin with the invocation of the Holy Spirit. Every *satsaṅg* has hymns, which plead for the showering of the Holy Spirit, and while singing those hymns the community join together with loud voices, with clapping of hands and beating of *kartāl*. They believe that such occasions and their prayer as one community surely brings showering of the Spirit on them.

The staff members of the *āśram* gather in prayer on the eve of the Sunday or second Saturday. They use this prayer-time for the inspiration of the Spirit to give them the theme for the next day's preaching and the person who will preach. Anil Dev started his ministry of preaching the Word when he experienced the "showering of the Spirit" in such charismatic conventions. He and other members of the staff consider this movement as a gift of the Holy Spirit and a sign of the Spirit's working. The decisions they take after invoking the Spirit is regarded as authorised by the Holy Spirit. They trust that it is the Spirit that brings the people into the movement. The members in the *āśram* believe that the individuals are given the gifts of the Spirit in order to serve the community according to the nature of these gifts.

1. Charism and leadership: Gift of the Spirit

The Christ-devotee movement considers all charisms and abilities as gifts of the Spirit. The understanding of the community about the role of the Spirit is visible in the process of recognising someone as *aguā*. In Charismatic circles, the accent usually has been on the spirituality of the leader rather than on his other abilities or skills[9]. The *aguās* are those who show the abilities of leadership and have the charism to guide the community and lead them in prayer. The criteria for selection or recognition are not based on caste, social standing or education but on

---

[9] A. Anderson, *Spreading Fires: Missionary Nature of Early Pentecostalism* (London: SCM Press, 2007), 260.

charism. Those who have experienced some kind of miracles of cures, remain earnest about the faith, show readiness to spread the message of Jesus, and are devout and faithful, are given preference. Therefore, we find *aguās* from different *varṇas*/castes including the *dalits*. Mostly, the women show more interest in the matters of religion and its practice. Hence, there are more female *aguās* than men.

2. *Uniting power of the Spirit*

In this movement, the members of all *varṇas* across the caste/*varṇa* barriers are brought together by the Holy Spirit as one community. Once they come into the movement, they are taught to love one another following the example of Jesus. There is no hierarchy or honoured position for anyone based on his or her birth. They experience a kind of equal dignity in the movement and enter into a communion, albeit with room for wider improvement. Christianity, which was considered as the religion of the outcastes, has become instrumental in bringing the people of several castes into communion. Thus, on the one hand, the Christ-devotee movement has opened up Christianity to the members of other castes/*varṇas*, and on the other hand, it has made possible for people from all castes to worship together.

CHRIST-DEVOTEES – A BOON TO THE CHRISTIAN MISSION

In India, especially in the northern part, where the Christian mission is often met with antagonism from several fundamentalist quarters, the Christ-devotee movement offers a different model of being disciples of Christ which seems to be in tune with the cultural ethos of this nation. This movement has created an ambience and an atmosphere where faith in Christ and proclamation of faith in Christ is not rejected but welcomed and embraced.

The Christ-devotee movement can be seen as a gift of the Spirit for the Indian churches to present an alternative model of being the church in India. Taking into consideration the situation in India and its cultural differences, this gives us a concrete model acceptable to the people at large. It is a unique place where people accept Christ and publicly proclaim their faith in him, while remaining within the fold of the Hindu culture. Formerly, there were individuals who accepted Christ and tried to live as his disciples in an Indian way, but here people in large numbers have committed themselves to the faith in Christ while retaining their Hindu identity.

In the body of Christ, there is no room for divisions based on origin. Up to now in the North Indian context, mostly the *dalits* have accepted Christianity and people from higher *varnas*/castes have kept themselves away from the Christian faith. In the Christ-devotee movement, people from all castes, including the high castes and, in some cases, even Muslims are joining the movement. The Spirit is bringing together people of all castes forming them into a community based on Christ.

Baptism into Christianity implies in India a change from one social community to another with social and legal implications. It is not limited to a personal religious choice. Therefore, baptism is opposed vehemently by Hindu groups.[10] In the Christ-devotee movement, the devotees are not forced to change their social and cultural community, and are not transferred from "Hindu Personal Law" to "Christian Personal Law." At the same time, the churches need not opt out of their obligation to preach the gospel in order to make disciples for Christ. Thus, it gives us an excellent opportunity to live Christian commitment according to a new model that is relevant to the Indian context.

It is an opportunity to respect Indian culture. As Donald McGavran says, each culture has an inalienable dignity and right to exist; no man has the right to change it.[11] The Christ-devotee movement provides an opportunity to share the Christian faith without being arrogant towards other religions and cultures. It opens a window to preach the faith in Christ, while not advocating the western culture.

The Christ-devotee movement has integrated into itself several charismatic elements which are the gifts of the Spirit. The charismatic elements have given much solace to the Christ-devotees as well as the ordinary Christians. The spiritual revolution that the charismatic

---

[10] H. Staffner, "Conversion to Christianity: Seen from Hindu Point of View" in M. Dhavamony (ed), *Evangelization Dialogue and Development* (Roma: Universita Gregoriana Editrice, 1972), 235.

[11] Cf., D. McGavaran, *The Clash Between Christianity and Cultures* (Washington: Canon Press, 1974), 2.

elements bring into the church is, thus, an opportunity for the church to renew itself.[12]

Finally, it seems the Spirit of God is poured out on those who are not within the fold of any of the Christian denominations. At Pentecost, the Holy Spirit came down on the disciples in the form of what seemed to be the tongues of fire that separated and came to rest on each of them. Immediately, their message crossed the boundaries of language. The festival pilgrims and residents of Jerusalem heard their native languages being spoken by the group of (mostly uneducated) Galilean followers of Jesus. Not surprisingly, the experience left them feeling bewildered, amazed, astonished, and perplexed (Acts 2:6, 12). Some even sneer about it, accusing the speakers of being drunk (Acts 2:13). Later, even the first Jewish Christians were amazed at the outpouring of the Holy Spirit on Gentiles (Acts 10:45). Today also one might be amazed at the outpouring of the Holy Spirit on Christ-devotees who have not received the baptism of water. The forest fire is able to jump gaps such as roads, rivers and fire gaps and has the potential to change direction unexpectedly. Let the fire of the Spirit help the churches and the ecclesial communities in India to jump the gap between Christians and Hindus and let the Spirit as "wind" enable us to cross the barriers between cultures. Pentecost resulted in the formation of a new community, eventually called as Christians, which replaced the Jewish ethnic thinking.

---

[12] P. Hocken, *The Challenges of the Pentecostal Charismatic and Messianic Jewish Movements: The Tensions of the Spirit* (Farnham/Burlington: Ashgate, 2009), 58.

14

INDIGENOUS SPIRITUALITY AND THE HOLY SPIRIT IN A PLURALISTIC CONTEXT

Atola Longkumer[*]

> "*Beholding what the Spirit is doing in the world sets us at the beginning of a path, a new path.*
> *New discoveries, new challenges, new potentialities await.*"[1]

The Holy Spirit became centred in Christianity in the late modern period. It is not to say that the Holy Spirit has been on the periphery of Christianity. While the Holy Spirit as the third person in the Trinity and its role has been intrinsic to the belief, identity, and historical development of Christianity in all its variety,[2] at the beginning of the late twentieth century, a renewed theological discourse and observation of phenomenological manifestations of the Holy Spirit as expressed

---

[*] **Atola Longkumer**, DTh, is Professor of Religions at SAIACS, Bangalore. She also serves as the Book Review Editor of the journal, *Mission Studies*.

[1] Velli-Matti Karkkainen, *Pneumatology: The Holy Spirit in Ecumenical, International, and Contextual Perspective* (Grand Rapids, MI: Baker Academic Books, 2002), 117.

[2] Alister McGrath, *Christian Theology: An Introduction* (Oxford: Blackwell Publishing, 1997); Daniel Migliore, *Faith Seeking Understanding: An Introduction to Christian Theology* (Grand Rapids: William B. Eerdmans, 1991), 233-234.

in the growth of Pentecostal/Charismatic Christianity is perceived.³ The theological interpretations and understanding around the Holy Spirit have also not been without divisive contentions in the history of Christianity.⁴ In the recent era, there has been renewed interest and appreciation of the role of the Holy Spirit in the life and work of the church, not least in its missional task of witnessing to the living God as revealed in the life and work of Jesus Christ. Incidentally, the centring of the Holy Spirit in Christianity in the late modern period has taken place, simultaneously, as Christianity is embraced and experienced as a significant agent of transformation in the Global South contexts, whereas it wanes in the erstwhile Christian lands – the Global North cultures comprising the West.⁵ The making of the Holy Spirit, as central to the mission of the church, is demonstrated in the global events of Christianity and mission documents of the global Christian organisations.⁶ Three major global Christian organisations have emphasised the significance of the Holy Spirit in their mission documents and declaration. The Council of World Mission and Evangelism/World Council of Churches (CWME/WCC) in its mission statement of 2012 has emphasised the centrality of

---

³ Allan Anderson, *An Introduction to Pentecostalism: Global Charismatic Christianity* (Cambridge: Cambridge University Press, 2004); Grant Wacker, *Heaven Below: Early Pentecostals and American Culture* (Cambridge, MA: Harvard University Press, 2001); Karla Poewe (ed), *Charismatic as a Global Culture* (Columbia: University of South Carolina, 1994); Kirsteen Kim, *The Holy Spirit in the World: A Global Conversation* (Maryknoll: Orbis Books, 2007), Kirsteen Kim, *Mission in the Spirit: The Holy Spirit in Indian Christian Theologies* (Delhi: ISPCK, 2003); Amos Yong, *Beyond the Impasse: Toward a Pneumatogical Hermeneutics of Religions* (Grand Rapids: Baker Academic Books, 2003); see also, Karkkainen, *Pneumatology*.

⁴ Henry Chadwick, *East and West: The Making of a Rift in the Church* (Oxford: Oxford University Press, 2003). Here, the chapter on Filioque is situated within the larger context of Augustine's exposition of the Trinity, see, 27-33. See also Anthony C. Thiselton, *The Holy Spirit: In Biblical Teaching, Through the Centuries and Today* (Grand Rapids, MI: William B. Eerdmans, 2013).

⁵ Andrew F. Walls, *The Missionary Movement in Christian History: Studies in the Transition of Faith* (Maryknoll: Orbis Books, 1996); Lamen Sanneh, *Whose Religion is Christianity?: The Gospel Beyond the West* (Grand Rapids, MI: William B. Eerdmans, 2003); Dana L. Roberts, *Christian Mission: How Christianity Became a World Religion?* (Oxford: Wiley Blackwell, 2009); Philip Jenkins, *Next Christendom: The Coming of Global Christianity* (Oxford: Oxford University Press, 2002).

⁶ Kirsteen Kim discusses the role of the South Korean theologian Chung Hyun Kyong in bringing to fore the discussion of the Holy Spirit in the global ecumenical context. Despite igniting a controversy, among the members of the World Council of Churches, Hyun Kyong's performance of a Korean dance calling on the Han Spirit, as part of the response to the Assembly's theme, "Come Holy Spirit, Renew Your Creation" brought to fore the discussion of the Holy Spirit as vital in the mission of the church. See Kim, *The Holy Spirit in the World*, viii-xiv, 55-58.

the Holy Spirit in the mission of the church. Titled, *Together towards Life: Mission and Evangelism in Changing Landscapes*, the document underlines the significant role and function of the Holy Spirit in the witness to the reconciled life in Jesus Christ.[7] *Cape Town Commitment* is the title of the Lausanne Movement document prepared by theologians and evangelical leaders at the Third Lausanne Congress on World Evangelization, Cape Town, South Africa 2010. Mission as initiated, inspired, empowered and made complete by the Holy Spirit is stated categorically in the Cape Town commitment. *Evangelii Gaudium* (Joy of the Gospel) the other document on Christian mission and witness, as an exhortation by Pope Francis, also emphasised the crucial role of the Holy Spirit in sharing the good news of the gospel.

The renewed emphasis and appreciation of the place of the Holy Spirit in the life and witness of the church call on expressions and experiences in local contexts. In the present project centred on India and its pluralistic nature of society as a canvas to explore the manifestation of the Holy Spirit, I will highlight a chapter from the history of Christian mission among the indigenous people, the Nagas of northeast India. Taking a history of the religions perspective – Christianity, indigenous/shamanic[8] – the chapter illustrates a context wherein the Holy Spirit took a central role in indigenising Christianity among the Naga people.

The Naga response to Christian mission and the form of Christianity that emerged can be explained through the centring of the Holy Spirit in evangelisation as well as in shaping an indigenous type of Christianity. Placing the Holy Spirit and its experience disrupted a gendered Christianity introduced by the missionaries, ushering freedom particularly to women who formed the periphery participants. Centring the Holy Spirit in Christian life and witness broke boundaries and borders set by the imported Christianity and the experience of the Holy

---

[7] Jooseop Keum (ed), *Together towards Life: Mission and Evangelism in Changing Landscapes* (Geneva: WCC Publications, 2012); Lausanne Movement, Cape Town Commitment, see https://www.lausanne.org/content/ctc/ctcommitment (accessed 10 March, 2017). For the Evangelii Gaudium, see http://w2.vatican.va/content/francesco/en/apost_exhortations/documents/papa-francesco_esortazione-ap_20131124_evangelii-gaudium.html (accessed 10 March, 2017).

[8] James Cox (ed), *Critical Reflections on Indigenous Religions* (London: Ashgate, 2013); Graham Harvey (ed.), *Indigenous Religions: A Companion* (London: Cassell, 2000).

Spirit enabled women to participate as local preachers which otherwise as a privilege was unavailable to them beyond the women fellowships.⁹ Fracturing the gendered Christianity and enabling women to serve as leaders in the nascent Christian community, also added another important dimension to Naga Christianity. The "substratum" Naga primal spirituality which was shamanic with relatively no gender barriers to function as a shaman, found expression in the Holy Spirit enabled participation of the women in the community religiosity.

MULTI-RELIGIOSITY OF INDIA AND THE HOLY SPIRIT

It is common knowledge that India is not a homogeneous nation and cannot be represented by a few dominant images or notions. India cannot be described in monolithic terms, and therefore it entails that the diversities in different layers are reckoned in a missional engagement in the country. India is quintessentially a diverse country with multiple languages, plurality of religious beliefs and practices, different socio-economic classes, and diverse cultural worldviews exist in the nation.¹⁰

Plurality of cultures has been a way of life in pre-colonial India. The annals of history bear witness to the fact that modern India has been a region of multi-religiosity, and plurality of religions is part of its heritage from antiquity. Historians of religions inform us about this fact, for instance, Wendy Doniger of University of Chicago in her book, *The Hindus: An Alternative History* narrates the interactions of many religions in India, as she writes, "Hinduism interacted creatively with, first, Buddhism, Jainism, then Judaism, Christianity, then Islam and Sikhism, as well as with tribal religions and other imports (such as Zoroastrianism)."¹¹ Indeed, Hinduism as known today did not exist as a structured and institutionalised religion prior to the project of the Orientalists and

---

⁹ For a discussion on the practice of women fellowships among Naga Christians, see Atola Longkumer, "Tetsur Tesayula: Christian Mission and Gender among Ao Nagas of Northeast India" in Christine Lienemann-Perrin, et al. (eds), *Putting Names with Faces: Women's Impact in Mission History* (Nashville: Abingdon Press, 2012), 187-206.

¹⁰ Among the myriad of publications on India and its intricacies, for the most compelling references, see Edward Luce, *In Spite of the Gods: The Rise of Modern India* (New York: Random House, 2008); Ramachandra Guha, *India after Gandhi: The History of the World's Largest Democracy* (New York: Harper Collins, 2007).

¹¹ Wendy Doniger, *The Hindus: Alternative History* (New Delhi: Penguin/Viking, 2009), 45.

the missionaries.¹² The fact that many so called "world religions" – Hinduism, Buddhism, Jainism and Sikhism – have their origins in India bears witness to a context of tolerance, plurality and fluidity to meaning-making pursuits. Zoroastrianism, Judaism, Christianity, and Islam have significant impact upon the people and cultures of modern India, tracing back to their history of arrival and encounter with the people and cultures of the region.

According to tradition, Christianity took roots in India in the southern state of Kerala as early as the first century AD with the arrival of Thomas, one of the twelve disciples of Jesus along with the spice merchants from Arabia.¹³ Zoroastrians found a safe haven in India and flourished producing a rich heritage for the nation. These historical facts bespeak of an open, tolerant people accommodating different religions and thereby engendering plurality of religion in this part of the world.

The practice of modern Hinduism with its diversity in rituals, difference in emphasis, variation in local contexts also adds to the argument that modern India has a substratum culture of accommodation of many local cultures and rituals. Hinduism of today is different from the Rig Vedic religiosity, e.g., women's role in religiosity, which bespeaks of the adaptability of the Hindu religion. The evolution of Hindu religion as a construct of modernity, which has been reified at a certain historical period, is itself one that has seen a complex process of interaction and absorption as expressed in the following quotation from R. Champakalakshmi, a historian.

> The making of India's religious traditions has been one of the most complex processes in the development of its culture and civilization. Hinduism, as this religious tradition is known, defies definition as a religion, nor can it be described as a way of life. It certainly is more than both. It is the result of a complex interaction between Vedic and Puranic Brahmanism and innumerable indigenous cults, that is, regional and local beliefs, practices, cult forms and ethnic associations, many of

---

[12] Richard King, *Orientalism and Religion: Postcolonial Theory, India and 'the Mystic East'* (London: Routledge, 1999); Geoffrey Oddie, *Imagined Hinduism: British Protestant Missionary Constructions of Hinduism, 1793-1900* (New Delhi: Sage Publications, 2006).

[13] Leonard Fernando and G. Gispert Sauch, *Christianity in India: Two Thousand Years of Faith* (New Delhi: Viking/Penguin Books, 2004); Robert Eric Frykenberg, *Christianity in India: From Beginnings to the Present* (New York: Oxford University Press, 2008).

which are still unexplored, ultimately contributing to the emergence of a pan-Indian tradition, with interesting regional manifestations and variations.[14]

The complex religious traditions of India include also Christianity, which is as diverse as the nation itself. Christianity in India comprises of multiple contexts with diverse church traditions, different historical periods, and a myriad of local contexts. Christianity and its history and encounters with cultures in India, therefore, cannot be discussed in one voice with a single perspective. The local cultures in the country and their encounters with Christianity took place in different historical periods, with diverse socio-economic conditions with disparate Christian missions. Beginning with the tradition of Thomas, the Jesuits, the first Protestant missionaries (from Halle, Germany) to Tranquebar, the evangelical chaplains in the imperial army, the Serampore trio, the ABCFM (American Board of Commissioners of Foreign Missions), followed by the many denominational missionaries, and many indigenous mission efforts by the converts themselves, Christianity was established firmly, albeit, remaining a minority religion compared to the dominant religions.[15]

Christian theologians in India have also emphasised the role of the Holy Spirit in the development of theological discourse that reckons with Indian religio-cultural traditions.[16] It must be clarified that these Indian theologies drawing on the Holy Spirit, however, are limited to the brahmanical religious traditions that are philosophical and emphasise upanishadic concepts in interpreting the role of the Holy Spirit.[17]

Among the diversity of Christianity prevalent in India, in a plurality of contexts, Christianity practised among the indigenous people – the Naga – provides a religiosity, influenced by the residue of the religious substratum of pre-Christian notions and practices. A helpful

---

[14] R. Champakalakshmi, *Religion, Tradition, and Ideology: Pre-colonial South India* (New Delhi: Oxford University Press, 2008), 2.

[15] For a macro history of Christianity in India, the following are helpful resources, Samuel Hugh Moffet, *A History of Christianity in Asia*, vols. 1 and 11 (Bangalore: Theological Publications in India, 2005); and most recently, Frykenberg, *Christianity in India*. Apart from these, there is a growing literature on micro historical studies of particular contexts.

[16] Kim, *Mission in the Spirit*; Kim, *The Holy Spirit in the World*, 67-102.

[17] Kim, *The Holy Spirit in the World*, 96.

survey of the understanding, experience, and interpretation of the Holy Spirit across historical periods and multiple contexts is summed up by Velli-Matti Karkkainen affirming that the diversity of the experience and manifestation of the Spirit calls for an openness to the "new discoveries, new challenges, new potentialities" prevalent.[18] Local contexts such as the Naga Christianity illustrate the new potentialities of the role and working of the Holy Spirit.

NAGA CHRISTIANITY

> Let an Angami or Ao Naga array himself in his special tribal custom with crossbands of red and yellow, with woven blanket of gay pattern, with feathered head dress and spear or bow and arrows, and he bears a striking resemblance to his red (*sic*) brother of North America. Even the hue of his skin is the same deep red bronze, and the habits and customs of the tribes are such as might readily be understood by the Indian (*sic*) braves across the seas.[19]

The above quotation is a significant description of a Naga male as encountered by the earliest Christian missionaries in the late nineteenth century. Indeed, the description does betray the cultural naiveté held by many of the missionaries in their assessment of the people they evangelised.[20] While being aware of the cultural biases of the missionaries, the description of an Angami or Ao Naga with their traditional attire does mediate to the modern reader or modern Naga a fragment of the pre-Christian identity of the Naga. Since the Naga people have oral based cultures, the earliest written records of their religio-cultural practices are the colonial impressions and Christian missionaries' reports which provided detailed ethnographic and administrative records. To be sure, these earliest written records are not without the perspectives and biases of the time as much as oral narratives are themselves infused by the matrices of power hierarchy of the community.

---

[18] Karkkainen, *Pneumatology*, 176, 177.

[19] Letter of Alice Findlay, Subject File Assam, Archives of the American Baptist Historical Society (ABHS), Valley Forge, PA.

[20] Linda Tuhiwai Smith, *Decolonizing Methodologies: Research and Indigenous Peoples* (London: Zed Books, 1999). For the sustained "othering" of the natives, while portraying a collective image of the "heathen" by the colonising West, see David Chidester, *Savage System: Colonialism and Comparative Religion in South Africa* (Charlottesville: University Press of Virginia, 1996).

Indigenous Spirituality and the Holy Spirit in a Pluralistic Context

An indigenous people of the Indo-Myanmar region, the Naga people were colonised by the British and christianised by the Baptist missionaries from America at the beginning of the nineteenth century. While most of the Naga tribes profess Christianity today, there are still a few that practise and live in the traditional way. Encounter and embrace of Christianity for the Naga people has been tremendous. Robert Eric Frykenberg, an eminent historian, writes about the Naga Christians in the following words:

> These were peoples who, for ages untold, had never been Sanskritized or Islamicized and who were only too eager to escape from conditions of brutality and insecurity. This having been so, Christianity has simply become an accepted and vital part of a Naga ethnic identity, as this was 'constructed' (or 'invented') during the past century. As such it has separated them from peoples from whom they fervently want to be separated – namely, Hindus and Muslims.[21]

Naga people's response and embrace of Christianity is arguably a pivotal historical event, it initiated a new era and even a new identity in the modern period. In a nutshell, it can be said that the conversion to Christianity converged the Naga people with the modern world, as Frykenberg summed up, "modern education and literacy in Roman script has not only given them [Naga] easy cultural access to all of India but to the entire Anglophone world."[22]

Encounter and espousal of Christianity transformed the Naga people from an oral based shamanic religiosity to modern agents as literate and equipped for capitalistic economy. Despite the colossal changes below the surface of the Naga Christian spirituality, that is generally Baptist, there exists the lived Christianity, influenced, conditioned and defined by the substratum religiosity of pre-Christian Naga traditional religiosity. The most vivid manifestation is the Spirit infused spirituality. Distinct from the practise of Christianity as inherited from the Baptist missionaries at the beginning of the late nineteenth century, today's Christianity as observed among the Naga people bears resemblance to the shamanic religiosity. The Christianity that was espoused by the earliest converts to the evangelisation of the Baptist missionaries was marked by

---

[21] Frykenberg, *Christianity in India*, 422.
[22] Frykenberg, *Christianity in India*, 429, (Parenthesis added).

the ritual of baptism and membership in the church; a Christianity that was centred on the church and under the leadership of a male pastor. The reading of the Bible and singing of traditional hymns formed the core of their Christian spirituality. In a general way, the type of Christianity prevalent among the Nagas is church as the central institution, the church that is embedded in a patriarchal culture with male leadership – pastor and the deacons. Sometime in the last quarter of the century, the type of Christianity defined by the preaching of the word and with confident male leadership underwent a metamorphosis, wherein, intense prayers accompanied by ecstatic dancing and utterances emerged. In this phenomenon of an obviously charismatic Christianity, women became active participants and leaders. From the periphery of the community, women who exhibited the charismatic traits were sought out for prayers, intended on determining the will of God.

Christianity among the Naga people underwent the translation process into a religio-cultural context that was familiar and defining for them. Andrew F. Walls has narrated the process of translation of Christianity into local cultures highlighting the "revisioning" of the understanding of the gospel in relation to the specific context. Walls affirms that the "Christian mind" in its understanding and living of the gospel is influenced by the preceding culture and history; thereby, it makes "all churches culture churches."[23]

The analysis of Christianity in its relationship to local culture or the *vice versa* of local cultures imprinting on the expression of Christianity is available in fine academic work in many contexts, in fact the emerging area of world Christianity as an academic discipline is a product of this recognition of cultures indelibly defining the contours of Christianity.[24] The localising of Christianity can vividly be observed in the Naga Christianity. Categorised as scheduled tribe with indigenous cultures Naga Christians and their lived Christianity provide another aspect of the Spirit influenced Christianity apart from the other theological discourse by theologians in India. The centring of the Holy Spirit and its function

---

[23] Walls, T*he Missionary Movement in Christian History*, 8.

[24] For a resourceful discussion on the theme with insights from multiple contexts and voice, see Jonathan Y. Tran and Anh Q. Tran (eds), *World Christianity: Perspective and Insights* (Maryknoll: Orbis Books, 2016).

of freedom is markedly observed in the areas such as participation of women and recognition of the Spirit influenced spiritualities that define Christianity among the Naga people. To understand the working of the Holy Spirit in all its varieties, the context specific experiences of the Spirit need to be heard. Interestingly, Karkkainen states that any "talk of the Spirit must be always contextual and therefore culture specific."[25]

THE HOLY SPIRIT AND NAGA CHRISTIANITY

Historically, Christianity has a complex relationship with women across different periods and cultural contexts. While there were capable women actively involved in the community, Christianity has been undeniably a patriarchal religion with an androcentric theology drawn from a male-centred sacred text.[26] Scholarship continues to shed more light on the complex participation of women in the history and traditions of Christianity. For instance, excellent research in Mission studies are unearthing a goldmine of women's active participation in the transmission of the new religion and the values associated with it so much so that it can be said that Christianity is a religion of women. Dana Robert affirms this as she writes,

> [a]round the globe, more women than men are practicing Christians.... Christianity is a women's religion. The ratio of female to male Christians is approximately two to one. Within Catholicism, sisters outnumber brothers and priests by more than 50 percent...In the late nineteenth and the twentieth centuries, in both Catholicism and Protestantism, the majority of missionaries were women. However, until recently overview histories of mission have scarcely analyzed women's roles or acknowledged that women typically make up the majority of active believer.[27]

The recovery of women in history, the insertion of women's experience into theological discourse, the critique from feminist scholarship and the recognition of women's participation in the community

---

[25] Karkkainen, *Pneumatology*, 9.
[26] The classic texts for the paradigm shifting argument for feminist critique of androcentric theology are Rosemary Radford Reuther, *Sexism and God Talk: Toward a Feminist Theology* (Boston: Beacon Press, 1983); Elizabeth Schussler Fiorenza, *In Memory of Her: A Feminist Theological Reconstruction of Christian Origins* (New York: Crossroad, 1985).
[27] Robert, *Christian Mission*, 118.

can be said to be intrinsically linked with the Holy Spirit. The place, role and function of the Holy Spirit have both provided resources to articulate feminist theologies that interrogate a theology that is androcentric, as well as provided the freedom for women to participate as leaders in the community.[28] In other words, the understanding of the Holy Spirit has been central to women emancipation. On locating the role of the Holy Spirit in enabling women to break male-biased barriers, Karkkainen cites the example of a German mystic Hildegard of Bingen, an itinerant preacher and capable administrator of a religious community apart from being a prolific writer. The theological insights and visions that Hildegard received are *via* the Holy Spirit, as recorded: "From infancy you have been taught, not bodily, but spiritually, by true vision through the Spirit of the Lord. Speak these things that you now see and hear…speak and write, therefore, now according to me and not according to yourself."[29]

Estrelda Alexander and Amos Yong provide a well-documented study of women and their role in the emergence of the Pentecostal movement. The experience of charisma freed women from the restrictions of the society to function as religious figures, however, the routinisation and institutionalisation of the charisma into Pentecostal denomination brought restriction upon the participation of women. The important point to note is the freedom to lead, preach and assume leadership for women in the charismatic communities.[30] In overcoming the conventional ecclesiastical practices undergirded by an androcentric theology towards inclusive communities, the openness to the role of the Holy Spirit cannot be underestimated.

The Holy Spirit understood as a feminine aspect of the Trinity and the freedom experience of the Holy Spirit opened the bolted doors of the patriarchal church.

---

[28] Liturgical revivals are also enabled by embrace of the Holy Spirit, a feminist in nature, this movement for liturgical renewal balances the unhelpful dualism made between mind and body, sacred and mundane, etc, see Rosemary Radford Ruether, *Women-Church: Theology and Practice of Feminist Liturgical Communities* (Oregon: Wifp and Stock Publishers, 2001).

[29] Liber vitae meritorum, cited by Karkkainen, *Pneumatology*, 50.

[30] See, Estrelda Alexander and Amos Yong (eds), *Philip's Daughters: Women in Pentecostal-Charismatic Leadership* (Eugene, OR: Wipf & Stock, 2009); see Beverly Mayne Kienzle and Pamela J. Walker (eds), *Women Preachers and Prophets: Through Two Millennia of Christianity* (Berkeley: University of California Press, 1998); see also Derek and Dianne Tidball, *The Message of Women: Creation, Grace and Gender* (Nottingham: Inter-varsity Press, 2012), 199.

As documented and analysed in a variety of contexts, this is observable also in the experience of the women in Naga Christianity. One of the striking features of Naga Christianity is the phenomenon of "prayer warrior" characterised by intense and emotional prayer on behalf of others. Understanding and locating this phenomenon within the larger framework of Charismatic/Pentecostal Christianity by analysis will perhaps serve as a major key in illuminating Naga Christianity and its relationship with the indigenous spirituality.

Having said this, it is important to note that the Naga Christianity is not a Pentecostal denomination, it is Baptist in its denominational identity, tracing its roots to the mission work of the American Baptists of the nineteenth century. The denominational identity of the Naga Christianity is more complex than the conventional labelling and historical roots. Put simply, the social conservatism and biblical literalism prevalent among the Naga Christians make them closer to other conservative Baptists than the American Baptist, the roots of their Christianity. This denominational identity is significant to the understanding of the nature of Naga Christianity that is akin to Charismatic spirituality. While its mission roots are in the American Baptist mission, Naga Christianity in its expression, particularly the place and participation of women, is more complex in a socio-political conservative milieu.[31]

The phenomenon of prayer warriors, vividly active in performing the religiosity of intense prayers for persons in need, seeking divine intervention is not an occurrence in a "brick and mortar" Pentecostal church but a faithful member of the local Baptist church. The centrality of emotional prayers is accompanied with the other manifested features such as talking in tongues, wringing their hands, ecstatic dancing, and going into trance. The important point to note is the invocation of the Holy Spirit in such performance of prayer and the claim by the individuals who experience this state to be in possession of the Holy Spirit. The prayers can be simple, uncomplicated and conventional, yet they provide a site of observation giving direction to understand heartfelt religious experience. Here, amidst prayers, speaking in tongues experiences occur

---

[31] I have discussed this in detail elsewhere, see Christine Perrin-Lienemann, et al. (eds), *Putting Names to Faces*, 187-206.

when prophecies are told, the ailments are "diagnosed," and "treatments" are prescribed. Women are usually the most active performers of these intense prayers. In this phenomenon attributed to the Holy Spirit, women apparently are more attuned to the empowerment of the Holy Spirit.

Prayer carried out in intensity, captivated by the Spirit, is most visible in Naga Christianity that demonstrates the charismatic dimension of spirituality akin to the underlying shamanistic religiosity. In prayers, the spiritual gifts are demonstrated and the liminality of the women is defined. In that, the ability to perform the intense prayers sets aside the women as those able to lead and guide the faithful. A woman hardly with some primary school level education can be recognised as someone who can "exegete" the Bible and mediate the deep truths of God's will for his people. The pastor with a theological education becomes a mere institutional figure of the church. Hence, it can be argued that the ability to perform intense, emotional prayers can become the medium of negotiated empowerment for the Naga women in a patriarchal religious ethos. Marie Griffith has argued for the role of prayer in empowering women in her book *God's Daughters: Evangelical Women and the Power of Submission*. In this excellent study of the Aglow Women Fellowship, Griffith analysed "their religious narrative and prayers" and observed the negotiated power and identity of the Aglow women within a conservative Christianity. She writes that:

> [t]hrough prayer, a woman who feels angry, despairing, or powerless in her everyday life may experience a sense of intimacy with God as her loving father, friend, and husband. Through prayer she perhaps feel that someone hears her cry and cares about her pain, and that he will not only comfort her but will heal her suffering and fill her with joy. She can also feel herself to be stronger, more capable person than she was before; imbued with a new 'self-esteem' …that only through the surrender of prayer can a woman be completely healed, transformed, empowered, and set free.[32]

---

[32] Marie Griffith, *God's Daughters: Evangelical Women and the Power of Submission* (Berkeley: University of California Press, 1997), 19. See also Edith Blumhofer, "Women in Pentecostalism," *Union Seminary Quarterly Review* 57/3-4 (2003), 101-122. Blumhofer provides the template of the earliest Pentecostal/charismatic communities, wherein the experience of the Holy Spirit was sufficient for women to participate in religious services such as exhortation, preaching, even organising mission projects beyond the community. And objections to their participations were countered by the Spirit's enduement.

Prayer, thus, can be liberating, empowering for women, as the Naga women also apparently experience when captivated by the Holy Spirit.

As noted earlier, Naga socio-cultural backdrop is patriarchal in its gender relationship, however there is a relative freedom of participation enjoyed by women in the religious spheres. The gender roles and position can be described as qualified patriarchy, wherein the men and women functioned as complementary pairs in all aspects of the community except in the social decision making bodies. While in most Naga tribes women were neither kept in seclusion nor were they excluded from social festivities and community tasks, the decision making body was comprised of male members only representing the clans of the village. In such a social context based on the clan structure, a woman could be a shaman if she exhibits the abilities of "dreaming" for the community. This religio-cultural backdrop of pre-Christian Naga Christianity has contributed to it in a complex form. While patriarchal ethos of both the Victorian gender roles of the missionaries and the local cultures mutually affirmed the centrality of men as leaders in the nascent Christian communities, Naga Christians and the American Baptist missionaries were pragmatic in their attitude towards women folk. The women were not kept isolated, rather women departments were promptly organised. Women were taken as Bible women to assist the missionaries. The gifted ones were even sent as evangelists to the neighbouring villages.[33]

Naga women, nevertheless, were not positioned as leaders. They could not be pastors and neither could they be deacons that comprised the governing board of the local church. Naga women in the new religion were on the periphery forming the margins of mute spectators and devout members. This marginality underwent a tremendous change with the onset of the renewal movements that emphasised the Holy Spirit and its manifestations. Grant Wacker's vivid description of women in the early Pentecostal movement in America can be applied to the experience of Naga women and their empowerment by the Holy Spirit: "[L]ike a kettledrum echoing up from the deep, God's call beckoned women to

---

[33] See Narola Imchen, *Remembering our Foremothers: The Influence of the American Women's Movement on American Baptist Women Missionaries in Northeast India* (Jorhat: Eastern Theological College, 2003); Narola Imchen, *Women in Church and Society: The Story of Ao Naga Women* (Jorhat: Eastern Theological College, 2001).

herald the Word wherever the Holy Spirit" manifested.[34] Experience of the Holy Spirit and confirmation of the experience by the intense prayer performance affirm their position as "leaders" and "exegetes" worthy to be consulted in all matters by the believers and ordinary citizens. In centring the experience of the Holy Spirit, women were centred and given the "divine ordination" rendering "all human ordination [to shriveled] into utter insignificance" as described by Elizabeth Sisson, a former missionary in India who was later empowered by the experience of the Holy Spirit to be an itinerant Bible teacher.[35]

Recognition of women as capable participants in the religious sphere can also be seen as a tentative dismantling of the rigid male hierarchy of church leadership of Naga Christianity. While the institutional governance and authority continued to be centred around the male pastor and the male-only deacon board, gifted women's voice of advice and directions were valued when it was authorised by the Holy Spirit. For instance, a perceived error in functioning by the decision-making body could be "corrected" by the prophecy or vision of a woman recognised as empowered by the Holy Spirit. For many believers, the Naga Christian socio-religious hierarchy was rendered insignificant, when the Holy Spirit was the source of authority. Furthermore, the dormant religiosity that defined the Naga people prior to the espousal of Christianity emerged in subtle forms as the empowerment by the Holy Spirit enabled the individual to possess and exhibit exceptional abilities of communing with God and interpreting difficult choices and experiences of life. Under the empowerment of the Holy Spirit, shamanic form of religiosity such as dream-seeking, prescribing healing, prophecy, and guidance for daily weighty decisions to be made for a contented living became a defining spirituality of the Naga Christianity.[36]

The centring of the Holy Spirit in ushering an inclusive religious community among the Naga Christians, wherein women were

---

[34] Wacker, *Heaven Below*, 165.

[35] Wacker, *Heaven Below*, 163.

[36] For the proposition that charismatic dimension of Christianity has traces of traditional religiosity such as African traditional religions, native religiosity, see Corky Alexander, *Native American Pentecost: Praxis, Contextualization, and Transformation* (Cleveland, TN: Cherohala Press, 2012); J. Raboteau, *A Fire in the Bones: Reflections on African American Religious History* (Boston: Beacon Press, 1995).

also recognised as capable leaders, albeit tentative and not without ambiguity, illustrates the reflex of religious community when the source of empowerment was the ineffable experience of the Holy Spirit. The empowerment of women and emergence of the residual indigenous spirituality remain ambiguous and peripheral. Like the Pentecostal denominations and their relationship with women leadership, Naga Christianity remains a male-centred spirituality, mutually fed by the ethos of the larger socio-cultural attitudes of discrimination of women. While experience of the Holy Spirit helped women to negotiate their role as "leaders," it is far from being the norm. It remains an exceptional phenomenon for only some extraordinary women who had overwhelming experience of the Holy Spirit.

HOLY SPIRIT AND INCLUSIVE CHRISTIANITY

If the experience of the Holy Spirit empowered women to function as religious leaders and conduits of the divine, the openness to the Holy Spirit is continually relevant towards an inclusive community. Understanding the inclusive nature of the Holy Spirit is critical to the opening of the ecclesiastical spaces and roles for women to function as equal participants in the mission of the Triune God. Where the Holy Spirit has led the faithful community in its theology and lived spirituality, it has disrupted conventional norms and has broken through boundaries and limitations set by human notions of hierarchy. *Together towards Life* affirms:

> What is clear is that by the Spirit we participate in the mission of love that is at the heart of the life of the Trinity. This results in Christian witness which increasingly proclaims the salvific power of God through Jesus Christ and constantly affirms God's dynamic involvement, through the Holy Spirit, in the whole created world. All who respond to the outpouring of the love of God are invited to join in with the Spirit in the mission of God.[37]

In realising the creative ways of the Holy Spirit in witnessing to the reconciled life Jesus Christ ensures for the whole of creation, the faithful community opens itself to ethos of inclusion and emancipatory practices. To continue with rigid convention and myopic interpretation of cultural

---

[37] Keum, *Together towards Life*, 4, 5.

ethos would be limiting the dynamic and creative witness of the Holy Spirit to the all-embracing God.

Where charisma has had the upper hand for authorisation and power, women have also found negotiated space to be liberated from religio-cultural suppression. Elaine Lawless, in her study on the life stories of Pentecostal women preachers in America, observes a re-scripting of women in the religious narrative and landscape. In the re-scripting, Lawless opines, the women's experience illustrates the ability "to disrupt the status quo, call it into question, and provide the means to weaken male power and authority and deflect religious injunctions intended to silence women's voices. It is indicative of the ways women take control of their lives and their voices, subvert the dictates of a male hierarchy, and violate man-made codes which restrict them."[38] The capability to be subversive and disrupt imposed marginality comes with the encounter of the Holy Spirit. The Holy Spirit is the agent and the source of affirmation and enlightenment, the medieval woman mystic Hildegard of Bingen was instructed by the Holy Spirit and in late modern Christianity, where women have been in the periphery, the Holy Spirit empowers them to serve the community. If women preachers in Pentecostal Christianity defied restrictions and did what was directed by the Holy Spirit, then the Holy Spirit is indeed an inclusive Spirit. Hence, all members of the Christian community convinced and called to partake in the mission of God need to be accepted, equipped and recognised to share in the witness to the gospel.

Women's active participation in the mission of the Church continues to be a challenge in Naga Christianity. There are no overt restrictions against their pursuits of theological education and serving the peripheral positions of the church, but the recognition and acceptance of women as capable leaders of the church and the community at large still

---

[38] Elaine J. Lawless, "Rescripting their Lives and Narratives: Spiritual Life Stories of Pentecostal Women Preachers," *Journal of Feminist Studies in Religion* 7/1 (1991), 53-71. The discussion of women shaping and being shaped by the Pentecostal/Charismatic movement continues to be a critical relevant theme as indicated by the plethora of research undertaken in the area, for instance, a recent volume brings together a number of scholars pursuing the theme, see Margaret English de Alminan and Lois E. Olena (eds), *Women in Pentecostal and Charismatic Ministry: Informing a Dialogue on Gender, Church, and Ministry* (Leiden: Brill, 2016).

remains a challenge. If we noted that the experience of the Holy Spirit and the visible manifestation of the encounter did give a relative space and voice for Naga women, it was more an exception and not a collective transformation towards inclusive community. In the early chapters of western mission histories, women who felt called to serve as missionaries could only fulfill their evangelistic fervour by finding husbands who were missionaries,[39] and such paradigms and strategy continues among the indigenous Naga Christians. Women remain either complementary to the male leadership or continue to be the performers of the peripheral roles. Naga Christianity needs openness to the working of the Holy Spirit to accept the full participation of women called to the service of the church. In a general perspective of Christianity and its prospect for the future, mission historian Andrew F. Walls states that creative, innovative theologies will arise from the Christianities of the Global South in its interactions with the cultures and challenges of the contexts. One of the challenges is surely the question of women's participation in the transformation of communities through witness to the gospel. The context of plurality of cultures and peoples, such as in India, calls for creative and inclusive witness where an uncritical espousal of cultural conventions might hinder the creative and all-embracing empowerment of the Holy Spirit who makes all things new.

---

[39] Dana L. Robert (ed), *Gospel Bearers, Gender Barriers: Missionary Women in the Twentieth Century* (Maryknoll: Orbis Books, 2002).

Index

A

Advaita 158, 160, 162, 169
Alister McGrath 205, 259
Allan Anderson 71, 72, 85, 90, 91, 100, 114, 260
Allan Race 156
Amos Yong 7, 101, 102, 113, 155, 204, 260, 269
Andrew F. Walls 260, 267, 276
Anti-Conversion 19, 229, 230, 231, 234, 236, 237, 238, 244
Apologetics 9, 18, 101, 203, 205, 208, 209, 210, 211, 213, 219, 220, 221, 222, 223
Apostles' Creed 66
Atman 169
Augustine 139, 144, 200, 260

B

baptism 1, 10, 52, 70, 87, 88, 89, 103, 115, 123, 124, 125, 126, 176, 177, 178, 194, 200, 220, 245, 247, 254, 257, 258, 267
B.B. Warfield 69, 138, 139

C

Cardinal Ruffini 124
Cardinal Suenens 124, 125, 129, 130
Caste System 9, 19, 226, 227, 228, 231, 234, 236, 237, 238, 244
Chad M. Bauman 95
Charismata 15, 69, 90, 103
Charles Parham 71
Charles Taylor 206, 207
Cheryl Bridges Johns 88, 89, 131
Christological 6, 10, 42, 43, 113, 120, 155, 159, 161, 162, 195, 208
Christopher J.H. Wright / Chris Wright 7, 14, 21, 37, 43. *See also* Christopher J.H. Wright
Clinton Arnold 40, 42, 43, 44, 47, 48. *See also* Arnold
Contextualization 5, 7, 8, 9, 18, 119, 120, 210, 273
Conversion 16, 17, 19, 48, 50, 77, 79, 80, 87, 93, 95, 96, 100, 115, 126, 127, 128, 129, 137, 149, 150, 151, 184, 186, 188, 194, 216, 222, 229, 230, 231, 232, 234, 236, 241, 244, 266
Covenant 14, 23, 25, 37, 38, 40, 42, 44, 45, 46, 47, 49, 50, 52, 55, 58, 132
C.V. Matthew 233, 234, 235

D

Dalit 84, 86, 94, 95, 97, 160, 179, 226, 230, 231, 237, 238, 256, 257
Dana Robert 260, 268, 276
David Hardiman 93, 98
Donald McGavran 78, 98, 257
Donald Miller 96, 98
Donum Superadditum 61

E

Emil Brunner 11
Epistemology 212, 213, 214, 223
Eschatology 6, 38, 41, 47
Estrelda Alexander 269
Evangelical 15, 67, 75, 76, 78, 79, 82, 105, 108, 113, 148, 153, 179, 187, 188, 271

Index

Exclusivity 1, 8, 155

F

Francis Sullivan 129, 130, 131

G

Gary Tyra 7, 15, 16, 105, 107, 111, 112, 114, 115, 116, 117, 119, 120
Gavin D'Costa 160, 166, 192, 196
George Khodr 159, 171
Gospel 1, 2, 6, 8, 10, 12, 19, 23, 31, 32, 34, 35, 36, 40, 42, 44, 45, 47, 49, 50, 51, 52, 53, 55, 57, 58, 59, 61, 62, 63, 64, 73, 76, 77, 82, 89, 100, 108, 110, 113, 115, 117, 120, 126, 133, 146, 147, 148, 149, 150, 151, 152, 157, 179, 184, 186, 188, 192, 194, 195, 197, 198, 201, 210, 211, 214, 216, 234, 235, 239, 242, 251, 257, 260, 261, 267, 275, 276
Gregory of Nazianzus 66, 67

H

Harvey Cox 72
Hindu *Rashtra* 229, 230, 231
Hindutva 95, 100, 183
Homoiousios 66
Homoousios 2, 66, 176
Hypostases 66

I

I.H. Marshall 37, 53, 61, 64

J

Jacques Dupuis 9, 17, 153, 155, 156, 160
James D.G. Dunn 17, 214
James Forbes 205, 221, 222
James K.A. Smith 206, 215
John Calvin VIII, 17, 138, 139, 140, 141, 142, 143, 144, 145, 146, 147, 148, 149, 150, 151, 187, 188
John Hick 158, 159, 160, 161, 191
John McIntyre 217, 220, 221
John Webster 198

K

Karl Rahner 17, 179, 188, 189, 191, 192, 193
Khrist Bhakta 246, 247, 250, 253
Kingdom of God 7, 11, 31, 34, 43, 47, 58, 90, 101, 102, 124, 154, 250
Kirsteen Kim VIII, 9, 17, 152, 154, 155, 156, 160, 169, 182, 260, 264

L

Lesslie Newbigin 76, 196, 197, 198, 199
Louis Berkhof 69, 70

M

Margaret Y. MacDonald 36, 40, 43, 46
Marie Griffith 271
Mark C. Taylor 222, 223
Mark Heim 101, 160, 189
Martin Heidegger 215, 216
Marxist 1, 229
Max Turner 37, 50, 52, 61, 63
Meredith McGuire 133
Messiah 37, 38, 39, 40, 41, 42, 43, 44, 45, 46, 47, 48, 49, 50, 51, 52, 55, 56, 57, 58, 59
Messianic secret 49, 50, 58
Metanoia 3
Michael Gorman 51, 55
missio Christi 13, 224

Index

missio Dei VIII, 9, 13, 17, 38, 40, 41, 43, 44, 58, 61, 79, 80, 81, 82, 108, 116, 152, 153, 154, 155, 159, 164, 224

Missional pneumatology 13, 15, 16, 20, 107, 108, 109, 116, 121, 182

missio Spiritūs VIII, 9, 13, 17, 152, 153, 155, 224

Mky Habets 7, 10, 203, 204, 205, 210, 212, 222

Murray Dempster 89

Myron Penner 208, 209

N

New covenant 14, 37, 38, 40, 42, 46, 48, 49, 52, 58

Nicene Creed 2, 66, 154, 158, 161, 176, 190, 203

Niceno-Constantinopolitan Creed 67

N.T. Wright 40

O

Ousia 66

P

Pandita Ramabai 72, 226

Paterfamilias 56, 57

Paul Hiebert 76, 95

Paul Knitter 156, 158, 159, 160, 161, 163, 166, 169

Paulo Freire 131

Pax Christi 14, 46, 47, 48, 52, 58

Pax Romana 47, 52

Pentecostalism 13, 16, 65, 70, 71, 72, 73, 74, 75, 76, 77, 79, 82, 83, 84, 85, 86, 88, 91, 96, 98, 101, 114, 115, 116, 122, 126, 131, 139, 255, 260, 271

Pietism 77

Pluralism 9, 17, 61, 98, 100, 101, 106, 114, 149, 153, 155, 156, 157, 159, 160, 161, 162, 165, 166, 185, 191, 192, 225

Pneumatic missiology 13, 15

Pneumato-centric 15, 100, 104, 161

Pneumatology 6, 9, 13, 15, 16, 17, 20, 61, 65, 66, 70, 72, 73, 76, 77, 79, 82, 101, 107, 108, 109, 110, 111, 113, 116, 121, 138, 154, 155, 156, 158, 159, 163, 164, 166, 169, 172, 173, 179, 180, 181, 182, 185, 203, 210, 216, 217, 220, 221, 259, 260, 265, 268, 269

Pope Benedict XVI 17, 128, 135, 136, 191, 193, 194, 195, 196, 197, 198

Pope Francis 128, 136, 137, 261

Pope John Paul II 17, 126, 132, 191, 193, 194

Pope Paul VI 17, 118, 191

Pope Pius XII 127

Predestination 139, 145, 149, 151

R

Raimundo Panikkar 160, 189

Redemption 7, 38, 39, 161, 198, 207, 210, 217, 224

Reformation 39, 67, 68, 69, 75, 77, 126, 138, 148, 149, 204

Richard B. Gaffin, Jr. 138, 139

Richard Shaull 88

Robert Eric Frykenberg 88, 263, 264, 266

Robert Faricy 130, 131

Roger Hedlund 85, 86, 94, 95

Roger P. Schroeder 16, 106, 107, 109, 115, 116, 117, 118, 119, 120

S

Sanskritisation 227

Satsang 19, 248
Secularism 19, 163, 206, 228, 229, 230, 231, 244
Servant-King 14, 21, 22
Shakti 177, 183
Siga Arles 94
Sola Scriptura 75
Soren Kierkegaard 9, 203, 216, 218, 222, 223
Soteriology 15, 17, 37, 39, 45, 46, 70, 222
Spirit Christology 66, 160, 161, 162, 204, 205
Stanley Hauerwas 208, 209, 210
Stanley J. Samartha VIII, 9, 17, 153, 155, 156, 157, 158, 159, 160, 161, 163, 164, 165, 166, 167, 168, 169, 170, 171, 172, 173, 174, 175, 176, 177, 178, 179, 180, 181, 182, 183, 185, 186
Stephen B. Bevans 16, 48, 106, 107, 109, 113, 115, 116, 117, 118, 119, 120, 121

T

Tetsunao Yamamori 96, 98
T.G. Gombis 38, 40, 41, 43, 49, 53, 54, 57
Third Article (Theology) VIII, 6, 7, 9, 18, 203, 204, 205, 211, 212, 223
Thomas Aquinas 209
Thomas F. Torrance 2, 3, 4
Timothy C. Tennent 7, 8, 15, 16, 60, 106, 179
Timothy Smith 209
Tony Richie 100, 101, 102, 103
Trinitarian 5, 6, 9, 10, 13, 18, 20, 41, 42, 58, 60, 66, 67, 106, 123, 158, 160, 161, 162, 164, 189, 190, 204, 205, 210, 211, 220, 223, 224
Trinity 5, 11, 61, 66, 67, 69, 70, 73, 101, 107, 124, 138, 150, 153, 155, 159, 160, 161, 162, 164, 166, 175, 176, 177, 182, 204, 205, 207, 210, 211, 216, 220, 221, 223, 260, 269, 274

V

Velli-Matti Kärkkäinen 101

W

Wendy Doniger 262
William Menzies 67, 87, 262
William Seymour 70, 71

Y

Young-Gi Hong 90

www.ingramcontent.com/pod-product-compliance
Lightning Source LLC
Chambersburg PA
CBHW050340230426
43663CB00010B/1935